CULTIVATING A
MATH
COACHING
PRACTICE

A Guide for K–8 Math Educators

AMY MORSE

Foreword by Deborah Schifter

A Joint Publication

CORWIN
A SAGE Company

EDC
Education Development Center, Inc.

Copyright © 2009 by Corwin

All rights reserved. When forms and sample documents are included, their use is authorized only by educators, local school sites, and/or noncommercial or nonprofit entities that have purchased the book. Except for that usage, no part of this book may be reproduced or utilized in any form or by any means, electronic or mechanical, including photocopying, recording, or by any information storage and retrieval system, without permission in writing from the publisher.

For information:

Corwin
A SAGE Company
2455 Teller Road
Thousand Oaks, California 91320
(800) 233-9936
Fax: (800) 417-2466
www.corwinpress.com

SAGE Ltd.
1 Oliver's Yard
55 City Road
London EC1Y 1SP
United Kingdom

SAGE India Pvt. Ltd.
B 1/I 1 Mohan Cooperative
  Industrial Area
Mathura Road, New Delhi 110 044
India

SAGE Asia-Pacific Pte. Ltd.
33 Pekin Street #02-01
Far East Square
Singapore 048763

Printed in the United States of America.

Library of Congress Cataloging-in-Publication Data

Morse, Amy.
Cultivating a math coaching practice: a guide for K-8 math educators/Amy Morse.
    p. cm.
"A joint publication with the Education Development Center."
ISBN 978-1-4129-7105-8 (cloth)
ISBN 978-1-4129-7106-5 (pbk.)
    1. Mathematics—Study and teaching (Elementary school) 2. Mathematics—Study and teaching (Middle school) 3. Mathematics teachers—Training of. I. Title.

QA11.2.M67 2009
372.7—dc22   2009004461

This book is printed on acid-free paper.

09   10   11   12   13   10   9   8   7   6   5   4   3   2   1

Acquisitions Editor:	Dan Alpert
Associate Editor:	Megan Bedell
Production Editor:	Cassandra Margaret Seibel
Copy Editor:	Codi Bowman
Typesetter:	C&M Digitals (P) Ltd.
Proofreader:	Wendy Jo Dymond
Cover Designer:	Scott Van Atta

MATH COACHING PRACTICE

*This book is dedicated to Lily, Lila, and
Chloe—the three wonders of my universe.*

Contents

Foreword

Cultivating a Math Coaching Practice: A Guide for K–8 Math Educators is a book by, for, and about coaches and their supervisors. Amy Morse—who, in the 1990s, worked as a math coach for an urban school district and since then has supported the professional development of math coaches in various school systems throughout the country—recognized a growing need and has created this book to provide it.

Many schools are setting ambitious goals for mathematics instruction. Rather than exclusively focusing on speedy and accurate calculation, teachers are now being asked to structure activities and facilitate discussions that help students make connections among mathematical concepts, various types of representations, and real-world contexts. In addition to the content of number and operations, young, elementary students are to delve into the study of geometry, data, and early algebraic concepts. There is much greater emphasis on mathematical *understanding* in several mathematical realms, in addition to computational fluency.

To achieve a practice that embodies these ambitious goals, teachers must develop a qualitatively different and significantly richer understanding of mathematics than most now possess. They must come to see learning as the result of students' active efforts to make things comprehensible for themselves, and they must come to recognize common places where children need to stop and work through conceptual issues implicated in the mathematics to be learned. Teachers must acquire new pedagogical habits and routines, and where school systems have adopted new mathematics programs to align with new goals, they must learn to use a new curriculum effectively. The demands on teachers are considerable.

Even where strong professional development programs are in place, translating new insights into classroom practice is a difficult, and often a frustrating, process. The many demands on teachers' time, conflicting district policies, and the pressure of standardized tests may all reduce the actual effect that professional development has on instruction. Implementation efforts may be put off indefinitely. Initial efforts that do not meet with instant success (the norm rather than the exception) are often abandoned. A more profound and longer-lasting impact can be realized when programs integrate classroom support with professional development.

In recognition of this, many school systems have created the position of *mathematics coach* or *mathematics specialist*. The mathematics coach provides regular classroom consultation offering support as changes are introduced into the classroom, sustaining teachers' learning in the context that matters most.

However, with a new role established in the school system, many new questions arise: When coaches enter a classroom, what do they look for and how do they interact with teachers and students? What and how do coaches communicate with teachers before and after lessons? What are the responsibilities of mathematics coaches? What authority do they have? With whom do they negotiate? And most important, what must a coach understand to coach effectively?

Cultivating a Math Coaching Practice is an important resource for coaches and their supervisors who ponder such questions. Filled with cases written by mathematics coaches, it provides images of coaches in classrooms, coaches in meetings with teachers, coaches in discussion with principals, and coaches sitting alone working on issues of their practice. And it suggests some answers.

First, coaches must understand that the practice of coaching requires thoughtful reflection and continued learning. They must be prepared to learn mathematics, analyze student thinking, examine curriculum, and consider alternative teacher moves.

Second, coaches must work on developing strategic moves for teacher learning: How do you bring teachers' attention to mathematics content, to significant aspects of student thinking, and to the impact of their actions in the classroom? How do you help teachers develop the skills and habits of preparing for a lesson, of eliciting student thinking, and of analyzing student work?

Third, coaches must navigate the administrative structures of a school. What structures are in place that provide teachers and coaches the opportunity to reflect together? What niches can be used to open up a space for communication between teacher and coach? How can a coach negotiate with school administrators to align structures and policies more closely with the goals for mathematics instruction?

Cultivating a Math Coaching Practice provides a mechanism to initiate the processes of learning, reflecting, and navigating required for effective coaching. That is, this book is material for the professional development of mathematics coaches and brings readers right into the heart of the central issues of practice. For new coaches, it will help them prepare for the situations they are about to confront. For experienced coaches, it will support them in deepening their practice, by helping them become more effective in their work. For coaches who meet together, *Cultivating a Math Coaching Practice* can support the development of a culture of collegial inquiry, sharing and discussing dilemmas that arise in their work. For those who read the book on their own, it provides a connection to the community of coaches engaged in this important enterprise.

Deborah Schifter
Education Development Center
October 2008

Acknowledgments

My heartfelt thanks go to the teachers, math coaches, math specialists, and math leaders across the country who have contributed to and helped shape all parts of this book. I especially appreciate the contributions of the Boston Public School elementary coaches with whom I spent many "growing" years and whose inquisitiveness, thoughtfulness, and tenacity I admire. To the generous and brave coach-authors from across the country whose work is represented in these chapters and whose writing has kept me company over the past three years, I thank you.

Linda Davenport, Liz Sweeney, Lisa Y., Carol, Arusha, Francesca, Nicole, Marisa, Nancy, Megan K–P, Virginia Bastable, Angie Stephens, and Kay Caruso, your contributions sing loud and clear. Deborah Schifter, Polly Wagner, and Jan Rook, it is your encouragement and your many kindnesses—and the wisdom you so freely share—that makes all the difference.

I am deeply indebted to the many years of support from ExxonMobil Foundation for the projects focused on cultivating case writing as a tool for professional development for coaching. This book also represents work supported by a National Science Foundation grant ESI-010228. Any opinions expressed herein are those of the author and do not necessarily represent the views of either Foundation.

PUBLISHER'S ACKNOWLEDGMENTS

Corwin gratefully acknowledges the contributions of the following reviewers:

Carl Ameen, Math Coach
Silvio Conte Community School
Pittsfiled, MA

Beth Skipper, PreK–3 Math Coach
National Council of Teachers of Mathematics (NCTM)

Jenny Sue Flannagan, Director of Martinson Center for Math
Virginia Beach City Public Schools, VA

Elizabeth Marquez, Math Assessment Specialist
Educational Testing Services

Elizabeth Alvarez, Citywide Math Coach
Colman Elementary School
Chicago, IL

Kathryn Chval, Assistant Professor of Mathematics Education
University of Missouri

About the Author

Amy Morse is a national leader in designing and providing professional development for math coaches and district leaders responsible for coaching programs. In 1997, Amy joined Education Development Center (EDC) where, as a project director, she works on teacher and coach development programs. In this capacity, she worked for many years with the Boston Public Schools Elementary Math Department to design and facilitate the professional development for the district's elementary math coaches. At present, she directs Professional Development for Math Coaching institutes for EDC's Math Leadership program (http://www.mathleadership .org). Amy travels extensively, working as a consultant to school districts in various stages of implementing a math coaching strategy and is the director of the Center for the Professional Development of Coaching and Math Leadership at EDC.

Introduction

As she walked down the hallway toward the fourth grade classroom, Polly glanced at her watch. Two minutes until the start of another classroom observation. She stops, hoists up onto her shoulder a book bag teeming with papers and curriculum materials, and turns to tell me one last thing.

"I explained to her," she said, "that it is a privilege to be in her classroom, to be with a teacher who cares so much about kids. I also told her that it took all the courage I could muster to tell her the truth.' I said, 'It isn't enough to love them and go page by page in the math book.' I continued, 'It's November, and we are going to have to work hard together to help you really understand the math you are teaching and to help your students learn more deeply.'"

Polly hesitated again as she reached the classroom door. "Sometimes it's a thrill to be a coach, and sometimes it's so hard I just want to break down and cry—right in the middle of a grade-level meeting. Sometimes I really nail it, and other times I leave wishing I had listened more carefully. But"—she smiled—"I keep coming back."

As I put my hand out to say my thanks for allowing me to shadow her for the morning, she held my hand and said softly, "Sometimes, I am stunned by how so very real this work is."

Over the past decade, I have listened carefully to hundreds of stories of coaching. Stories, such as Polly Wagner's, that were written and shared in formal district professional development settings and stories told in short bursts in hallway conversations. Stories written as a way to think through puzzling circumstances or to view, with a coach lens, a classroom math investigation . . . stories recounted with a sense of wonder or in a voice of despair in coach meetings, in chopped sentences and phrases online on listservs, and in large group gatherings such as math and coaching conferences. Each of these descriptions of coaching has engaged me enormously: I have developed a huge appetite for understanding this very intersection of learning where coaching is enacted, in this new form of on-site math professional development support for adults.

For many years, I have worked with coaches and with those who are responsible for organizing coaching programs and system structures that support coaching efforts. I have had the privilege of working on a weekly basis with elementary math coaches, over the course of many school years, as they navigated uncharted waters. It is their work, and the wisdom and generosity of their district leaders, which set this collection of coaching materials in motion.

Math coaching is still relatively undefined. While successfully instantiated in some sites, it is in its infancy in education. Overall, we do not have a shared vision for coaching goals, for what the role implies—nor are we yet clear about the characteristics of the structures that make coaching an effective strategy for developing classrooms where children are deeply engaged in, and successful in learning, important mathematics. We do not have a clear sense of guidelines regarding the intersection of coaching and supervision. In fact, across a single district, we might even have different titles for the same job—or common titles for jobs with an entirely different focus.

We do know that coaching is not simply "fixing" or "advice-giving." Indeed, one coach describes, with chagrin, the tendency to fall back on "seeking something to change and telling the teacher to change it."

Coaching *is* a matter of listening intently in classrooms to articulate students' ideas in ensuing discussion with the teacher and, at the same time, facilitating an exchange with the teacher that helps him sort out what he intends for students to learn, how his students' ideas intersect with those mathematical ideas, and then, the implications for his next teaching moves and agenda. Coaching does not always occur after the math class is over; often, a coach is in a position to work with the teacher to examine the mathematics of the upcoming lesson, anticipate what is likely to occur, and make plans for how to construct and teach the lesson with math goals and his own students' learning in mind.

To be well prepared to offer this level of support, collaboration, and guidance, a coach needs to understand her role deeply and engage frequently in opportunities that effectively build the knowledge that is required for enacting that role.

Given the rapid growth of coaching in schools, this is a very exciting time! We are just learning what coaches know, or need to know, and how they "get there" in terms of coaching practice and, then, what promotes the continued development of a coach's work. There is much to be learned by observing coaching, collecting data about the ways coaching strategies function to serve teachers and students, and by listening carefully to coaches as they describe their challenges, insights, and ways they respond in their work.

Cultivating a Coaching Practice is a contribution to the effort to both strengthen and deepen coaching work. This professional development material includes math activities, focus questions for discussion, planning activities, extensive facilitator notes, and, most importantly, cases of practice authored by coaches. These authentic stories, recounted in the voices of novice and of experienced practitioners, provide us with a rich and complex landscape of images of coaching and learning.

Working with these materials allows us to explore and study significant principles and themes of practice that lie at the heart of math coaching. Selected from hundreds of cases, in these episodes and journals surface coaching themes typical across urban or suburban settings, across schools that represent a range of success with regard to student achievement, and across math curriculum programs. In using these materials, you will have an opportunity to carefully think through the implications of these themes for coaching within your own site and at your own level of experience.

THEMES OF COACHING

The cases and related activities in this book relate to the big ideas of coaching and what is entailed in successfully developing and supporting a strong math program in schools. The job of coaching is multilayered, engaging an assortment of individuals in a variety of district positions, and it requires leadership that is firmly grounded in mathematics and in the fundamental belief that learners have mathematical ideas. As teachers become teacher leaders and take on responsibilities outside of their classrooms, they discover a new vantage point from which to understand what is learned in math class and the very way learning and teaching works. The cases in this book relate to the following themes:

Learning Mathematics

Coaches encounter new math ideas through their careful observation and analysis of student learning and through the same observation and analysis of teacher learning.

Authority

Authority in coaching is a powerful aspect of enacting the role. Negotiating issues of authority and leadership and building relationships for collaborative work requires skills that, for many, develop over time.

Focusing on Mathematics

It's about the mathematics—coaches facilitate complex discussions with adults that require skills in maintaining a focus on mathematics, math learning, students' and teachers' math ideas, and math teaching practice.

Strategically Aligning Coaching Goals With District Structures

Coaches are charged with identifying opportunities and structures for aligning their coaching moves with their goals for teacher and student learning.

DEVELOPING A REPERTOIRE OF COACHING MOVES

To meet the needs of the different constituents with whom coaches work—and the varied entry places of these people—coaches need to develop skills for considering a range of moves and models of coaching based on a growing understanding of the mathematics in the classroom and the ways teachers learn and teach it.

Analyzing School Contexts and Learning Goals

Coaches build understandings of what it means to analyze and articulate school contexts well enough to develop workable goals for schools—and of what is entailed in differentiating coaching based on the school particular and the teachers and administrators in it.

Building Collaborative Relationships in Support of Learning Goals

Learning how to bring others in, to be successful in creating opportunities and invitations that align both with school collaborators' skills and potential with astute coaching goals is a foundation of the leadership skills coaches cultivate.

Each of these themes is surfaced through the case scenarios in this book. As you delve into the particular issues in your coaching site, the discussions and insights that grow out of understanding more deeply the themes and principles of the role will help guide your work in thoughtful and meaningful ways.

HOW TO USE THIS BOOK

Cultivating a Math Coaching Practice provides resources for 12 to 14 sessions that vary in length from two to four hours. The book is separated into two sections; the first section includes 12 chapters for participants' reading, so each participant will need her own copy of the book. The second section is a facilitator guide that describes timed agendas and offers detailed support for facilitation of every session. Successful facilitation of the cases and related activities is predicated on the idea that facilitators carefully prepare for each session by reading the case, doing the math activity or planning activity, and writing out responses to each of the focus questions. Engaging with the materials this way is essential for anticipating participants' responses and taking ownership of the session agendas.

Materials

A set of materials for each session includes:

- *Case*—Authored by a math coach, the case provides an authentic account of coaching practice, dilemmas, and insights. A Case Description and a Notes to the Reader preface the case and orient the reader to the case themes.
- *Session Activity*—Each case is accompanied by a related Math Activity designed to strengthen coach math content knowledge or a Planning Activity designed to support thoughtful consideration of next steps in one's coaching practice.
- *Focus Questions Activity*—Small- and whole-group discussions focus inquiry on important elements of each case.
- *Facilitation Notes*—Written for the session leader, these chapter-by-chapter notes provide bulleted session goals, case descriptions, session overviews, detailed agendas, and practical facilitation support. In addition, Facilitation Notes include specific examples of participants' questions, responses to cases and activities, and anecdotes describing facilitator responses.

Organization

The material in this book is designed to complement a variety of professional development settings. Time allotted for district coach professional development varies in length and in intervals between meetings; the flexibility of these materials is meant to address this. Each chapter represents a stand-alone session; it is not essential to move through the book chapter by chapter. The order of chapters set forth in the Table of Contents, while representative of the trajectory of a developing coach practice, is not set in stone. A facilitator can choose the order of cases in response to a particularly relevant topic at play at his site. Reading the case descriptions (prefacing each chapter and repeated in the chapter Facilitator Notes) and related Facilitator Notes will provide useful information with which to make these types of decisions. For instance, Chapter 8, Cultivating Relationships with Administrators and Other Leadership Colleagues, focuses on inviting collaborators into the work, communicating with the principal, and articulating learning goals for the teachers in the school. This material is most appropriate to use after the school year has begun—perhaps midyear—when coaches have had time to determine schoolwide coaching goals, establish relationships with teachers and administration, and are surefooted enough to determine an agenda for leadership and collaboration with others. And yet, you may be working in a context where these relationships and goals have been established in the first year or previous years of coaching; in that case, it may make sense to begin a new school year with this chapter. The first six chapters include Math Activities that support establishing a practice that includes engaging in mathematics with colleagues and other teachers, while chapters that include Planning Activities may be most effective after new or experienced coaches become familiar with new school sites and have begun to develop goals for their work.

Whether you choose to begin by examining the issues highlighted in Chapter 1 or with Chapter 6, the accompanying Facilitator Notes will provide a comprehensive guide for every part of each session. To provide structure for the participant, the case is placed at the front of each chapter followed by Focus Questions and a Planning or Math Activity. Some session agendas, however, have participants begin with the Activity as groundwork for reading the case that is the central focus of the session. The Facilitator Notes describe the order of the agendas, the logic of how each session unfolds, and guidance for leading discussions.

These materials represent central issues in coaching and are offered as rich territory for discussion, reflection, and planning. These materials are designed to be accessible and challenging for novice teacher leaders with little coaching experience and also for practicing coaches with skill and knowledge gained over many years. The authors of these cases offer stories of practice to be mined for new perspectives and ideas at many levels.

If you are a coach using this book without benefit of formal group and facilitated sessions, you will find it helpful to read the Case Description and the set of Focus Questions before you read each case. This pre-reading will draw your attention to the themes and issues highlighted in the chapter and provide a useful orientation to the material.

The authentic voice of the coach runs through this book. We have a great deal to learn, still, about this new arena of teaching and learning, and so it makes good sense to listen with an attentive ear to coach voices telling their stories. Here, we return once again to Polly's voice as she describes the role of coaching—the practice this book is designed to cultivate.

A coach's role is to support teachers to be the best practitioners they can be, to watch for and share moments of brilliance from both teachers and students, to be curious about the mathematical ideas students and teachers have, to figure out ways of engaging in those ideas with teachers in dynamic ways—to push and to listen at the same time, to recognize and acknowledge the privilege of entering a teacher's classroom, to hold steady to what you believe is right for children and the school—even when it's hard.

1

Observing, Studying, Analyzing, Planning

Preparing to Coach

Chapter Elements

✦ Case: Moving Between Models

✦ Math Activity: Models, Fractions, and Percents

✦ Focus Questions Activity

CASE DESCRIPTION

The Moving Between Models case offers an example of a reflective practitioner who studies the curriculum, the central mathematical idea in the classroom, the students' work as they engage in a new concept, and the implications for her coaching. Lila, the author, wrote the case midway into her second year as an elementary school coach. Specifically, she raises questions, both mathematical and pedagogical, about the relationship between fractions and percents and the issues that influence children's reasoning as they begin to work with ways to represent rational numbers.

The coach uses her case writing to help her learn more about the mathematics she encounters in the classroom and, at the same time, to help her analyze her next coaching moves and supports for the teacher.

The case offers an interesting perspective on the role of coaching. All coaching does not happen in the moment; certainly, there is a significant amount of preparation coaches undertake for individual classroom visits and meetings or workshops. The case raises a question for discussion: What is the nature of *preparing to coach?*

NOTES TO THE READER

As you read the case, write questions or comments in the margins and note the line numbers of sentences or paragraphs that interest you or raise questions for you.

Case 1	Author: Lila

Moving Between Models

1   In the past week, I've been in two fifth grade classrooms where the students are working through the ideas in the new curriculum unit. Both visits brought up a lot of questions for me about the ways students (and adults) think about fractions and percents and how they move between
5   different models for these ideas.

Ms. Henry's class has had very little experience with this math curriculum prior to this year, and there is quite a range of understanding of fractions. She started off the math class by asking the students about the relationship between fractions and percents.

10   "Both talk about parts of a whole thing; it's just different ways to describe different parts of a whole thing," said Teddy.

"Both need to have equal parts that you cut them into and with percents there has to be 100 little parts," said Leonardo.

"We are learning about both of them," said Kayla.

15   Later, when we asked them to think about fractions that are the same as 60%, many said $\frac{60}{100}$. No one offered another fraction that represented the same amount. Many students could also write $\frac{27}{100}$ as 27%. I kept in mind that these are easily mimicked responses as the students began working on the day's story problems—ones that required more complex thinking
20   and synthesis of ideas. The students' work with these problems was pretty widely variant and so interesting.

For one problem, students were asked to consider a class of 40 students, groups of which leave the classroom to do different things. One section of the problem says that 10 students left the class to go help first
25   graders, and students are asked to calculate "what percent left the room?"

Ms. Henry's students' answers ran the gamut from $\frac{10}{10}$ to 10% to 25%. Similarly, although many students knew that if five students were absent that meant $\frac{5}{40}$ was absent, many said it meant that 5% were absent.

I became really intrigued. What accounts for the range of responses? And what about the equating of the numerator of a fraction with its percent equivalent, regardless of the denominator? What are these students' understandings and images for fractional parts and percents? How are their mental models of these ideas linked to their responses? What do they need help understanding in order to link, with more consistent success, the notions of fractions and percents?

All of this was still swirling around in my head a few days later when I spent some time in Mrs. Mittal's room at another school. The fifth grades in this school are pretty far behind in the pacing guide, so the session we saw was just the second activity. At this point in the unit, students calculate the shaded portion of a grid of one hundred squares and express that portion in terms of fractions and percents.

Because Mrs. Mittal was opening her classroom to several third and fourth grade teachers, she facilitated a previsit meeting for the visitors. Mrs. Mittal gave each of us a copy of her map of the session; she planned to start with some review warm-up material that included having students find factor pairs of 42.

In observing this class and, in particular, thinking about the work of Amari, one of Mrs. M's most vocal students, some ideas about the fractions and percents work kind of came together for me. So I want to begin by outlining Amari's work with the finding the factor pairs of 42 because it raised some interesting questions for me later on in the class. The students were doing this work on their whiteboards that they wave in the air to signal that they're done. When it was time to share, the class listed most of the factors pairs, including (6, 7) which were then scribed on the front board. Mrs. Mittal called for any other pairs.

"3 and 14!" Amari cried.

"How did you know?" Mrs. Mittal asked.

"Because if you have, like 6 and 7 . . . like six groups of seven things, well, it makes sense that if I had half as many groups I've got to have twice as many things in them to equal the same amount!"

Amari was loving her idea. Other students were confused, and Amari explained again. One student expressed frustration in not understanding the idea Amari discovered and was applying, and Mrs. Mittal suggested the two get together over break time to talk about it.

We moved into the beginning of the fraction and percent activity, where the students play a sort of rigged up game of "Guess My Rule" and brainstorm ways to express how many of the six students in the front of the room fit Mrs. Mittal's "rule" (students with zippers). They listed the following on the board:

3 out of 6

3

6

50%

Amari stared at the list, pretty distressed. "That's wrong," she said. "It's 3%, no, 30% . . ." but her voice trailed off.

"Why do you say that?" her teacher asked.

"Because it's 3 out of 6, and that's 30%, I mean $\frac{3}{6}$ is half, so $\frac{3}{6}$ is 30 . . ." Her voice trailed off as her own thinking started to feel "off" to her.

"Go back," said Mrs. Mittal. "Think about what you just said."

"$\frac{3}{6}$ is half . . . I see. We said that $\frac{1}{2}$ is 50%." Amari smiled and sat back, satisfied.

Way more happened after this, but I started to think about the flow of Amari's thinking. She understood 3 out of 6 as half, and she knew that half was 50%. But what was her understanding of 50%? While she seemed to understand that half could also *be written* as 50%, this feels different from understanding that $\frac{3}{6}$ is *equal to* 50%. So what models of these ideas were happening in her mind? Were they linked or still too disparate for her to move easily from one to another?

It made me think a lot about the different models of fraction/fractional ideas they're working with and that are possible to think about when working with the idea of portions. When Teddy mentioned his thought that fractions and percents both deal with parts of a whole, his thinking seemed based on an area model of portions—he was cutting up a square. The students have also established an area model for percent—a grid of a hundred squares (at least Ms. Henry's have; Mrs. Mittal's will be). They've worked with the notion of a set as well (How many students out of six are wearing stripes?) and used fractions to represent that. And they link that kind of idea to percents, but not necessarily because they see that grid of one hundred squares as a collection or set. In other words, I think it takes some time to apply that square area model to the notion of a set. What does it take to really see the link between the two?

I'm wondering if there's a step there that takes a lot of processing for students who do not really believe that fractions can refer to portions of groups of whole objects as well as to a piece of one whole object. How do students make the transition between an area model of a square of one hundred things and the thought of each of those squares representing one or part of a collection or a chance or whatever? How do they move between the notion of a whole as a discrete object to be sliced and a set of unsliced objects? What's in place that lets them see that $\frac{3}{6}$ is 50% because it can be seen as part of a set as well as part of a whole? This becomes weirder when I think that this can feel as if we are either extrapolating the set of 6 to a mythical set of 100, or subdividing the 6 into smaller bits so that we have 100 bits.

This makes me think of numerical ideas and multiplication, where we are also asking students to make that link between an area model and a collection—that a row of 4 squares in a 4 × 6 array actually could represent the legs of an elephant and that one square thus is representing one leg.

The notion of multiplication and manipulating groups was so clear to Amari. What led her to track so easily *the groups/number in a group* idea but have trouble when considering a collection and a portion of it? How do these ideas relate to quantity? What is it that she understands about quantity and constancy in the multiplication that isn't in yet in place with the "portion out of 100" idea? What makes a student ready to see that?

How do students keep track of the nature of the whole and move between different ideas of them?   125

It seems important to consider whether the array model is one that Amari uses when working with multiplication as she starts this work with percents. If not, then how *does* she think about it? And if not, is Amari's muddlement knit to the fact that her models of number and numeracy and   130
multiplication are different? Is it that bags-of-candies kind of model that many people use? Four bags with three candies each/three bags with four candies each? If Amari doesn't use the array model for these ideas, it makes sense to me that she doesn't immediately knit the ideas of fractions and percents together.

So for Amari, as well as for the students in Ms Henry's class, what are   135
the implications for teaching if this is the case? What if the students haven't yet internalized/understood the idea of percents as a collection of 100, or if they are thinking of it in terms of a cut-up whole into a 100 but haven't yet thought about each square as representing one thing? Is all of it made more complicated by the seeming arbitrariness of considering per-   140
cents only in terms of 100 after the relative freedom of considering any number of parts to a whole when they worked with fractions? How does it all link to the idea of quantity and counting and tracking? What and how will the teachers and I learn in the coming weeks about students' models and the implications for, or influence on, students' reasoning?   145

As I think about these questions, I realize that they'll inform my next moves as a coach as well. Because, right now, I am thinking that an essential step in building an understanding of fractions is for kids to have ample and explicit opportunity to make connections between different fraction contexts and models, to compare them to make sense of the relationships   150
between them. How do elements of one model relate to elements of another? How do fractions arranged on a line relate to a set of fraction strips? How is 25% percent on the grid like ¼ on the number line? Like ¼ of 100 cookies? How are they different? Because it is in such acts of comparison, I believe, that generalization is possible; that is, I believe that com-   155
paring models and situations helps kids make sense of the essence of fractions even as they come to understand the different contexts for their use. And for teachers to best support their kids in understanding these ideas, they need to feel comfortable with them as well.

So, as a coach, I need to make sure the teachers I work with have ample   160
opportunities to think about these ideas—in fraction *and* in whole number contexts. ("How is using the array like skip counting on the hundreds chart?") This means that I'll need to make strategic use of looking at student work sessions, perhaps asking for specific samples or even bringing in work from other grade levels that scaffold and support such think-   165
ing. I also would love to facilitate teacher visits such as the one to Ms. Mittal's room, where the kids' thinking gives us so much fodder for thought. I can also envision using grade-level meetings to work through activities in the math unit and make connections between them, as well as math activities designed specifically for adult learners that invite teachers   170
to make sense of the ideas.

But I also know that it is so important for me to hold a longer view of this work in mind; it's only our first year working together with this

175   curriculum, and new understanding and ensuing shifts in pedagogy take time to take hold. But isn't this process what it's all about, for our students and for ourselves? All of us are learning.

Isn't that the best part of this work?

Case 1   Moving Between Models

Math Activity: Models, Fractions, and Percents

Here are a few math problems that help illustrate ideas in this case. Think carefully about your responses to these problems, note ideas you are relying on to solve them and draw models or representations on paper. The idea is to pay close attention to the mental images you construct that help you to solve these problems.

1. Jeffrey is showing 8 horses at the horse show in Northampton. He will have 5 of them in a jumping competition. What models might describe the fraction that represents the number of Jeffrey's horses in the jumping competition?

2. What percent of Jeffrey's horses are in the jumping competition? Describe a model that reflects that percent answer.

3. Jeffrey will bring a bag of oats to feed 3 horses at the show; the others eat only hay. One bag of oats is enough to feed 16 horses.
   a. For Jeffrey's 3 horses, how much of the bag will he use up?
   b. What are your ideas about modeling this fractional amount?
   c. Considering the same expressed as a percent, what model represents the amount?

Case 1   Moving Between Models

Focus Questions Activity

1. In lines 10–28 at the beginning of class, the coach describes a variety of student responses to translating fractions to percents. Consider these responses and discuss the logic of these early ideas.

2. Consider the student, Amari. To put Amari's struggles into context, the coach describes the flexibility of her thinking about multiplicative relationships. Refer to lines 49–60, and in your own words, describe Amari's mathematical idea. How general is the idea she states?

3. Amari appears confused about whether $\frac{3}{6}$ is equal to 50% or 3% or 30%. What is your interpretation of the coach's analysis?

4. Consider in your own words the questions the coach is contemplating in lines 102–134. What ideas about fractions and percents do students need to have in place to "move between models"?

5. What questions and insights does this case raise as you think about Amari's sorting out of numerical relationships and future work for Amari and her classmates?

6. Consider the coaching implications for Lila and these questions about your own coaching context:

   • What mathematical ideas and what pedagogical ideas do you think are important for teachers to work on?
   • What structures or opportunities in your own setting might allow for coaching with regard to these ideas?
   • What resources might you use for planning your coaching work with this teacher or with groups of teachers?

2

Discerning and Responding

Coaching in Real Time

Chapter Elements

+ Case: Analyzing Multiplication
+ Math Activity: How Do You Know?
+ Focus Questions Activity

CASE DESCRIPTION

Lisa, the coach-author, first encounters a fourth grade classroom where the students are no longer working on the school curriculum; rather, they spend the math class hour working on drill and practice. She listens carefully to the teacher who expresses her dismay at her students' work and the tensions she feels about the upcoming state test. The teacher's concerns have moved her to revert to classroom work that focuses on solving many problems with little, if any, emphasis on explaining or exploring reasoning and development of strategies for solving problems. Rather than intervene, Lisa takes it all in as she weighs her coaching choices. Through the description of her coach day, Lisa presents an image of a coach who sees her role in multiple dimensions. In this case, she describes a teachers' meeting she designs based on what she's observed and then skillfully facilitates at the close of the same school day. The case sheds light on how a coach might perceive her role with respect to teachers' learning.

NOTES TO THE READER

In this session, first you will have a chance to work on the Math Activity (page 20) in a small group as a way to preview the math issues raised in this episode of coaching. Next, when you read the case, write questions or comments in the margins and note line numbers of sentences or paragraphs that interest you or raise questions for you.

Case 2	Author: Lisa

Analyzing Multiplication

1   "No, we haven't started the new math unit yet. And in addition to doing that unit, I have to focus on calculation, Lisa." I could see the tension in Mrs. Martin's face, and her voice had a stressed, anxious tone. Last time we met, we'd had a conversation infused with humor, and we looked at
5   students' work with eager interest. What had happened here? My guess? It's that state test looming.

Mrs. Martin looked at me and said with some measure of despair, "My students can't get beyond a score of 2 because they make calculation errors. We do the state test in math in a little over a month, and I have to
10   get them prepared."

I thought to myself, "Isn't that what the new math unit is going to do for your students? Why are they now doing just drill sheets on calculating in multiplication and division?" Suddenly, the students are giving over their own strategies and relying solely on the standard algorithm. On the
15   drill sheet, space for their work is limited. It would be hard to describe any other solution strategy given the way the problems on the sheet are set up. Yet, posted around the room are many examples of the students' use of cluster problems for supporting multiplication—evidence of more thoughtful work than what I see today. I remember that in the past, I've
20   heard Mrs. Martin comment that students seem reluctant to use strategies using landmark numbers when they are in testing situations. From the work she had her students doing, it appeared that panic has set in. I wonder if the test anxiety she is experiencing stems from a lack of trust in the strength of her students' thinking. Or could it be that she's not so sure of
25   how to make the connections between the strategic thinking her students have developed and the rigor of solving test problems? If students are making calculation errors that undermine their success on the test, how do we get underneath that and meet it? What do I do to support Mrs. Martin and her students in the moment—and what really lies underneath this
30   sudden shift back to old ways of working with mathematics? In this exchange and in this classroom visit, I choose to listen and observe. I know I'll be seeing Mrs. Martin at a math meeting later today.

From Mrs. Martin's fourth grade class, I go next door to fifth grade. I can feel the excitement in the air! The class is working on an activity from the number strand module. The activity is in the section on multiplication and division. I join the class as students are sharing their strategies for determining if 27×8 will equal more than 100, more than 200, or more than 300. The teacher has recorded problems students used to help think about this. For instance, Manuel offered that 20×8 would show that 27×8 must be more than 100. Mr. Gordon recorded April's suggestion that 25×8 would show that it must be more than 200. Other similar problems had been recorded on the board. During the discussion, Mr. Gordon reminded students that at this point he wasn't looking for the exact answer to 27×8, rather their sense of how large it is. The sharing of strategies and ways of thinking about the problems continued. There were so many helpful problems recorded on the board that by the time Mr. Gordon asked them to find the exact answer, students had tools to show many ways of finding that $27 \times 8 = 216$.

He then asked the fifth graders to consider 27×13. Is that more than 100? More than 500? Students talked to their partners and worked individually to decide and discuss their reasoning. Many students talked about 10 groups of 27 being 270 so 13 groups would have to be over 100 but under 500. Several then started thinking about how much 3 more 27s would be and determining multiples of 27. In determining that 27×13 was going to be less than 500, Tyrone said, "Since 8 groups of 27 is equal to 216, then 27×13 would have to be under 500." As he continued to talk, he wrote his developing argument on the board. He wrote,

Since $16 \times 27 = $ double (8×27) and $2(8 \times 27) = 2 \times 216$, it's under 500 because it is just a bit more than 2×200.

The students raised their thumbs to indicate that they followed Tyrone's reasoning and agreed.

Mr. Gordon now gave the class a problem with two possible ways to estimate a reasonable answer. The students were to determine, without calculating, which one would yield the closer amount. Here is what Mr. Gordon wrote on the board:

Problem: 47×32 Which is closer? 40×32 or 50×32?

Partners discussed this together. Hands were in the air. Students were eager to share their findings. There was widespread agreement in the class that 50×32 would be closer. Megan said 50×32 was closer because it was only three 32s away from the actual problem instead of seven 32s away in 40×32. More students offered related comments, and the whole class concurred that Megan was right.

The next problem the teacher offered resulted in controversy. Again, the students had to choose which would be closer, but they found this set more challenging.

Problem: 39×22 Which is closer? 40×22 or 39×20

Many were sure that 39×20 was closer; I was so caught up in the discussion that I didn't record all the commentary. Mr. Gordon looked at me as if to say he was unsure where to go with this and then asked me for some assistance. In the moment, I wondered, was it that he was unsure of the correct answer himself or was he wondering what the next step should be? I reminded the students that in many of their previous explanations to problems they had talked about *groups* in justifying their answers. I asked them to think about the idea of groups now.

Together, we worked through the problems; we looked at how much larger 40×22 is in terms of groups of 22 and how much smaller 39×20 is in terms of groups of 39. This direction helped many students reconsider their first response. There was no time to check in with everyone because today's class time was over. Mr. Gordon and I talked briefly then about coming back to this tomorrow and working on similar problems offered on the page:

Problem: 312×9. Which is closer, 312×10 or 300×9?

Problem: 123×38. Which is closer, 123×40 or 120×38?

This work seemed to generate lots of energy in the class and helped them see the power in looking closely at multiplication. The last problems really challenged them in terms of thinking about groups and how the relationship between the factors affected the product. It seemed to be work right on target for developing ideas about the operation.

If only Mrs. Martin could have seen this. So many of Mr. Gordon's students had been in her fourth grade class last year. These students are now using landmark numbers and "easier," related multiplication problems to solve harder problems. I feel sure the experiences in fourth grade helped build this ease and flexibility.

Our common planning time meeting for Grades 3 through 5 teachers was to take place in the afternoon and seemed an excellent opportunity to analyze multiplication ideas together. Both Mrs. Martin and Mr. Gordon would be present. The six teachers gathered for our 40-minute planning time in the lunchroom at 2:00. I had been rethinking my agenda for that meeting since I'd been to the fourth and fifth grade classes earlier in the day—especially since my visit to Mrs. Martin's class. So we started our meeting by looking at some of the "Is it true? Is it equivalent?" items from the extra 30-minute packets developed by the math department. I deliberately chose a few items from third, fourth, and fifth grades that focus on items dealing with multiplication or division. I felt we needed to consider reasoning with groups.

The teachers were very engaged. The problems we worked on led to comments about the importance of understanding the idea of groups in multiplication.

After that, I had them look at some questions dealing with multiplication from their own fourth and fifth grade curriculum units. From the fourth grade,

Problem: 56×4. Is it more than 100? More than 200? Why?

Problem: 28×15. Is it more than 100? More than 500? Why?

For the problem, 28×15, the teachers raised ideas about how 25×20 or 10×30 or 10×28—along with an approximation of half of 10×28—could help students answer the questions about estimating the product.

And for fifth grade work, I thought it would be a good idea to look at the problem that had challenged Mr. Gordon's class earlier in the day:

Problem: 39×22. Which is closer, 40×22 or 39×20?

Teachers thought for a while. There was some discussion. Then, Mr. Meads shared that 40×22 must be closer, but he had trouble verbalizing why. There was a long pause in the discussion, so I asked the teachers to think again about groups and how each problem changed the groups from the original problem.

We worked together to determine that 40×22 was different from 39×22 by 1 group of 22 and that 39×20 was different by 2 groups of 39. This was much the same work that we had done in the fifth grade class. Then, just as we were about to wrap up the meeting, Ms. Birt, a fourth grade teacher, suggested that an estimate would be closer if the factor changed by a smaller number.

I was glad to hear Ms. Birt's idea. Working with a hypothesis like hers would give us a way to examine something more than individual problems. It would give us ways of talking about multiplication beyond "in this particular instance," and now, I really wanted the teachers to continue this investigation. Our time was up, and the library was soon to be used by the afterschool program. Because I have a chance to meet with this same group for about 20 minutes on Thursday before our school leadership meeting, I repeated Ms. Birt's statement and asked the teachers to reflect on whether they thought this statement would always be true. I wanted to be certain that our session would end with a question about this idea—and not with the notion that this was, in fact, true. Specifically, I suggested that they consider whether the size of the groups would affect her hypothesis, "Let's say," I continued, "If you were dealing with some large groups." We agreed to try some problems on our own, and we'd each bring sample problems on Thursday. The only one of these teachers I'll see before then is Mr. Meads. I'm glad to know the two of us can spend a bit of our planning time working on a couple of these kinds of problems together.

As the teachers headed out, Mr. Gordon and I had a chance to linger for a few minutes with Mrs. Martin. He and I shared a bit about the work his students had done today. She smiled as she heard about the way her students from last year are now using facts and numbers they are comfortable with to help them do more difficult multiplication problems. Following the work we'd just done together, our brief conversation about her former students seemed to relieve some anxiety about the upcoming test. I hope it gave her more confidence in believing that working in this way with students would yield sturdier thinking about multiplication than taking them through pages of drill and practice. I knew there was more we wanted to discuss about developing fluency with math facts, but as always, we would come together again, and it was time pack up my books and bring this coaching day to a close.

Case 2	Analyzing Multiplication

Math Activity: How Do You Know?

Consider the following problems by paying close attention to the ideas you rely on to think through the questions—rather than focusing on solving for the exact answer. Write a brief explanation of your thinking and include any diagrams or other models that helped you sort out or illustrate your ideas. Solve each problem, and then share in your group before moving on to the next.

1. 13×62

    Is it more than 500? More than 700? How do you know?

2. 39×22

    Which is closer, 40×22 or 39×20?

3. 312×9

    Which is closer, 312×10 or 300×9?

4. How many eggs are in 38 dozen? Which is a closer estimate, 40×12 or 10×38?

Case 2   Analyzing Multiplication

Focus Questions Activity

Exploring the Math

1. Mr. Gordon has asked the students to reflect on the size of 27×8. How do Manuel's and April's responses 20×8 and 25×8 relate to 27×8?

2. Consider Tyrone's argument about 27×13 in lines 53–59. What ideas does Tyrone draw upon to develop his reasoning?

3. In lines 136–140, Ms. Birt offers a generalization about the problems. Referring to the choice between two estimates, she suggests, "An estimate is going to be closer if the factor changes by a smaller number." Just as the teachers in the case are asked to do, explore Ms. Birt's idea. Is this always true? What do you learn?

4. The coach capitalizes on the idea of groups as a way of focusing student—and teacher—attention. Looking ahead to the mathematics students will encounter, what's mathematically relevant about this work? Or similarly, what are the ideas that come up in first and second grade that support these kinds of ideas?

Exploring Implications for Coaching

5. In lines 11–32, the coach is working to make sense of what's going on in Mrs. Martin's math class. For two years, the school has been using a curriculum that encourages strategic thinking based on conceptual understanding of the mathematics. Mrs. Martin has, until recently, been using the materials with her students. Consider possible implications for coaching given each of the different hypotheses Lisa describes.

6. Review the case and make note of line numbers that indicate actions and decisions Lisa makes in the varied contexts of her day. In your review, consider the implications for each of her coaching moves. She uses particular resources to support her agendas; in what ways do these choices matter?

7. Given this case, consider how Lisa might characterize her role and coaching responsibilities? How does Lisa's perception of her role affect the decisions and outcomes of her coaching throughout the day?

3

Strategic Coaching

Goal-Centered Modeling in the Classroom

Chapter Elements

+ Case: "It's 30 Less and 90 More": A Case About Listening to Children's Ideas

+ Math Activity: Angles and Angle Measurement

+ Focus Questions Activity

CASE DESCRIPTION

The case, written by an experienced elementary and middle school coach, describes teacher and coach interactions based on fourth grade geometry ideas and students' work in class. The coach negotiates the teacher's requests and expectations and considers her own goals for the teacher's learning. As she works to frame a coaching experience that will get at the heart of important ideas of teaching practice, in this case, she lays out her own beliefs about guiding principles of teaching and learning. It is from these beliefs that she devises a structure for her collaboration with the teacher in the geometry class. The case presents an opportunity to "peer in" closely at student work and to analyze the logic of students' ideas as they explore angles and measurement. The case also stands as an example of strategic coaching, by capturing an image of core elements of the role as they are enacted in a single math class.

NOTES TO THE READER

In this session, you will first have an opportunity to work with a small group on the Math Activity (page 32) that highlights the same ideas the students in this case are working on. Next, as you read the case, write questions or comments in the margins and note line numbers of sentences or paragraphs that interest you or raise questions for you.

Case 3	Author: Tina

"It's 30 Less and 90 More": A Case About Listening to Children's Ideas

1   Mr. Gallagher, a fourth grade teacher, is enthusiastic about mathematics and loves to teach. Fairly quickly though, I got the sense that while Mr. Gallagher is comfortable with his own mathematics, he seems to spend more time on his math *teaching* and less on his students' math *learning*. He

5   enjoys talking, and although he is enthusiastic, he can expend a lot of time and energy trying to keep control of the lesson. I think this is interesting; it is an interesting disconnect that also gives me a place to consider how to frame the goals I have for our work together. I thought about it for a while and began to see it as if I centered my work on my own coaching and

10   coaching strategies and left the teacher's ideas in the background. I could do this or that "thing" when I worked with Mr. Gallagher, but if the pedagogical "thing" isn't in relation to the mathematics of this classroom and this teacher, well, I don't think I've had much of any real effect.

   Mr. Gallagher can sometimes appear to be overwhelmed by the respon-
15   sibilities of preparing for and managing a fourth grade class. Perhaps, as a consequence, he rarely remembers I am scheduled to visit his class, even though we have set dates weeks ahead of time. To my chagrin, our meetings are often very much "of the moment" rather than guided by either of our long-range goals. No matter how hard I try to stay grounded, he initiates dis-
20   cussions with concerns that are peripheral to the classroom mathematics. I'm working on having the first word, but so often, he barges in late to a planned meeting already talking as he comes in the door. He might start off by talking about how other teachers do not like the curriculum or how the principal doesn't "get it" or that a parent misunderstood his math homework
25   assignment. I find myself fighting feeling scattered when I talk with him.

   Recently, in the hallway during an informal conversation about scheduling, Mr. Gallagher mentioned that he'd like to take a look at student work with me. This was a surprise, as he usually doesn't connect with what I might be able to do *with* him—in fact, getting to an agreement of what we might do in collaboration has been a stretch. In the moment, I sensed that he and I would come to this looking at student work with differing agendas. He would want me to look at it and agree that his students didn't get something and then tell him what resource or activity to do to "make it all work." And *I* would be coming at it as a way of studying his students, of getting a handle on what they were struggling or successful with, what logic they were using to solve problems, and what math ideas would be important to consider or questions to focus on in the next activities. I even wondered if he saw looking at student work as a way to separate himself from my view—in that, if we focused on the kids, he might not have to think about his teaching. In our discussions, he has been focused on thinking about the mechanics of the lesson, deciding when to chart ideas, complaining about how long the introduction of a lesson should be, wondering what to say when, worrying that he gets off track too easily, loving to go off track when necessary, questioning the scope and sequence, fighting with himself, and defending his decisions all within the same breath.

And so I decided to take this opportunity to reframe the discussion by centering on the students' ideas—while supporting the idea that his teaching influences the ways that students engage with the mathematical concepts. A goal I have for my work with Mr. Gallagher is to help him learn how to listen more carefully to students' ideas and to have those ideas inform his instruction. His interest in student work would make an excellent starting place. Now, we have a piece of work we can both sink our teeth into. I wondered aloud if we might talk longer and, as luck would have it, he had 10 minutes right then.

We moved into the empty teachers' room and sat down. I told him I thought looking at student work was a really important thing to do. He responded by asking if I would also model some lessons for him; he wanted to "watch me juggle the mechanics of the lesson so he could see how someone else would do it." I was impressed by his sincerity and his interest in helping his students. I thought carefully about how to support his enthusiasm and his request. While I was sitting with him, I considered how to proceed. If I modeled a lesson, he might focus on *what* I said and did rather than the reasons behind my choices. But I also thought I might be able to teach a class—one that would help him to focus on how students thought about the concepts embedded in the lesson rather than the structure of the lesson. In the moment, I suggested that rather than me modeling the lesson, he might launch the class and together we would make the rounds of students as they worked in pairs. I would be responsible for initiating discussion with students while they were working, and he could focus on the students' responses without having to also be responsible for doing or saying whatever would come next. He would be able to take his time to watch students develop strategies without having to hold everything it takes to teach a class. In effect, I wanted to "model" how to differentiate through the questions I posed, when I posed them, and how I paid attention to the responses. This idea appealed to him.

Mr. Gallagher and I met the following day (like clockwork—we are on to something!) to go over the upcoming lesson about 2-D geometry and angles. I asked him what he wanted the students to learn about the core mathematical focus of the activity he would be asking them to work on. This was a new kind of discussion for us. Usually, our discussions centered on how he wanted the lesson to unfold, so it wasn't surprising to me that he now had a hard time bringing words to what he wanted students to learn. Instead, he chose to respond by focusing on how his students had done on the last assessment question, "What is a quadrilateral?" He quickly became emotional in an angry sort of way—though it was hard to tell whether he was feeling his own failings or because the students had let him down. He said he had expected them to do much better; "Their responses were lackluster." He said, "And our classroom conversations had been so rich." He described his disappointment at the list-like nature of student responses and his dismay that the students' responses lacked depth.

I made a choice not to push on my original question. I asked if he had the student work at hand. He did. We spent the next few minutes, each of us quietly looking through the papers. I found myself much less concerned by the results than he seemed to be. In his teacher handbook are examples of benchmark work on this assessment—and to my eye, many of his students' work satisfied the mark.

"What had you hoped to see in the assessments?" I asked.

"Well," he said, "I, uh, I . . ." He fingered through the papers as his voice trailed off. I wondered again if the preamble about students and disappointment served as a way of keeping us from really delving into the mathematics he is teaching. He repeated that he was disappointed because his classroom discussions had felt rich (Had they been, I wondered, or had he spent much of the time talking and not really listening?), and now, this collection of work looked "well. . . perfunctory."

I decided to back up from the quadrilateral assessment question to ask, "What do you think your students would say about angles? What might they offer as explanations for what an angle is or how an obtuse angle is different than an acute angle?" I knew I was asking three questions in a row, but now it seemed like a strategy for keeping us in the math and on the point.

As he began to talk, I realized that he was talking about what he knew and what he wanted the students to know, but I wasn't sure that he had any data about his students' thoughts. I became intrigued with all the student ideas that weren't represented in our discussion. I wondered whether the students were confusing *lines* with *angles* as I had seen lots of students do in other classrooms. Would some students in his class, as is typical in early discussions of angles, describe a narrow acute angle drawn with long sides as larger then a short-sided obtuse angle? Had students had a chance to get up and actually simulate an angle or measure of a turn with their bodies? As the juxtaposition of his math knowledge and the silence of his students' voices became more apparent to me, I could feel an excitement about what we might find out together if we listened to his fourth graders. And, as we talked, Mr. Gallagher said aloud that he was realizing he didn't know the answers to these questions about his students. He turned to me and said that at the start of the class he wanted to find out what the students thought about angles. This would be his "launch."

Math Class

Later that morning, I walked into fourth grade just as the math class was about to begin. Mr. Gallagher shifted the students from the literacy lesson by saying, "Okay, here we go. It's time for math, and I have a question for you. "What is an angle? Who can tell me what an angle is?" He looked out over the class and waited while students put their books away and turned their attention to their next lesson. On the board, Mr. Gallagher had drawn a triangle and drawn an arc through one of the angles. (See Figure 3.1.)

Cara raised her hand and said confidently, "It's the part inside that fits. It's like . . . not the line part . . . it's the whole part inside."

Mr. Gallagher nodded and called on Michael. "It's that line and the part inside," he replied as he traced the triangle.

Next, Josh offered, "Umm . . . like, well, an angle is kind of like a closed shape." He points to the area within the arc that cut through one angle of the triangle. "With angles you'd want all the lines to touch. If you don't have angles your shape would look like this" (see Figure 3.2).

Figure 3.1　　　　　　　　　　　　　**Figure 3.2**

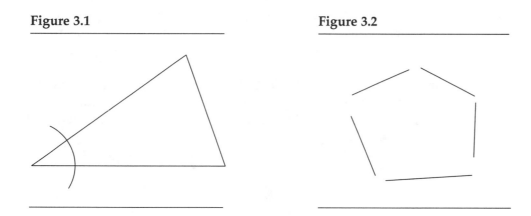

Mr. Gallagher was looking at his watch and checking the clock on the wall. He called on students, but as students talked, he called on one right after the other. They did not engage in an exchange of ideas or a building on each other's thoughts. It was interesting that even though he asked the question, it seemed hard for him to listen to his students' responses. Or maybe, I wondered, he just didn't know what to do with what he *was* listening to? Even so, one student, Mary, was listening to the other fourth graders. She raised her hand and offered a new idea.

"I don't think of it like that at all. I think it's in there (she draws a V shape in the air with her finger). I don't know if it has to be a part of the shape or not."

I am interested in the comments. I wonder if this might be the first time the students have talked about angle as an idea or even spoken out loud about how they interpret such an important concept. Some students seem to see an angle as the space between the lines: "it's the whole part inside." No students mention the length of sides or point to the sides as angles. No comments unearthed typical complex notions students often have about the length of lines in relation to the space inside. I wondered if this meant they were clear about these things or whether this short introduction hadn't been engaging enough to bring to the surface more complex ideas—or confusions. I wonder about Mary's comment. She seemed to be thinking about angles that aren't a part of a shape. I like how she references other kids' ideas, which alerted the others and me that she's listening and considering

130

135

140

145

150

155

160

their ideas. I wonder if Mr. Gallagher had pursued her idea, whether the
issue of measuring the turn of an angle could have been addressed.

165   Mr. Gallagher has said, before, that he tends to get annoyed with Mary and
has a hard time connecting to her because she is so "often out in left field."

After this brief discussion the students worked independently to form
90-degree angles with two or more shapes using brightly colored, plastic
polygons of different shapes and sizes. The polygon manipulative set is

170   made up of different sized rhombuses, rectangles, triangles, and hexagons.
As they worked, I moved from one pair of students to another. When
Mr. Gallagher wasn't dealing with other classroom issues, he was by my
side. Many students were able to identify 90-degree angles in right triangles and rectangles. Doing so, they pointed to the corner of the shape.

175   Their conception of angle still seemed ambiguous to me. Their efforts to
compose 90-degree angles with *two* or more angles with the plastic polygons revealed different ways of thinking about and interpreting this task.

Some students formed 90-degree angles by placing two right triangles
together in such a way that the negative space created a 90-degree angle

180   (Figure 3.3).

Many students put together shapes to create designs but seemed to
lose track of the angle they were trying to create (Figure 3.4). Perhaps, they
were getting interested in the colors and shapes the polygons formed.

Figure 3.3

Figure 3.4

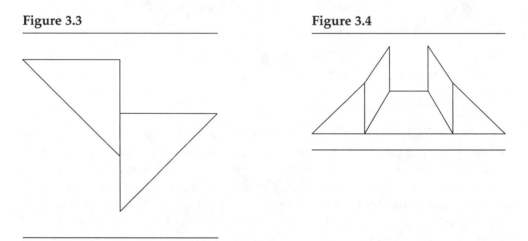

Others had a hard time seeing whether the angle was smaller or larger

185   than 90 degrees (Figures 3.5 and 3.6). Some knew what they had created
didn't measure 90 degrees, but they couldn't distinguish whether it was
smaller or larger than 90 degrees. I wondered whether they were getting
confused by which angle to focus on, the inscribed angle (Figure 3.5) or the
exterior (or supplemental) angle (Figure 3.6).

Figure 3.5

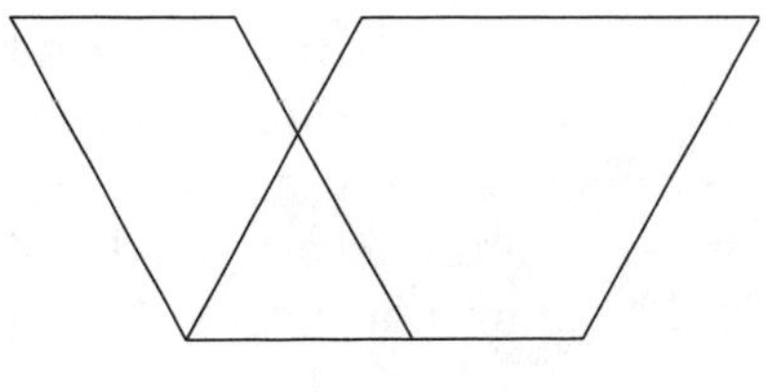

Figure 3.6

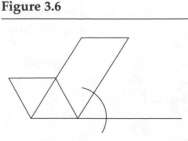

Bobby, in particular, seemed to have difficulty composing the right angle. His partner made two different angles. One used a rhombus with a triangle (Figure 3.7), while another used the same rhombus but a different triangle (Figure 3.8). One formed a 90-degree angle while the other did not. I noticed Bobby hadn't touched the shapes much, and he hadn't used a right angle from one of the rectangles to compare the constructed angles against. He just looked at them and said, "Aren't they both the same?"

After students had worked to sort out 90-degree angles, the students began thinking about ways to figure out angle measures for individual polygons. Kelan put two 45-degree angles together and said each one was half of 90. Some kids put three slim, brown rhombuses together to figure out that each one was 30 degrees (Figure 3.9). Samantha said, "Since the shapes are equal, I know each one is 30 degrees." All the while, Mr. Gallagher followed me from group to group and watched in silence.

Figure 3.7   **Figure 3.8**

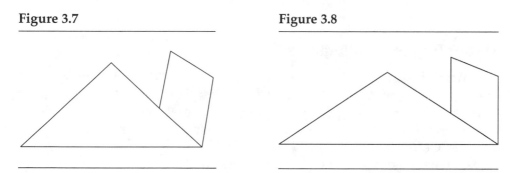

We sat down at a table with Chloe and Emerald. Chloe wondered aloud about the measure of the obtuse angle in the brown rhombus (Figure 3.10).

Chloe is a student who stays after school once a week to get additional math support from Mr. Gallagher. She is soft spoken and tentative about her ideas. Emerald is much more confident than Chloe and likes to take over. I sensed that Emerald's not pushy, rather she's completely engaged in this challenge. The two girls look at the angle. While Emerald is looking for shapes to put together to make the angle, Chloe puts the shape in her hand.

Chloe: It's 30 less and 90 more.
Emerald: No. It's 60 plus 60 which equals 120 and then another 30 equals 150. (She has put together three polygon angles to form this conclusion.)
Chloe: Okay.

She seems to give in to Emerald's view, but I want her to describe it more fully. I was interested in Chloe's idea. I didn't know what she meant immediately, but because she said it quickly and she was so specific about her numbers, I wanted to hear more. So I asked Emerald to wait.

Me: Chloe, tell us more about what you are thinking.

She proceeded to line up the shape in such a way that she formed an invisible line extending from the angle (Figure 3.11).

Chloe: See, right here is the 30 less. (She points to the empty space—the exterior angle.) So you take it away from the line that is 90 and 90, (she pauses and thinks for a moment) . . . 180, take away the 30 and you get . . . (pausing to think and write the equation) . . . 150.

Figure 3.9

Figure 3.10

Figure 3.11

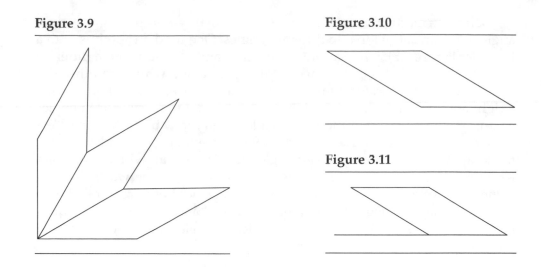

Debriefing Mr. Gallagher's Class

After class, as we are walking to the library to discuss what we'd each learned from the students, Mr. Gallagher says he had never thought about constructing an angle measure by looking at the negative space, by *subtracting*. He said he had never heard, or expected to hear, a child come up with Chloe's idea.

As we talked, it became clear to us both that not being at the center of math class was a new experience for him. But he told me how important listening to Chloe had been for him, the experience of really hearing Chloe's idea. He said he was afraid that he'd been missing those ideas, and he was so thankful that I had been there—primarily for Chloe—but also for him.

"There was something so powerful about being able to listen to students. I feel as though I don't spend enough time with each student daily. Following you around today allowed me to see what I might get from looking at student work in a more regular, daily way. Now, I have to think about this afternoon and our whole-group discussion."

He, typical of all our conversations, ran with his thinking. He said almost without taking a breath, "I'm good at roaming around from student to student, but I don't think about how to connect students' ideas. I need to think more about what to do next. I'm not sure which students' work to share in the whole group . . ." I interjected, "And in what order to share them."

Mr. Gallagher returned, "Yeah, I always share whatever *I* like; I have to admit I hadn't thought about whole-group discussions before. I hadn't been thinking of what goes into it, I just start it. I hadn't thought about calling on a student because of their work. . . . I call on them because they raise their hand or I want to know if they are paying attention or if they can answer the question."

I was almost breathless myself listening to him. It is powerful for teachers to take a step back and really hear their students talking about mathematical ideas as they are thinking out loud. Clearly, Mr. Gallagher had been ripe for this chance to pay such close attention. He said, "I know how to listen to kids, but I'm feeling as though I may be missing pithy things or just not doing anything with what they've offered."

After listening to each of these students and knowing that Mr. Gallagher and I had seen these together, we decided that we would meet over lunch and think about how to conduct the whole-group sharing discussion later in the afternoon.

I wondered for myself which students I would want to have share, what ideas I want to come forward, what connections between different kids' ideas I would promote, and, really, what I wanted to get out of that discussion. Given Mr. Gallagher's habit of steering us off the mathematical course, I was determined to have a collaborative discussion that focused specifically on the ideas that came up in class and how to keep them at the center of the student whole group discussion. To that end, I took off for the lunchroom with my notebook and proceeded to capture on paper as much of the details, the specifics of what we'd seen together as I could. I would get the first word in, and my first question would be, "We are going to look back at what we just experienced, so let's look at these notes. If we look at these six kids, one at a time, what can we learn about the students' ideas about angles?" And then, from there, I hope we can build a discussion plan that will help all of us keep learning.

Analyzing My Own Work

I really believe that there is no better route to improving math instruction than by helping teachers learn how to listen to students' mathematical ideas—to develop a sense of what to listen for. This belief guides my work. The strength of my conviction and what teachers come to see as the sensibleness of it, can help many pay closer attention to what students say. Once they start listening, they realize how rich their students' own ideas are. I want teachers to see that the classroom itself is singing with possibilities.

Instead of modeling lessons so my teaching is at the center, I work to "model" listening for and listening to student ideas. I capture student ideas in the form of narratives for teachers. I write down student dialogue and share it with the teacher. We work together to analyze and discuss what we are learning. Sometimes, teachers have heard the same student comments I have written down, but often, they realize they skipped over the student's idea in favor of the next thing in their plan book. Sometimes, teachers have heard and even responded to students' ideas but giving them the opportunity to explore the ideas further during our debrief time allows the teacher to articulate what they understood from the student as well as what he or she might do next. What did the student mean? What does the student understand? Misunderstand? How was what we heard connected very specifically to what we wanted them to learn? By carefully considering and analyzing students' ideas and student dialogue, we can peel back to how well and to what extent the mathematics of the lesson has been learned.

In the planning meetings I have with teachers, I always ask teachers to describe the mathematical goals of the lesson and unit. I ask if these goals make sense given what the teacher wants the students to learn. I think it's important to focus on the mathematics of the lesson and consider what came before and what will come next to contextualize the lesson we'll both be considering.

Although it is a central focus of my job, encouraging teachers to articulate their mathematical goals in their own words and for them to be able to do it is something we strive for. It requires, *for both of us*, a grasp of the math and experience with the ideas—and so gaining ground with this work is a goal of our meetings and our work together.

Case 3	"It's 30 Less and 90 More"

Math Activity: Angles and Angle Measurement

1. Using two or more angles from the set of polygonal shapes (see Figure 3.12), make some 90-degree angles.

2. Examine your set of polygonal shapes. Find a 90-degree angle in one of the shapes. Using this angle size as a measure, determine the size of the angles in all the surface polygons in your set. Record the measurements.

3. Choose two shapes from your collection. Determine the size of the exterior angles of each of these shapes. Record the measurements.

4. Make a list of what you notice about

   - The sum of the interior angles of a shape,
   - The sum of the exterior angles of a shape, and
   - The relationship between a shape's interior and exterior angle measures.

Figure 3.12

Copyright © 2009 by Corwin. All rights reserved. Reprinted from *Cultivating a Math Coaching Practice: A Guide for K–8 Math Educators,* by Amy Morse. Thousand Oaks, CA: Corwin, www.corwinpress.com. Reproduction authorized only for the local school site or nonprofit organization that has purchased this book.

Case 3 · "It's 30 Less and 90 More"

Focus Questions Activity

On Your Own

Spend a few minutes reflecting on the case through these lenses:

- Understanding the students
- Understanding Mr. Gallagher
- Coaching goals
- Avenues for learning

As you review the case, mark line numbers citing students' ideas, insights into Mr. Gallagher's ideas about his own teaching, and how he thinks about learning and doing math. Look for reflections from Tina, the coach, about her goals and note the principles of coaching which help inform her decisions.

In Your Small Group

Discuss the following:

1. What happened in the In Math Class section? What do we learn about students' ideas about angle? What does Mary offer?

2. Consider Bobby (lines 190–196). What is he confused about?

3. How do students in the class determine the size of angles? What does Emerald understand? What does Chloe understand?

4. What do we learn about Mr. Gallagher? What is the coach paying attention to in order to learn about Mr. Gallagher? What questions does she ask?

5. What are the learning goals for this teacher? Why?

6. What is the coaching strategy? Describe the coaching model Tina employs.

7. How would you answer the questions in lines 263–276, that Tina poses for herself? What goals would *you have* for this debrief? What would you like to see happen next?

4

Reaching a New Teacher

Math as the Conduit

Chapter Elements

✦ Case: A Case of Coaching: Multiplication and Division Journal Entries

✦ Math Activity: Looking Beneath the Surface

✦ Focus Questions Activity

CASE DESCRIPTION

A Case of Coaching is a set of journal entries written by a second-year coach as she works to cultivate a successful coach-teacher relationship with a new teacher. During her visit to the fourth grade math class, the coach, Ellie, is surprised to discover that her own ideas about division are less than solid. In preparation to coach well, the author sets about studying types of division and sorting through related story problems. She decides to use this example of a self-directed investigation as an entrée to a collaborative study with the classroom teacher and, thus, begins a series of written communications that help form the basis for their working relationship.

NOTES TO THE READER

In this session, first, you will have a chance to work on the Math Activity (page 43) in a small group as a way to preview the math issues raised in this episode of coaching. Next, when you read the case, write questions or comments in the margins and note line numbers of sentences or paragraphs that interest you or raise questions for you.

Case 4	Author: Ellie

A Case of Coaching: Multiplication and Division Journal Entries

October—Grade 4, Garnet School

Journal Entry 1

1   Early in my second year of coaching, I'm trying to connect with the new fourth grade teacher, Ms. Ayvazian. She has transferred with her husband from across the state and had previously taught in a school using a math curriculum she described as "stuff we'd developed over years of
5   teaching; we each did our own thing." The math curriculum and expectations for teachers and for students here at Garnet are a far cry from self-made activities and quizzes, though it wasn't all that long ago that I would have used a similar description for the materials of my own teaching.

   In our brief initial conversation, Ms. Ayvazian talked about the chal-
10   lenges of finding her way around the city, getting her kids set up in new schools, and orienting herself to Garnet and to the principal here. When I decided to shift gears and ask how math was going—she has a pretty lively fourth grade, and I know a lot of her students from working with Mrs. Kane, their third grade teacher—she was less forthcoming. She did
15   say that the curriculum is "wordy" and that "the kids need some more straightforward work to do" and added, "especially, at the beginning of the year so they get in a good routine." She went on to describe a couple of students (Liz and Jan, who can give anyone a run for their money, I know), and pretty soon, I realized the conversation had drifted away from
20   math to kids' personalities and ways of being in the classroom, and in the newness of our getting to know each other, I didn't push back. I wondered what she meant about "get in a good routine" and what sort of content she had in mind for "straightforward work," but just as I was about to ask more, Ms. Ayvazian said she had a meeting with the school counselor to
25   talk about some of the students. I thought to myself, "This has been a 'touching base,' not a coach-teacher discussion. Or is there a difference?"

   I walked away from the conversation thinking about what it means to be new somewhere and all the subtle and not-so-subtle things you have to figure out to feel oriented and settled in a new school. I wondered about
30   an approach to begin working with Ms. Ayvazian and what to be keeping in mind. The math program here requires more of a teacher's involvement

in the content and strategic planning for class and also a commitment to, and ability to, understand students' ideas. For Ms. Ayvazian, this may likely be a huge shift; it was for teachers here, and we're only just beginning our second year. So what, once again, I ask myself, does it mean to be a coach? How do we choose which path to go down, and how do I draw our attention to what will matter most?

Journal Entry 2

Mulling over our conversation, I thought about what made many teachers at Garnet uncomfortable with the changes in math when we started. There were complaints about the way the math book is set up and about the types of questions and activities students are supposed to engage in. In brief exchanges in the first couple of weeks in school, Ms. Ayvazian had waffled in her response to my support—as though if she accepted it or sought me out, maybe she would be admitting that she's less than certain of what she's doing and how well she's doing it—which can be really hard when you're new. And maybe, it was just about getting settled in her new circumstances; I really do understand that. But her comments today made me think there is more to it, and I feel a responsibility, to both Ms. Ayvazian and the kids, to get moving now. I think this is a tricky place for some teachers; we (and I include myself, especially in my newness as a coach) want to be good at what we do and want to be *viewed* as good at what we do, and in the usual set up of school cultures, struggling with new material is perceived somehow as "having a poor practice."

At the Price School, where I coach one day a week, there is a different tactic going on. There, one vocal leader, a fifth grade teacher who's been at the school for two decades, has decided she doesn't like these changes in the math program. Teachers, who are intimidated or anxious about the material, now have a chance to join up with the vocal oppositionist and her followers in resisting the curriculum. Focusing attention there, they can effectively avoid the awkward struggle and the consequences of being less than expert as they trumpet the view that the new curriculum "has huge gaps of content" or "isn't set up for students like ours." I know this version of undermining change—at least what it looks and feels like— because it's such a daunting challenge for me as a coach to get underneath that strategy and turn it around so we can all just start learning and focusing on kids' learning. I am still struggling, over there, against a pretty strong tide of opinion and school culture that seems to support this kind of rebuff to change, but my coach colleagues are there with me in spirit, and we are helping each other figure these things out. (I am so grateful I'm not the only coach in the world!)

But this isn't the deal with Ms. Ayvazian. She's neither an active resister nor someone who complains; I think she hasn't yet made friends with her colleagues and doesn't know quite what to make of working with a coach. Who wouldn't then tread lightly, after all?

Another dilemma of coaching, which I wasn't quite prepared for myself when I was a teacher working with a coach, is that collaborating with a coach makes practice public. While my aim is for the teacher to become a skilled "reader" of her students, what we (coach and teacher) do together toward that goal is "crack open" the classroom. We leave bare the

80   students' talk and work so we can examine it carefully. We dissect the
teaching agenda and the teacher's and my ideas so that we can look
together at what's going on with kids' learning. The whole experience
may actually take place just between the two of us, *but even just between the
two of us,* it's hardly what we would call private work. I have a lot of empa-
85   thy for how tough it is for some of us to get a coaching-teaching partnership going. *Are* there ways to just jump in without scaring someone off?

Anyway, at the end of that conversation, I did have a second to ask
Ms. Ayvazian what would make sense for me to do this first time when I
came to her math class. I didn't ask her if she *wanted* me to come to her
90   classroom, rather I decided to just go for it and start with, "*When* I come
into the classroom. . . ." It seemed that this helped her avoid having to
avoid me, and she thought about my question for a minute.

She responded by asking if I could come in and introduce the daily
number routine to her class. She said, "I just haven't gotten this started yet,
95   and maybe you could get it going?"

What a smart way for her to begin this, I thought. This way, she doesn't
have to endure my observing what's challenging to her, but she also has
accepted my assertive request to come into her class. It also calls for kids
working with *me* first before I observe them engaging with her!
100   I agreed and suggested we spend time together thinking about the best
way I should begin the routine. Here's the waffling part. Ms. Ayvazian
said that she really wanted to get this routine going as soon as possible *and*
that she couldn't meet with me for the next two days. Then she opted for
my assertiveness strategy. She said, "You come in on Friday and introduce
105   it, and then we can talk after school on Monday about how it went." And
without hesitating, she added, "Okay?" She said it not really like a question but more like a signal of our agreement. I took it. With very little ban-
ter, we'd both gotten what we wanted, and if the truth be known, I think
what we both wanted was to get started working.

Journal Entry 3

110   On Friday, I introduced the routine by using the number of the day
(October 17 was the date so the number of the day was 17). Ms. Ayvazian
has 28 students, and they were attentive and ready to begin. This math
practice may be new to her, but it was clear that the norms of the class
were well established and that the students were treating their math class
115   seriously. As it turned out, the kids did well for the first time—actually,
many did really well.

I asked the students to put away anything on their desks and to think with
me about the math problem. A minute or two of shuffling papers and books
passed, and pretty soon, all eyes were on me, including Ms. Ayvazian's!
120   I asked the students to come up with a number problem that had the
answer of 17. I told them they had a good, long, quiet moment to consider
possible number sentences equaling 17 and then I'd be looking for volunteers to share their ideas. I passed out a blank page of paper for each
student and said, "Consider how you might make 17. Think about it and
125   write down some solutions, some equations."

I walked around in the silent room looking at papers as the students
solved the problem. I saw mostly adding and subtracting and one person
using multiplication in his equation. I didn't get to everyone's paper, but

I saw Ms. Ayvazian walking around too. I felt pretty sure I could call on any one or two students and we'd take a walk through the number sentence he or she offered before time was up. Already, Jay-Lee was waving his hand around. After a minute or two, I called on Tess.

"I did; 34 − 17 = 17."

"Okay, Tess, anyone notice anything in particular about this equation? Yes, Maguel?"

"I did subtraction too. I knew that 17 + 17 was 34 too, so I added another 10 and got 44 − 27 = 17."

"Wow, okay. Deborah, can you say how Maguel's is like Tess's or how Tess's is like Maguel's?

"Well, they both subtracted, and they're the same except Maguel's is 10 more to start with and . . ." She stopped as she puzzled for a minute. I knew she would get it but I wanted to move on, so I decided to ask Christian if he could finish where Deborah was headed.

"Yeah, Maguel has 34 plus a 10 so he also has to add 10 to the 'first' 17 to end up with a 17. I get that. It's like you could take Tess's and say, 36 − 19 = 17. You just add 2 to both the starting and the number you are subtracting."

I liked this train of thought and knew it was a great exchange for Ms. Ayvazian and me to consider later.

"Okay, Jay-Lee, give us another idea of how to get to 17."

Jay-Lee looked up at me and said, "149 divided by 17 = 17." I was pretty taken aback with this division sentence right off the bat and gave a quick glance at Ms. Ayvazian. She was staring at Jay-Lee with a look of surprise. This class was trotting right along, I thought. I asked him how he arrived at this.

He used his hands a lot to describe his thinking. "Well," he said, "149 is the same as 100 plus 49. And so, in 100 there are 10 tens. In 49, there are 7 sevens. 10 plus 7 equals 17."

His matter-of-fact description was so compelling—and his quick response to the whole question had been so startling—I actually didn't realize at first that the answer wasn't right, couldn't possibly be right. Even still, because I was standing there trying to think in my head whether this explanation was sensible or not—and now, talk about practices cracked open—and in front of Ms. Ayvazian, who was no longer staring at Jay-Lee but was staring at me—I looked out at the class and suggested they work in groups on Jay-Lee's strategy to see what they would discover, and they, frankly, were intrigued to do so.

After a few minutes, I'd easily over extended my 10-minute problem of the day, so I asked the class to consider this solution to the problem in their homework for Monday. I said, "Let's leave Jay-Lee's response for now and let's hold open in our heads that we want to prove whether or not this is a valid way to come up with 17. The question for his example is, 'Does it work every time or even this time? Why or why not?'"

I wasn't sure if this was a satisfying way to end the discussion, but I needed time to consider it, and I wanted Ms. Ayvazian to do the same. And the kids too, of course. Ms. Ayvazian was teaching a literacy class next, so I told her I'd see her on Monday after school and we'd debrief.

Later in the day, I left her a note saying how interesting I thought Jay-Lee's explanation had been and how he was really able to consider breaking numbers up and how it will be interesting to consider how his ideas about division will get refined. "The answer was wrong, but his idea fascinated me," I wrote. I hoped she, like the kids, would feel compelled to sort it on their own.

Journal Entry 4

185   Imagine my surprise when I arrived at school Monday to find a note in my mailbox from Ms. Ayvazian!

She wrote,

190
195
200

> Thanks for coming on Friday. I've been thinking about the number of the day a lot this weekend. I was really surprised by Jay-Lee's work. At first, his strategy seemed so cool. When you asked the students how this worked, I was all ready to figure it out and was so impressed. When the kids were working on this for the next couple minutes, I wasn't paying much attention to them; I was trying to think about it myself. But it didn't make sense. Then, when RuAnne said she got it and was so happy with it, I began to wonder why fourth grade math is now so hard for me. But when later, I got your note and you confirmed that his answer was wrong, I could relax. You hadn't said why, but it helped to know that there was a reason I couldn't figure out how it worked. I thought about it this weekend and know that it's impossible to solve the problem that way or RuAnne's way. I feel confident about that! Unfortunately, I have to take my son to the dentist because he lost his retainer. So I can't meet until Thursday afternoon.

205   It was only Monday. I took a giant leap and decided to keep this communication open as if we were meeting on paper, and at lunch, I wrote back to her.

210

> Thanks so much for your message. You weren't the only one who was taken in by Jay-Lee's idea! I think one of the reasons that I was initially fooled by this strategy was the simplicity of how it appeared to work. While other kids in the class were coming up with predictable expressions that equaled 17 ($15 + 2$, $25 - 8$, $100 - 83$, $(5 \times 3) + 2$, and so on), here was someone who saw that there was something about the number 149 that was in some way connected to 17. Somehow, this child saw a relationship that others did not see.

215

> His strategy intrigued me enough that I had to take time to try to figure out what might be logical about his thinking. After you and the class had moved on to literacy, I spent the next half hour or so in the teachers' room working on this problem myself. This is how I thought about it:

> Why couldn't you do it this way?

220

> What was misleading about this strategy?

> Is 149 divided by 17 the same as $100 + 49$ divided by $10 + 7$?

> What does this division problem ask you to find out?

First, because of what I know about sharing and partitioning situations used in division, 149 divided by 17 could be looked at it two different ways: 225

One way to see it is, "How many groups of 17 are there in 149?" (Partitioning)

Another way is to divide 149 into 17 groups to see how many would be in each group. (Sharing)

I looked at strategies that I might use to solve the problem and 230 worked to compare them to the way the student might approach the problem. I came up with the following examples as a way to help me think these through:

Sharing

I have 149 baseball cards, and I want to share them among 17 friends. First, I could estimate. I know if I gave each friend 235 10 cards . . . I'm over my limit because $17 \times 10 = 170$. I know that 149 divided by 17 is less than 10.

$170 - 17 = 153$

$153 - 17 = 136$

So each friend would get 8 and there would be 13 left over. 240

Now, if I use a strategy similar to the Jay-Lee's, I might take 100 cards and split them up into 10 groups so that 10 kids will each get 10 cards . . . and if I take the other 49 and split them up into 7 groups, then I can give out 7 more to 7 kids, that is I wouldn't be dividing the cards equally between all 17 kids. So what I know about division and sharing 245 tells me that this is not sharing the cards evenly between 17 friends.

Partitioning

I have 149 cards, and I want to put them in bags, each of which will contain 17 cards. How many bags of 17 cards can I get from the 149 cards?

$17 \times 1 = 17$

$17 \times 2 = 34$ 250

$17 \times 4 = 68$

$17 \times 6 = 102$

$17 \times 8 = 102 + 34 = 136$

I can't get another group of 17 in bags, so I have 8 bags with 13 cards left over. 255

Going back to one other student's strategy of splitting up the two numbers in the problem: If I split up the 149 into 100 and 49 and divided each by 10 and then by 7, I would get

100 divided by 10 is 10, so we would have 10 bags of 10

49 divided by 7 is 7, so we would have 7 bags of 7. 260

This would give us NO BAGS of 17 at all.

(Continued)

(Continued)

Or you could combine the 7 bags of 7 with 7 bags of 10 and have 7 bags of 17 and 3 bags of 10. So what does it mean to divide 149 by 17? We want to see how many groups of 17 will make 149 or if we divided 149 into 17 groups, how many of in each group will we have? There is something about keeping the concept of 17 as a whole that's important to remember.

But I realized that there is something similar to this last student's idea that I can do. Let's say, I want to make the problem easier to see how many whole groups of 17 there are in 100—then how many whole groups of 17 there are in 49—then how many whole groups of 17 are there in the leftovers. This would keep the wholeness of the 17 intact. I think it's important to note that the divisor remains whole here, but the dividend can be broken into more manageable pieces.

I thought about these division problems and the relationship between multiplication and division. Dividing 149 by 17 means how many groups of 17 can you put together to make 149 ($17 \times \_\_ = 149$) Both are using groups. In multiplication, the number of groups and number in each group are what is known and the total is what I'm looking for. In division, the total is known and I'm trying to find out either how many groups or how many in each group (sharing model and partitioning model).

This problem intrigued me in lots of ways. It really got me to think about division in a methodical way, and I hadn't done that quite this way before. At first blush, I really didn't understand why this boy's strategy didn't work. Just a bit, I wanted it to work because it looked so darn simple. It just seemed to me that there must be some logic in the way he was thinking about the problem. However, knowing that 10×17 would be way more than 149 was my clue that it didn't work. Then, it all unraveled from there! I look forward to seeing you Thursday—the ideas in your classroom have really given me food for thought!

Ms. Ayvazian and I ended up at our meeting on Thursday just doing division problems together and talking them through. We used smaller numbers, we used story problems, and we did 149 divided by 17 to compare the strategies we could use. When I wrote her the note, I knew I was giving her tons of information, and none of it was overtly an invitation for her ideas, but it really was just that. I meant to establish that math was provocative, that it was logical and interesting, and maybe most importantly, that given some interesting student thinking, we could learn a lot.

We seemed to have hit it just right—a student's idea that caught us by surprise, and it seemed, the fact that we were surprised was an expression of our shared interest in what fourth graders do. We were able to share our curiosity about the problem in a way that smoothed a path toward collaboration. What else will we discover in these students' math thinking? What else can we learn about the math curriculum together? What was it that cut through the awkwardness and the gawky stages for us of beginning a collaboration about learning and practice? Is there something in here that maps on to my other coaching challenges?

Case 4 A Case of Coaching

Math Activity: Looking Beneath the Surface

The problem is 48 ÷ 4. Below are two solutions to this problem. Investigate each and figure out why a solution works or doesn't work.

(a) 40 ÷ 4 = 10	(b) 24 ÷ 2 = 12
8 ÷ 4 = 2	24 ÷ 2 = 12
10 + 2 = 12	12 + 12 = 24

Sebastian, a fourth grade student in your class, says, "17 × 17 = 149," and his small-group members nod in agreement. You give everyone a minute to consider what Sebastian said. Martina's hand goes up. She argues, "It can't be right. But it's kind of right. It's like adding and multiplying. I mean, how do you know which is which, in a way? I know it's not right."

a. What's the logic in Sebastian's statement?
b. What's important to consider about Sebastian's thinking and about Martina's response?

Case 4   A Case of Coaching

Focus Questions Activity

Examining the Mathematics

1. Using 136 ÷ 15, write two story problems, one that describes partitioning and one that describes sharing. With cubes, model the two division problems. How are the stories and the models the same and how are they different?

2. Ellie uses what she heard in class as a way to carefully revisit her own ideas about division. What does she find out for herself and how do the students' ideas contribute to her investigation?

3. In Journal Entry 3, what math ideas are Tess, Maguel, and Deborah playing with? Describe Jay-Lee's idea.

4. What questions or ideas about the students' math might you raise in a debrief with the teacher? How might you frame these questions or ideas?

Examining Coaching

5. In the first two journal entries, Ellie describes her encounter with Mrs. Ayvazian. She reflects on coach and teacher relationships using the expression, "cracking open one's practice" as one descriptor of the work. What does this mean, and what are the implications for establishing collaborations?

6. Ellie describes her very deliberate consideration of division that she chooses to, subsequently, pass on to Mrs. Ayvazian in the form of a letter. What happened as a result? What makes Ellie's choice work?

7. Consider next steps for Mrs. Ayvazian. List your ideas and discuss how they relate to what you want her to learn, or to be working on, next?

5

Preparing for Thoughtful Dialogue

Chapter Elements

✦ Case: Considered Coaching: Transcript 1, Transcript 2, Transcript 3

CASE DESCRIPTION

The Considered Coaching case examines one coach's responses to a math exchange between the teacher and students in a second grade classroom. Rosa, the coach, has set out to more fully understand ideas about *number sense*. As a way of capturing these ideas as they play out in math class, Rosa, with permission from the teacher, brings her laptop to class and transcribes a brief round of mental math. As she types the students' and the teacher's dialogue in one column on the screen, she also records her reactions to what's happening in class in a second column. The Considered Coaching case is set up in three parts: (1) the original classroom transcript with no commentary, (2) the same transcript with reflective commentary, and (3) the same transcript again with the coach's first responses to the transcript. The title word "considered" becomes central in discussions about the transcript and the implications for coaching. Rosa explores the difference between her immediate take on the students' ideas about number and the teacher's facilitation and then the more reflective, and substantially more useful, exploration of the transcript as she prepares for a thoughtful dialogue with the classroom teacher.

NOTES TO THE READER

This chapter consists of three classroom transcripts (two of which include the coach's commentary) and step-by-step directions to follow. In this classroom scenario, students are working to create number sentences that equal 17. As preparation for reading, try creating a variety of your own number sentences for 67.

Step 1

Consider Transcript 1 of student and teacher dialogue from a classroom working on a math-of-the-day problem. With this transcript, you will find a blank grid on the right where you can write your own impressions of two things: the mathematical ideas of number sense and the interactions between teacher and students. First, read the transcript and write notes solely about the mathematical ideas that may be present in the dialogue—these can be observations and/or questions that come up for you as you read. Second, go through the transcript and note your observations about the dialogue.

TRANSCRIPT 1

This second grade class is working on number of the day: 17. The teacher asks for volunteers to share their mental math.

Teacher-Student Interaction	My Thoughts
Student 1: 6 + 4 + 7. Teacher: Good. S1: 6 + . . . T: (interrupts and prompts) "I know that . . ." S1: I know that 6 + 4 is 10 and 7 is 17. T: Good, good.	
Student 2: 7 + 3 + 7. T: Okay. How do you know? Prove it to me. S2: I know that 7 + 3 is 10 and 7 is 17. T: How did you do it? Did you count up? S2: (nods) T: Like in your head? 10, 11, 12, 13 . . . ?	
T: Anyone else? Student 3: 8 + 2 + 2 + 3 + 2. T: What did you do? S3: I knew that 8 + 2 is 10 and that 2 + 3 + 2 is 7. So . . . T: (interrupts) So what did you do? S3: (quiet) T: Did you break up the 7? S3: . . . Ye—ah. T: So you are using a strategy. . . . You are doing some good thinking here . . . (T begins to write on the board): You have used combinations of 10, counting up, and breaking numbers up. . . . What do we call these? Students: Strategies! T: Yes. A strategy is a way to figure something out.	

Teacher-Student Interaction	My Thoughts
T: Anymore? Student 4: 9 + 1 + 7. T: So 9 + 1 = 10 and 7 is 17. You counted up? S4: Yeah. Student 5: I know, I know! 10 + 2 + 5. T: Okay.	
Student 6: 5 + 5 + 5 + 2. T: How did you do this in your head? S6: I know that 5 + 5 is 10 and plus 5 is 15. T: So you are skip counting by 5s?	
Student 7: 10 + 1. . . . (pause) T: What are you doing in your head? . . . S7, what are you doing? Tell me what you are thinking? S7: 6! T: So you did it in your head. (T moves on)	
Student 8: 9 + 5 + 3. I added 9 + 5. That is 14 plus the 3 is 17. T: So you knew it was 14 and then you counted up.	
T: So let's make it a little more difficult. What about using addition and take-away? Student 9: 10 + 10 − 2 = 17. T: So . . . 10 + 10 is 20. Now count back. What did you get? 18? S9: Oh, so it's 18. T: So you need to take away one more. (Writes on the board: 10 + 10 − 2 − 1 = 17 draws a number line and illustrates jumping back and moves on).	
Student 10: 6 + 6 + 9. Six plus six . . . is 12. Plus 9 is 18. T: No . . . close . . . count up. S10: . . . 12, 13, 14, 15, 16, 17 . . . T: Okay. A few more and then we are going to do something different.	
Student 11: 20 − 3 − 1 + 1. T: Is this a true statement? (She points to the number line she has drawn on the board.) Start at 20, go back 3 − 1 + 1 . . . is 17! Awesome! So you made a connection with S9's math sentence? But you don't know how you did it. (Teacher moves on to another student.)	

(Continued)

(Continued)

Teacher–Student Interaction	My Thoughts
Student 12: $4 + 4 + 4 + 4 + 1$. T: How did you do it? S12: I counted in my mind. T: I need to understand. . . . (T records on the board) S12: I know that $4 + 4$ is 8 and $8 + 4$ is 12 and $12 + 4$ is 16 and 1 is . . . T: So you know that $4 + 4 + 4 + 4$ (circles this on the board) is 16. But you can also break it up in your mind: $4 + 4$ is 8 and $4 + 4$ is 8. That equals 16. And $16 + 1$ is 17. Good thinking. T: Sometimes, we just know a sentence. Like $21 - 4$. I just know it is 17. Like last year, the kids' favorite one was $35 + 15 = 50$. And so I learned it. I just know it.	
At this point 25 minutes have gone by. She now turns to the next activity.	

Step 2

In groups of three, discuss your responses to the following questions:

1. Examine the students' suggestions. What mathematical ideas might students be drawing from to develop the problems offered in this mental-math activity?
2. What do you see in this transcript that could be relevant to a discussion with the teacher about number sense and about the students' thinking?
3. What questions does this 25-minute snippet from a classroom raise for you about teacher-student communication? Identify specific places in the transcript that trigger your thinking. What do you see in the transcript that could be relevant to a teacher-coach discussion about *math talk* in the classroom?

Step 3

Read Transcript 2, which includes Rosa's reflective thoughts as she analyzes the transcript. When your group has finished reading, discuss the following questions:

1. Examine the thinking offered by Students 1, 2, and 3. Read the author's comments and discuss ways these equations may be related. Why might a coach choose to debrief these equations under the umbrella topic of number sense?

2. The author suggests that the problems offered by Students 4 and 5 are related. What mathematics might the teacher and the students consider in analyzing these equations?

3. Consider Rosa's reflection, "Highlighting strategies is not the same as highlighting number relationships." What does this idea suggest to you? Where in the transcript do you see evidence of the teacher highlighting strategies? Relationships? What might the coach learn and what might the teacher learn from a discussion about this idea?

4. Trace the ways the teacher elicits students' engagement and responds to students' contributions. What do you notice? What ideas do you have about the potential for mental math discourse in the classroom?

5. Consider how to begin your discussion with the teacher. What is your goal for this first conversation? How might you frame your conversation? And finally, reflect on the reasons for the particular framing and the focus of what you choose to discuss.

TRANSCRIPT 2

In my math coaching, my top priorities are to support elementary teachers and students in developing greater flexibility in number sense and fluency in communicating mathematical ideas. Over the past two years of collaborative school-goal writing, leadership meeting discussions, data analysis work, and coaching in many classrooms, these two priorities seem to be fundamental issues on the minds of many teachers. As a coach, I wonder what is going on with number sense in classrooms—is it, in and of itself, the reason for students' challenges and lower scores? What underlies the mathematics and the teaching that supports it?

I take responsibility here, too, in coaching and in figuring out what's going on. This year, a personal goal I have is paying very close attention to my coaching around these issues. This task elicits a high level of anxiety for me. . . . Am I doing a good enough job? Does my coaching help teachers identify and use mathematical opportunities for developing their students' number sense *and* ability to explain their thinking during lessons and in morning math? Do *I* see these opportunities myself? Do I have enough mathematical understanding and competence, keen listening skills, analytical ability, and mental speed? The list goes on. Yet, rather than continue with this self-doubt, I decided it would be helpful to look at what goes on while I am observing a lesson.

This is a transcript of second grade students making 17; the answer to their problem is 17. Both the school and the teacher are new to me in early September. I know that this teacher is just beginning to make strides in shifting her practice and is working to use the curriculum. I want to consider coaching that will support her work. I want to note in this writing opportunities to discuss number sense (for next time in class or that might happen in a debrief between the two of us). I also want to understand number sense more clearly from a student, teacher, and my own perspective—a personal goal for this year.

This second grade class is working on number of the day: 17. The teacher asks for volunteers to share their mental math.

Teacher-Student Interaction	My Thoughts
Student 1: 6 + 4 + 7. Teacher: Good. S1: 6 + . . . T: (interrupts and prompts) "I know that . . ." S1: I know that 6 + 4 is 10 and 7 is 17. T: Good, good.	How do we help students make their thinking explicit when they share? Here, for example, I wonder if this child separated 10 and 7 as a first step. If this were the case, S1's strategy of using 10 as a starting point would seem an important number-sense idea to bring up for discussion. I am not sure if the use of 10 as a landmark number gets across in his explanation as is. A teacher question could be, "Why did you choose 6 and 4?"
Student 2: 7 + 3 + 7. T: Okay. How do you know? Prove it to me. S2: I know that 7 + 3 is 10 and 7 is 17.	S2 is also starting with a combination of 10. S2 also names her actions, but is she explaining why she chose those numbers to begin with? Why is the teacher asking the student to prove it? Does this student's explanation prove that 7 + 3 + 7 is 17? The interaction continues to be about what the student did, but the number sense behind her actions is not being made explicit.
T: How did you do it? Did you count up? S2: (nods) T: In your head? 10, 11, 12, 13 . . . ?	With this question the teacher sets up a yes-no situation. By stating what the child did, has the teacher inadvertently encouraged counting by ones? Maybe he is grouping, and thus, his mental math could look very different. The teacher tries to establish his counting strategies, but her line of questioning is neither highlighting nor exploring this child's number sense.
T: Anyone else? Student 3: 8 + 2 + 2 + 3 + 2. T: What did you do? S3: I knew that 8 + 2 is 10 and that 2 + 3 + 2 is 7. So . . . T: (interrupts) So what did you do? S3: (quiet) T: Did you break up the 7? S3: . . . Ye—ah. T: So you are using a strategy. . . . You are doing some good thinking here . . . (T begins to write on the board): You have used combinations of 10, counting up, and breaking numbers up. . . . What do we call these? Students: Strategies! T: Yes. A strategy is a way to figure something out.	Highlighting strategies is not the same as highlighting number relationships. It seems to me that these students are very comfortable with finding combinations. Yet, I don't get a sense of their thinking. I think the teacher is trying to make their examples fit into a strategy. In this case, T names breaking numbers up. This might be what the child did, but where is the evidence? T tries to make a connection between S2's (7 + 3 + 7) and S3's (8 + 2 + 2 + 3 + 2) by pointing to S2's combination and asking: Did you break up the 7? Again, this is a yes-no situation; the examples she chooses do not clearly represent the strategy the T names, and she, and not the child, is doing the talking.
T: Anymore? Student 4: 9 + 1 + 7. T: So 9 + 1 = 10 and 7 is 17. You Counted up? S4: Yeah. Student 5: I know, I know! 10 + 2 + 5. T: Okay.	Here is a yes-no set again. I wonder if this could be a place to pause and have a conversation about these two examples 9 + 1 + 7 = 17 and 10 + 2 + 5 = 17.

Teacher-Student Interaction	My Thoughts
Student 6: 5 + 5 + 5 + 2. T: How did you do this in your head? S6: I know that 5 + 5 is 10 and plus 5 is 15. T: So you are skip counting by 5s.	I wonder if the teacher is trying to get all the strategies on the board. This is repeated addition. This child might be comfortable with grouping by 5. I think here is another opportunity for a number sense discussion. How is this similar to 10 + 5 + 2? The student's ideas are not explored; rather, the student is told what he is doing.
Student 7: 10 + 1. . . . (pause) T: What are you doing in your head? . . . S7, what are you doing? Tell me what you are thinking? S7: 6! T: So you did it in your head. (T moves on)	The tone of this student is hesitant, struggling. The teacher asked for her contribution, but it seems the teacher dives in as soon as the child begins to speak. What does the teacher mean when she asks, "Tell me what you're thinking"? Do students understand the teacher wants them to explain their *actions* on numbers? Is *she* clear on what she is asking students to do? Maybe. Yet, by saying, "So, you did it in your head," to S7's "6," is she missing the opportunity to discuss number sense? I feel like the teacher has learned questions to ask and strategies to name, but here, the responses don't necessarily apply to the individual's thinking.
Student 8: 9 + 5 + 3. I added 9 + 5. That is 14 plus the 3 is 17. T: So you knew it was 14 and then you counted up.	The teacher names yet another strategy (using what you know). I am curious why the teacher continues to get examples but no one else besides her is talking about them. What kind of conversation could I have with this teacher to move her from a teacher-centered classroom to a student-centered one?
T: So let's make it a little more difficult. What about using addition and take-away? Student 9: 10 + 10 − 2 = 17. T: So . . . 10 + 10 is 20. Now count back. What did you get? 18? S9: Oh, so it's 18. T: So you need to take away one more. (Writes on the board: 10 + 10 − 2 − 1 = 17 draws a number line and illustrates the jumping back and moves on).	I do not have the benefit of knowing this teacher or this group of students. At this point, I am lost as to what the teacher's intentions are for this particular activity. There is so much class invested in this activity at this point! I wonder if asking this teacher what her goals were would be a starting point. Yet, I am not sure where to go from there. There are pedagogical issues, and I am also curious about this teacher's understanding of underlying mathematical activities. I feel at this point that the teaching is about teaching strategies and not about student reasoning numerically.
Student 10: 6 + 6 + 9. Six plus six . . . is 12. Plus 9 is 18. T: No . . . close . . . count up. S10: . . . 12, 13, 14, 15, 16, 17 . . . T: Okay. A few more then we are going to do something different.	

(Continued)

(Continued)

Teacher-Student Interaction	My Thoughts
Student 11: 20 − 3 − 1 + 1. T: Is this a true statement? (She points to the number line she has drawn on the board.) Start at 20, go back 3 − 1 + 1 . . . is 17! Awesome! So you made a connection with S9's math sentence? But you don't know how you did it. (Teacher moves on to another student.)	This teacher has named many strategies, used the number line model, and told students what they have done, but none of this can provide, or be attributed to, having evidence of students' number sense. The evidence I have so far is that some students can do the following: make number strings that add up to 17, feel comfortable with combinations of 10, know 10+ combinations, and can add on from a number counting by ones.
Student 12: 4 + 4 + 4 + 4 + 1. T: How did you do it? S12: I counted in my mind. T: I need to understand. . . . (T records on the board) S12: I know that 4 + 4 is 8 and 8 + 4 is 12 and 12 + 4 is 16 and 1 is . . . T: So you know that 4 + 4 + 4 + 4 (circles this on the board) is 16. But you can also break it up in your mind: 4 + 4 is 8 and 4 + 4 is 8. That equals 16. And 16 + 1 is 17. Good thinking. T: Sometimes, we just know a sentence. Like 21 − 4. I just know it is 17. Like last year the kids' favorite one was 35 + 15 = 50. And so I learned it. I just know it. At this point 25 minutes have gone by. She now turns the next activity.	How can I help this teacher understand the difference between her thinking and students' thinking? What is this teacher's number sense? How do I establish a conversation with this teacher who, at first impression, seems to feel very sure of her implementation and knowledge of the material? What questions would be helpful to begin a conversation about 1. evidence of student understanding, 2. building a mathematical community, 3. eliciting students understanding of number sense, and 4. using the collective student thinking to help each individual student move in his/her understanding?

Step 4

Read Transcript 3, which describes the author's first impressions as she sat in class and, simultaneously, recorded the classroom discourse.

1. How do the coach's first and second reactions differ? What does the coach's more considered reflection offer over the in-the-moment response?

2. In your own coaching, how do you differentiate between reactive coaching and considered (or disciplined) coaching? What strategies or beliefs support your efforts to work from a stance of considered coaching?

TRANSCRIPT 3

Teacher-Student Interaction	My Thoughts
Student 1: 6 + 4 + 7. Teacher: Good. S1: 6 + . . . T: (interrupts and prompts) "I know that . . ." S: I know that 6 + 4 is 10 and 7 is 17. T: Good, good.	**Combinations of 10.** That's good . . . how to communicate.

Teacher-Student Interaction	My Thoughts
Student 2: 7 + 3 + 7. T: Okay. How do you know? Prove it to me. S2: I know that 7 + 3 is 10 and 7 is 17 T: How did you do it? Did you count up? S2: (nods) T: Like in your head? 10, 11, 12, 13 . . . ?	Combinations of 10. That's interesting . . . "prove it to me." Does this prove it? She's telling the child what he did . . . ? Did he? Combinations of 10, 10 + __. Maybe his strategy is different. Can she tell from this interaction?
T: Anyone else? Student 3: 8 + 2 + 2 + 3 + 2. T: What did you do? S3: I knew that 8 + 2 is 10 and that 2 + 3 + 2 is 7. So . . . T: (interrupts) So what did you do? S3: (quiet) T: Did you break up the 7? S3: . . . Ye—ah. T: So you are using a strategy. . . . You are doing some good thinking here . . . (T begins to write on the board). You have used combinations of 10, counting up, and breaking numbers up. . . . What do we call these? Students: Strategies! T: Yes. A strategy is a way to figure something out.	Starts with combinations of 10. Interrupts again! No waiting! (She refers to the 7 from S2's example.) . . . his voice . . . he is not sure. I can't tell . . . are these clear to rest of the students? Give all students a chance to think about it. What questions could she use to elicit number relationships more explicitly?
T: Anymore? Student 4: 9 + 1 + 7. T: So 9 + 1 = 10 and 7 is 17. You counted up? S4: Yeah. Student 5: I know, I know! 10 + 2 + 5. T: Okay.	How do we know what she did? Too packed . . . time for getting into ideas? What's coming from the students?
Student 6: 5 + 5 + 5 + 2. T: How did you do this in your head? S6: I know that 5 + 5 is 10 and plus 5 is 15. T: So you are skip counting by 5s?	Let the kid explain! . . . I can't tell what student is thinking, really . . . teacher's voice dominates and explains. Interrupts.
Student 7: 10 + 1. . . . (pause) T: What are you doing in your head? . . . S7, what are you doing? Tell me what you are thinking? S7: 6! T: So you did it in your head. (T moves on)	. . . S7 stops and doesn't seem sure what to say next. ***Teacher hasn't left the blackboard . . .*** Can you see what she is doing? How do you know what she knows? S7's hands are under her desk . . . using fingers to count by ones to 17. No she didn't . . . this is too fast . . . teacher's goals . . . ?

(Continued)

Teacher-Student Interaction	My Thoughts
Student 8: 9 + 5 + 3. I added 9 + 5 That is 14 plus the 3 is 17. T: So you knew it was 14 and then you counted up.	Maybe this is what she did . . . but what questions would be better? . . . Elicit number relationships? What about the other quiet kids. . . . Who is benefiting?
T: So let's make it a little more difficult. What about using addition and take-away? Student 9: 10 + 10 − 2 = 17. T: So . . . 10 + 10 is 20. Now count back. What did you get? 18? S9: Oh, so it's 18. T: So you need to take away one more. (Writes on the board: 10 + 10 − 2 − 1 = 17 draws a number line and illustrates the jumping back and moves on.)	**Why does she tell them what to do? Who is doing the work?** Uses model . . . but missing conversation about number relationships embedded in choice of strategies. . . . Isn't this one goal of today's number? Is she doing this for my benefit?
Student 10: 6 + 6 + 9. Six plus six . . . is 12. Plus 9 is 18. T: No . . . close . . . count up. S10: . . . 12, 13, 14, 15, 16, 17 . . . T: Okay. A few more and then we are going to do something different.	Looking for right answer . . . obscures reasoning about number relations and using what we know to consider if answer makes sense. He is nodding with each count! By ones! What's happening here? Models, double-checking, naming strategies (beginning of lesson), models for thinking, paraphrasing students' thinking (not really) . . . Where is the reasoning about number relations?
Student 11: 20 − 3 − 1 + 1. T: Is this a true statement? (She points to the number line she has drawn on the board.) Start at 20, go back 3 − 1 + 1 . . . is 17! Awesome! So you made a connection with S9's math sentence? But you don't know how you did it. (Teacher moves on to another student.)	Uses vocabulary . . . is she trying to show me something about her teaching? **S12 looks puzzled.** **What!!!?** **Maybe she doesn't know?** **I can't follow . . .** *At this point, I was feeling like this was a show for me, a show of all the types of teacher moves that should happen in the course of a lesson. But there is no substance to the lesson.*

Teacher-Student Interaction	My Thoughts
Student 12: 4 + 4 + 4 + 4 + 1. T: How did you do it? S12: I counted in my mind. T: I need to understand. . . . (T records on the board) S12: I know that 4 + 4 is 8 and 8 + 4 is 12 and 12 + 4 is 16 and 1 is . . . T: So you know that 4 + 4 + 4 + 4 (circles this on the board) is 16. But you can also break it up in your mind: 4 + 4 is 8 and 4 + 4 is 8. That equals 16. And 16 + 1 is 17. Good thinking. T: Sometimes we just know a sentence. Like 21 − 4. I just know it is 17. Like last year the favorite one was 35 + 15 = 50. And so I learned it. I just know it.	He will tell you he added. . . . Another line of questioning maybe? . . . What question? Is this your thinking . . . or the students? Again, a number sense opportunity. . . . Place value. Why does she share this then?
At this point 25 minutes have gone by. She now turns to the next activity.	Too many examples without much pondering, reflecting, making connections, having other students explain each others' thinking, and so on. Look for openings in the lesson for number sense discussion.

6

Purposeful Planning and Facilitation

CASE DESCRIPTION

In the case, Coaching in a Group: Moving From 1:1 to 1:?, the coach-author, Chloe, describes her struggles as she branches out from one-to-one coaching to coaching groups of teachers in team meeting structures. This novice and, yet, deeply self-reflective coach describes her attempts to design agendas that matter and facilitation that captivates groups of teachers at a meaningful level. Chloe's case moves between descriptions of two group meetings, the planning and preparation for each meeting, and her reflections on her coaching. As she struggles, she also gains new insights that help her develop a stronger coaching practice. Novice coaches and experienced coaches, alike, will relate to the complexities of planning and purposefully facilitating group meetings described in Chloe's case.

NOTES TO THE READER

You may choose to read the Focus Questions (page 64) prior to reading this case as a way to orient yourself to the important issues the coach describes. As you read the case, write comments or questions in the margins and note line numbers of sentences or paragraphs that interest you or raise questions for you.

Case 6	Author: Chloe

Coaching in a Group: Moving From 1:1 to 1:?

1   It's one thing to work with one teacher 1:1. You know how it is; you are in her classroom, you share observations—sometimes in the moment—about the experience with her own students. You've met before to do the math together, and you meet afterward to examine the students' work and
5   engagement with the math activity. You collect data. You know her strengths, have a sense of where she is in her own mathematics understanding, and you have a feel for how she "sees" her students. You work together to build on these things and continue, together, to study the students' work and plan the next steps for their learning. For the coach,
10 there's preplanning, organizing, and follow-through—but it's always with this particular teacher in mind. An audience, or a collaborator, of one.

I'm quickly finding that it's another thing altogether to facilitate meetings and discussions with *groups* of teachers. Like most coaches, I have responsibilities for group meetings, and in particular, I'm puzzling over
15 the concept (and, yikes, my responsibility for) grade-level team meetings. I wonder about *leading* these meetings as I consider the facilitation of them an essential aspect of my coaching job. Frankly, I question really what I should *prepare*, what I should *do*, during grade-level meetings, and how to think about *organizing* meetings that are both engaging and purposeful.
20 In general, I'm new at this, and I'm determined, but I can't get a handle on this role, and I am having a hard time refining something without input from others. And by others I mean those of you with benefit of experience and the ability—the wisdom—to understand the bigger picture.

I've talked with other coaches about cultivating grade-level meetings as
25 a main forum for our work because, frankly, with the way school schedules are and the precious little time designated for professional development, it's not even physically possible to get to enough people by simply coaching 1:1 all the time. Meeting with groups seems like a strategic way to spread the resource of coaching more broadly. This means that planning an agenda and
30 the facilitation of these group meetings is key to my work, which is another reason I'm determined to get this moving in a productive direction.

I have lots of questions: What are goals to keep in mind for grade-level team meetings? What *is* a realistic goal for 90-minute monthly meetings? What does it mean to support teachers *as a group* working on mathematics—
35 how does one determine the agenda? Is there a way to make the meetings be *our* meetings rather than *mine?*

Since September, I've facilitated a few grade-level meetings, but if truth were told, the quality has varied, and I know these have to tighten up a lot; I'll be doing many more. In an effort to learn more deeply how to get these right—and starting somewhere—I offer a description of the first meeting. Maybe by writing them, with you as my audience, I can construct a perspective that's revealing!

First Meeting at the Signal School

For the past two years, the Signal School has been using, to varying degrees, the recently established district curriculum. I am a new coach at Signal, and as such, I am just beginning to establish relationships with the teachers. Team meetings are mandatory, system-wide, and run once a month, for 90 minutes. By a lucky fluke (surely not to be repeated), I was able to run two 90-minute meetings, two weeks in a row, at the end of September. All the first and second grade teachers attended the meetings, rather than the more typical one-grade-level version. As I prepared, I came up with lots of ideas for the first meeting. We could talk about goals for the year, we could look at student work, and we could examine the embedded assessments from the math book. We could talk about assessment as an inquiry topic. This first meeting was brimming with possibility. Wanting to have students "present" to keep us grounded, I took it upon myself to ask Marcy, a first grade teacher, to bring student work for all of us to examine at the meeting. I also decided to prepare a chart of issues I thought would be useful to address; it would serve as an agenda of sorts.

The meeting began at 8:00 with all eight teachers (four first grade and four second grade) coming into the section of the library the principal had offered as a meeting space. I was ready to start even before 8:00, and actually, for a first meeting we did okay with beginning relatively on time. We had a few moments of chatting "hellos," and I moved us right into looking at Marcy's student work. Even though it represented only one grade level, it seemed a good place to start. But already, I could feel a lack of interest; it seemed that no one appeared invested in *learning* anything from the work. Over the course of the next hour, the group's conversation meandered from "what students didn't learn in Kindergarten" to a discussion of a parent's request that her child learn long division in second grade. We had strayed, and I wasn't sure how to rein us back in on something useful. Because I had "Goals" written on the chart that I'd put up on the wall at the beginning of the meeting, we talked "goal talk" but only a few volunteered and the talk had no charge—no commentary, no building of discussion. I was at sea and grateful, at least, that no one was complaining outright or restless as much as they were, well, stuck there. What a terrible feeling it is to captain a sailing ship with no wind and, worse yet, no compass. I had prepared, but with what end in mind? How did what I had prepared make sense or even relate to this mixed-grade-level group of teachers? I didn't know why it wasn't working, and I didn't know with what or how to rally the group. As the teachers began to fall silent and the meeting time was coming to a close, I was realizing that asking these teachers to come up with authentic goals to offer would be difficult when the whole point of the meetings wasn't feeling clear (to any of us). I looked up, hoping I didn't look as discouraged and helpless as I felt, and asked,

85   "Are there topics you would like to consider next time we meet?" Looking back, I don't know if I was trying to open up ownership of the meetings or abdicate my role entirely.

After a quiet moment, Katya piped up and said she wanted to talk about pacing. Continuing with some vigor, she explained, "Pacing of the
90   district-curriculum guide was set much too fast last year, and it looks like it's not letting up this year either." Looking around the room, Katya offered this example: Her class had worked for quite a while on "combinations that make 10 and doubles," and then, in following the pacing guide, the class had been asked to "leap much too quickly" into working
95   with numbers as large as 100. She shook her head and said, "It's not a good idea to make us go so fast. The kids can't learn that much." Katya didn't elaborate on what might be more appropriate or about what her students need to know to transition in a more realistic fashion to the next level math idea. But she appeared to feel strongly that the pacing guide
100   was wrong for her students. It was a start.

Our time was up, and without giving anyone a chance to respond, Gina, a second grade teacher, looked at her watch and said, "We've really got to go."

Planning the Next Meeting

I contemplated this meeting as I planned for the second. What would
105   it take for a group of teachers who have been using the same curriculum for two years now to take new steps forward in their work, to go deeper into the work? Would it be useful to address some of Katya's concerns about pacing? Would there be a way to address the pacing-guide issue that could also be important for the other teachers in the group? Would there
110   be a way I could help shift our attention from pacing to how to assess student learning, for example?

I was determined to have a more fine-tuned agenda this time around. First, we'd start with a group look at Angela's whole-class Numbers Assessment. Next, we would take a step back to look at, across grades,
115   how students' ideas and understanding of numbers develops through first and second grade. I wasn't totally confident about being able to keep the second part tightly focused. Regardless of this niggling doubt, I decided it was important to try to expand the thinking of the teachers who appeared comfortable with the curriculum—though only at their own grade levels.
120   I hoped, with this plan and in consideration of Katya's concern, we would be able to touch on the pacing of the curriculum by way of investigating how students' number ideas develop over time.

The Second Meeting

Wanting voices other than mine to be heard from the beginning, I started by asking, "Does anyone have concerns, questions, or exciting things to
125   share about what has been happening in your classrooms?" A few quick comments were offered, but it was a brief volley of detail sorts of questions and a brief anecdote from Jay, and quite soon, we got down to the business of, again, looking at student work.

I introduced a "looking at student work" protocol so we could exam-
130   ine the papers with a structured, grounded approach. As promised,

Angela had brought several students' papers pertaining to Question 3 of the assessment:

> At the zoo, the children saw many animals. There were 2 birds in a tree, 4 snakes on the ground, 3 foxes in a pen, and 2 deer drinking water. How many animals did the children see?   135

Angela was surprised by the assessment question because "it was based on an activity her students had not done." She told us that it was extremely difficult for her students to do this problem and that she had spent a lot of time supporting individual students during the assessment. She continued, "There were too many numbers to add together and too much to keep track   140 of and remember." Angela told us that the complexity of it all was compounded by the fact that students tend to draw detailed drawings for these kinds of story problems and lose track of the mathematics.

We looked at the student work to learn more. In the first piece, the student had drawn elaborate pictures of animals all over the page. We   145 commented on Jolene's drawings and worked to figure out if she had, in fact, made drawings of *all* the animals in the story problem. As it turned out, Marcy pointed out that Jolene had drawn each animal but had never written a total number. We thought about how she might be making sense of the problem; did Jolene understand "finding a total number of ani-   150 mals"? She was, in a sense, rendering the story on the page, but was she solving the problem? We couldn't tell. The whole group agreed they would want to go back and ask Jolene directly how many animals the children saw at the zoo.

Emmett's drawing depicted linking cubes lined up in a row: 2 red,   155 4 blue, 3 yellow and 2 green cubes as representing animals. In addition, he had written the number 11 for a correct total. Angela and Jay commented on Emmett's ability for abstraction in using specific colored cubes to represent each type of animal. Katya compared Emmett's cube model to Jolene's animal pictures and wondered if it were possible that he under-   160 stood some things about number that Jolene had not yet formulated. When I asked what she meant, Marcy stepped in and said, "Well, Emmett is *counting up* the animals, but Jolene doesn't show that she's counting at all." After looking at a few more piece of student work that weren't particularly revealing, it was hard to know very definitively what these   165 students, other than Emmett, were able to say about *total amounts*. Megan shifted the talk to the role of the teacher during the administration of these assessments. Many were in agreement that less explicit students' work often prompted questions for the teacher. How much should the teacher ask? Is it legitimate to press the student during the assessment to show   170 more information on her paper? Should teachers give out manipulatives if the student isn't seeking them out? What *are* the boundaries of teachers' involvement anyway?

While we didn't come to consensus on these issues, I did feel that the discussion touched on important practice considerations. We were discussing   175 what the students were doing with the problem and, too, how a teacher might know what a student understands.

I introduced Part 2; we would examine the progression of ideas regarding children's development of number sense. I started this portion of the meeting by saying that because everyone in the group was currently teaching modules   180

185   on number, I thought it would be useful to consider the progression of students' ideas, understandings, and strategies with regard to number sense in the first and second grades. I told the group that in thinking about number, admittedly a broad idea, I had chosen to focus in on a set of important concepts for first and second graders. I encouraged the teachers to add others to a prepared chart of these categories that I, then, taped to the wall:

- Solving addition and subtraction story problems
- Considering number combinations
- Counting
190
- Making sense of the number system
- Number relationships/Numbers within numbers

195   We took a minute to look over the list, and I suggested we talk about how students' ideas and strategies might develop through the two grades with regard to the categories on the chart; I was counting on their experience and their expertise to help them generate discussion. I asked the group to first consider, "Solving addition and subtraction story problems."

At first, no one said a thing, and they looked confused. I waited, not wanting to lose my confidence in facilitating and stammer my way to a new question too soon. After, to me, an interminable wait time, Mary
200   finally asked, "Do you mean how kids solve them?" and I nodded. She then offered, "Drawing pictures."

And then there was another silence.

So it took a little while. There were lots of silences. I was realizing, belatedly, that if you just teach the curriculum without ever having a
205   chance to actually articulate what you are doing, maybe, the first shots at talking it through on an adult level is hard; the words are hard to pull together. I wonder what else might have helped get this going. I was also realizing that while I had images and thoughts in my head as I brainstormed the list by myself, it occurred to me that these were *my* ideas, *my*
210   thoughts, *my* brainstorm, and *my* resulting categories. How will I ever learn to connect to *their* ideas?

After a bit of quiet, the teachers began to contribute. They talked among themselves for a few minutes and took some time to generate a list of ways young students work with numbers in order to work through and
215   solve story problems. There was a discussion about the progression of these strategies, and I was relieved to see that as the meeting was progressing, the energy for thinking about how students are doing their work was higher than at the last meeting. The list looked like this:

- Drawing pictures (of the story)
220
- Using other objects to represent the objects in the story
- Counting on
- Using facts you know

Angela pointed to the Counting category. She said that there are lots of ways that students in both grades count in the early stages. There was a
225   fair amount of discussion among the group as a new list began to emerge:

- Counting orally
- Counting objects

- Recognizing quantity
- Counting on
- Counting by groups   230

Although I recognized that this was just a list, it did name strategies and ideas that we could all be looking out for in these early grade classrooms. Satisfied, for now, with the list for counting, we were also beginning to run out of time. I closed by again asking, "Is there anything in particular you want to discuss at the next meeting?" And, again, Katya   235 offered an idea. She looked right at me and said, "I would like to know what to do with struggling students." In that moment, I realized that Katya could steer us all over the place if I kept asking this question. I said that I would think about her request. And I knew I had to do more than just stop asking the question.   240

Reflecting on the Second Meeting

Were these new connections about students' work for the teachers? Was this useful or were teachers politely going through the motions of an exercise that I had contrived? And just how would I gauge that? What do I listen for or how would I measure any impact that follows? Now what?   245

I realize I don't have enough of a sense of where these teachers are in their thinking about math learning and teaching or about their students or about their roles. And so I don't have a clear grasp at all of where they might need to go next. If this is my job to figure out, how do coaches learn the answers?   250

Thankfully, though painfully (it's so hard to be new), it is becoming clearer each time that I need to determine a really centered focus and very specific goals for grade-level meetings. How *do* coaches think about intentions? About focus? About goals? About agendas? I hadn't realized how definitive I would need to become; a group's learning required such keen   255 awareness of what's useful and necessary, and I'm not sure how to discern these things. Maybe, if I thought back to my own teaching, if I connected to what helped me look deeply at my students' thinking and their work, if I looked at the curriculum and used it as a resource. . . . Would this help me determine a more cohesive and purposeful focus?   260

So in the end, I have fundamental questions about my work, and these are questions that I need to struggle through with other coaches. I find it hard to work in isolation with only my own best ideas as a guide. How can I tie into a bigger framework for professional development? This coaching business is a far cry from teaching my third grade class just last June. It isn't the   265 fact that I'm working with adults now (though more humiliating to fail in front of them than my students who were so forgiving and to whom I could return cheerfully the next morning at 8:00). More, it's stepping out of working with a predesigned math curriculum to figuring out what teachers need to work on and how to get fruitfully at that work. A coach is charged with   270 professional development design, articulating a focus, nailing down goals. I know this; I'm just finding my way there.

Case 6	Coaching in a Group

Focus Questions Activity

As you discuss the questions refer to the specific line numbers of Chloe's case.

1. New to both coaching and to the Signal School, Chloe plans an agenda for the first mixed-grade-level meeting. How would you characterize Chloe's understanding of her role and responsibilities as she plans an agenda and facilitation of the meting?

2. Consider the meeting as it unfolds. Citing line numbers, how do you see the teachers engaging? What questions come up for Chloe as she's facilitating?

3. As she reflects on the first meeting, what does Chloe take into consideration in planning for the next? Describe the ideas and intentions behind the decisions she makes. Explain how Chloe is thinking about Katya's agenda suggestion.

4. While Angela raises concerns about the assessment question in the first meeting, the group moves on to learn about how students attend to solving the problem. Just as the teachers would like to go back and to find out more about what Jolene does understand, formulate a few specific questions you might pose to these teachers in order to find out more about their understandings and ideas.

5. At the end of this meeting, Chloe wonders, yet again, what has been accomplished. Put yourself in the position of coach colleague for Chloe. What questions might you ask her that could help reveal the accomplishments of her plan and of the group discussions? What ideas do *you* have in mind that might help Chloe sort out some answers to "coaching in a group" questions she poses? These should not be advice disguised as questions, rather ones that would help Chloe think about this for herself.

6. Refer back to the beginning of the case. Can you identify elements of Chloe's 1:1 coaching, with which she feels competent and comfortable, that might directly relate to ways of thinking about working with more than one teacher at a time? What might Chloe take from her 1:1 work that will transfer in significant ways to successfully working 1:?

| Case 6 | Coaching in a Group |

Planning Activity:
Facilitating Group Learning

1. Before you begin a discussion in your small group, take a few minutes, on your own, to think carefully and write about the following:

   • Describe, from a coaching point of view, the purpose or direction for a group meeting you facilitate.

   • Describe, from the meeting participant's point of view, the purpose for the group meeting.

   In your response, you might reflect on the purpose for grade-level meetings, planning meetings, math team meetings, or debrief meetings of teacher visits to each other's classrooms. Focus on structures or opportunities for facilitating learning outside the realm of the, perhaps more familiar, one-to-one classroom coaching. Include both the teachers' points of view—even if they are murky—and your own as the facilitator—even if it is murky—so that you have a place to begin your group work. Explore, in writing, how you understand your expectations, and the participants' expectations, for this work. Are they the same? How do you know?

2. Take turns sharing your writing and describing both points of view. During this time, the members of your group will listen without commenting or asking questions. When each person has had a chance to talk, take a few moments and jot down new ideas or questions this raises.

3. As a small group, brainstorm responses to the overarching questions Chloe raises:

   • How do you determine an agenda? How do you take into account a plan that places participants' learning at the center?

   • How do you know your agenda will bring the group to the goal you have for their learning? What measure might you use to determine the success of your meeting?

   • How do you think about determining a balance of ownership for the meeting?

4. Choose one question from #3, and on chart paper, list your group's ideas.

7

Refining and Reimagining One's Coaching Practice

Chapter Elements

✦ Case: Learning About Counting, Learning About Coaching

✦ Focus Questions Activity

✦ Planning Activity: Cultivating Collaborative Study

CASE DESCRIPTION

In Learning About Counting, Learning About Coaching, the coach-author describes a Kindergarten classroom observation, interviews with several students as they engage in counting activities, and her subsequent questions about effective coaching debriefs. Elaine, a coach with past experience as a high school math teacher, becomes intrigued with the varied strategies for counting in Kindergarten, and over the course of one classroom visit, she is bursting with questions and a new appreciation for the children's effort involved in sorting out counting as an idea. She describes the ensuing teacher debrief, which, she soon realizes, falls short of its potential. As she reflects on the classroom experience and her facilitation of the teacher debrief meeting, she gains new insights about the questions she might have asked and about the level of teacher and coach learning for which she is aiming.

NOTES TO THE READER

You may choose to read the Focus Questions (page 76) prior to reading this case as a way to orient yourself to the important issues the coach describes. As you read the case, write comments or questions in the margins and note line numbers of sentences or paragraphs that interest you or raise questions for you.

Case 7	Author: Elaine

Learning About Counting, Learning About Coaching

November at the Meetinghouse School

1   Meetinghouse is a small school situated within a large urban district. The school serves three- to six-year-olds in six separate classrooms. There are two classrooms of three- and four-year-olds, two Kindergartens, and two first grades. What is unique about Meetinghouse is that in each of

5   these grade bands one of the classrooms serves as an inclusion classroom (a mixed class with students of varying needs) and the other is referred to as general education classroom. A classroom of 18 to 20 students, in the inclusion model, may include up to seven children identified with a .4 level of special needs. Paraprofessionals support each inclusion classroom,

10   and for a brief time in the early afternoon, there may be as many as three paraprofessionals assigned to the class. Other educational services, such as speech and language or occupational therapy, may also be provided to children other than the identified seven students with special needs. Teachers have a high investment in their students' learning and have espe-

15   cially been working on studying the needs of diverse learners; focusing on math content and on particular math teaching practices is new here.

I have been working at the Meetinghouse School with the Kindergarten teachers twice a month. I feel that our work is shifting from *building trust* to *looking at the content within the curriculum,* and now, we are melding

20   these two. The new math series was introduced last year and this year; for the first time, the school has math content and learning standards in place for these young students. Math coaching has been introduced, and I began working with the teachers at Meetinghouse School this fall; I am new to this teaching staff. The introduction of math coaching also

25   represents the first opportunity for teachers of young children to engage in content-specific support in their classrooms. Although I am not certified in special needs and, in fact, most of my mathematics experience has been

with much older students, I appreciate that primary students are capable of exploring mathematical ideas and that time devoted to the development of mathematical reasoning is valuable even for the very youngest children here.

My coaching schedule is still evolving, but basically, the routine is this: I meet with the two Kindergarten teachers before a math lesson, observe a lesson, and then, with all of us together again, debrief immediately after the math class. Over a six-week period, we each teach one class and participate in the structured pre- and postconversations with an eye toward examining the students' work as well as their *math talk*. At the same time, we aim to develop our own understanding of what's happening with the math and to learn to nurture mathematical understandings.

A lot is new in this Meetinghouse scenario. Kindergarten teachers are using a uniform curriculum for the first time, math-specific classes are taking place each day for a specific duration, and perhaps most importantly, there is group discussion about mathematics at this grade level. And for me? I'm not only new to the Meetinghouse School, I am just months into my new job as a math coach. I coach in three different schools each week, and I am still learning what it means to be a coach in reality—not just in theory!

Exploring Counting

Ms. Harding is waiting in the library as Ms. Bruggeman, the other Kindergarten teacher, and I gather to meet for our previsit discussion. We will be observing Ms. Harding's students today. The two of us join her at the table and listen as Ms. Harding describes the activity she is going to teach. The lesson will involve a whole-group meeting on the rug discussing a counting activity called Counting Bags. She wants to begin the math class with a demonstration of the activity with one student. Ms. Harding explains that she will then assign each child to one of several "math centers" where an activity is set up with counting objects and papers and markers for recordings. After 20 minutes at their math center, students will return to the rug to share their work. In planning meetings such as this one, Ms. Bruggeman, Ms. Harding, and I have been working toward thoughtfully articulating the learning objectives of each of the activities we offer students, and so next, Ms. Harding explains that the students will be encountering work designed to target the following: counting and the use of different counting strategies, representing quantities in different ways, and working in pairs. It has been, I think, through these math-focused discussions—new to the teachers—that we are all beginning to understand and identify (aside from just reading and accepting what it says in the teachers manual) the mathematical ideas embedded in these classroom activities.

Ms. Harding continued leading our discussion by describing the general tenor of the classroom over the past few days and offering updates on the emotional and physical well-being of the children. We spend some time listening to her reasons for pairing certain students; we learn about who she wants to watch carefully today. She offers a variety of explanations. Micah was agitated, and Eric was sad; Tina had cried for a long time after

75 her father dropped her off, and Jackie wasn't feeling well. By the end of our 30 minutes, we had gotten the update on life in the room 108. It was time to start class.

The three of us entered the Kindergarten classroom where an assistant teacher had been reading a book to the class. As soon as she entered,
80 Ms. Harding called everyone to the rug at the front of the room. Books are left on tables, chairs squeak as children push from their places, and there is the normal bumping and jostling and "classroom music" as young children change position, leave an activity, and figure out how to attend to the next business of what must sometimes feel like a very long day—or perhaps
85 the opposite—as though nothing else exists but this moment in time.

And so it took a few minutes to get everyone settled. David had to sit next to Ms. Harding with one hand on her leg for the whole activity. Each time he moved his hand off her leg, his focus wandered. Rafael became the teacher's helper so that he wasn't whispering and bothering Jasmine. Nye
90 had to be refocused several times before the meeting could get going. All the while, Marcus, on the rug to my left, was waiting patiently for "stuff to start."

Ms. Harding gave the students a verbal introduction to the counting lesson and then appointed Rafael to be her partner in demonstrating
95 Counting Bags. Rafael moved quickly to the front, sat down, and reached into the bag. He dramatically twisted his face away so as not to see the contents, felt around inside, and then counted to six without drawing out his hand. He then said he could tell the objects were crayons and drew, on a small white board, a visual representation of the number of crayons he'd
100 felt in the bag. Ms. Harding seemed a bit surprised when Rafael drew six squares to represent the crayons. She seemed to push at this idea, asking her students several times what other pictures they could use to represent the crayons.

Rafael said quietly, "You could use circles, too."
105 Alana offered, "How about sticks?"

Ms. Harding appeared to be searching for another answer. She looked out around the group and asked, "Is there anything that you can think of, looking at these crayons?"

Rafael seemed quite sure of himself. "You could use any shape," he said.
110 Ms. Harding, still watching the students, asked, "But what about drawing a picture of the crayons?"

A few students said something like "Oh," and she let it go and moved students to assigned seats at different tables where they would work for the next 20 minutes. I noted Rafael's and Alan's flexibility with this idea of
115 representation and wasn't sure what Ms. Harding was after and why she chose not to pursue the idea of any single representation standing for any single counted object. It occurred to me that she might be reaching for a realistic spread of what students might do; maybe she wanted the idea of drawing crayons to be made public because that version would be vali-
120 dated for all the children who would only know to do that. On a pad of paper I carried, I jotted this down to think about for our debrief conversation that would follow class.

The children moved quickly and quietly to their assigned tables and began working on the activities. While the assistant teachers and Ms. Harding
125 stayed at specific centers, Ms. Bruggeman and I moved about the room to observe children at work.

I watched two students, Catherine and Rafael, working together on a counting routine. They had one paper bag with cotton balls in it. Each child had a recording paper. Catherine had taken the cotton balls from the bag, put them on the table, and then counted each one, saying each number aloud. Rafael was listening to Catherine count, and he drew a representation and a number as she went along.

I watched Catherine for a very long time. She counted and drew. She would pick up a cotton ball and say the next number in sequence (3) as she placed it on the paper. She would lift the cotton ball and then draw where it had been, working very hard to make a circle the proper size to represent the cotton ball. After she had drawn all the cotton balls as she counted, she seemed unsure of her resulting total. She began counting and moving the balls to the circles and then to the side of the paper, one by one, to make sure she had counted accurately. She was moving her lips each time she moved the cotton ball. Several times, she was unsure of where she was and started over. The last time she was unsure, she was at the sixth ball. This time instead of beginning at 1 again, she counted five cotton balls that were on the side of her paper (removing the sixth one) and then counted with her pencil eraser touching each circle leaving it on the fifth ball. She then resumed her counting-and-moving-cotton-ball routine. She finally got to 10 and seemed satisfied.

As methodical as Catherine was to touch, count, reproduce, and record, Rafael was completely content to never touch the cotton balls at all. He made a shape to represent each ball and then, as Catherine counted and then went through her checking routine, he colored his shapes in with different markers. When Catherine had finished her recording, she turned to Rafael's work and talked to him. (Refer to Figure 7.1.)

Catherine: Why didn't you make circles? Yours don't look like the cotton balls.
Rafael: They don't have to look like them. I have ten squares. See. 2, 4, 6, 8, 10. (He moved his fingers up the page counting by twos.)
Catherine: They aren't all squares. Some are triangles.
Rafael: Yeah, these are triangles (pointing to his top row).
Catherine: No, one is a square.
Rafael: Oh yeah, these two are triangles (pointing correctly to the two triangles).
Me: How else could you show there were ten in the bag?
Catherine: With a number?
Me: What would that look like?
They both correctly wrote 10, without looking back at their work.
Me: Could you use any words to help show there are ten cotton balls in the bag?
Catherine: You could write 10, but how do you spell it?

We proceeded to sound it out and Catherine wrote TN. She looked at Rafael's paper and added an E, TNE. Then she crossed it out and wrote, "TEN."

I was impressed by the difference in the ways these two had engaged with the activity. I had watched Catherine closely and could feel her persistence and noted her clarity about the job at hand. I was also aware that Rafael had a very different orientation to the task. He, too, was clear about

180   the work he was doing—confident and unquestioningly representing cotton balls as triangles and alternatively with squares. It didn't just have to look like a cotton ball to represent a counted cotton ball. I thought about what he understood, what made sense to him, and the learning space between that and what Catherine was so clearly working through. At that moment, I was pleased to have been able to witness this very difference, to see what a simple task could draw out, and to help me learn about Catherine and Rafael and about steps in learning what it means to quantify.

I don't have a lot of words for this trajectory or "making sense," but I recognized it and found myself somehow humbled by it.   185

After leaving Catherine and Rafael, I went to visit the Counting Box activity at a different table. When I got there, Nye was working on counting buttons in the box. She picked up each button, placed it on her paper plate, and correctly said the numbers in sequence up to ten.   190

Ms. Brown, the assistant teacher, asked, "How many buttons do you have?"

Nye looked up from the plate of ten and replied, "Two."

Ms. Brown, wanting to remain neutral in judgment but wanting the correct answer, asked again, "How many buttons do you have?"   195

Nye began to count. "1, 2, 3, 4, 5, 6, 7. . . ." She looked up slightly at me and kept going but missed a button. ". . . 8, 9."

Ms. Brown gently persisted. "So let's see, how many buttons do you have?"

Nye came back with, "Two."

"Count again, Nye, okay?" she said.   200

Nye looked at the buttons and now said, "1, 2, 3, 4, 5, 6, 7, 8, 9, 10, 11."

"How many buttons do you have?" said Ms. Brown patiently.

"Two," she says looking from Ms. Brown, to me, to Ms. Brown.

Sensing that Ms. Brown wasn't sure about how to proceed, I took a stab at it. I asked Nye a slightly different question.   205

"Nye, I am confused. You have counted these buttons and I heard you count different times to 10, to 9, and now to 11. How do you know how many buttons there are?"

Nye held up two fingers and said, "Two."

Experimenting, I asked, "Can I change the number of buttons?" Nye   210
nodded, and I took all 10 buttons into the palm of my hand and then put 3 of them in a pile on her plate to count.

Nye moved the buttons as she counted, "1, 2, 3."

"So how many buttons are there on your plate?"

Nye looked at her plate and then her fingers. First, she had two fingers   215
up and then slowly raised a third finger. Her mouth looked like she was about to say two, but then she said, "Three."

"How do you know there are three?"

At this, Nye counted, "1, 2, 3."

"What if I change the number again?"   220

"Okay!" Nye had not tired of this exercise; she seemed as intrigued as we were. I put four buttons down in a pile for her this time.

"1, 2, 3, 4," she said.

"How many buttons do you have now?"

Nye looked right up at me and confidently said, "Two!"   225

I wasn't sure what to make of this exchange in the moment but, again, recorded it for discussion later. What was Nye's interpretation of, "How many do you have?" and why didn't it connect to her correct count? In Nye's mind, what does "two" describe? What does she understand, and what is she missing?   230

The time for the counting activities was drawing to a close as I thought about this. I took a walk around and scanned the various approaches children were taking. Some students had picked up objects and drawn random, seemingly unrelated, numbers of pictures; one boy couldn't

235 describe the connection between the pictures and the numbers of objects. There were students who wrote numbers and students who seemed not to know how to represent quantity in any other way than pictorial representation. There seemed to be a full spectrum of approaches to counting, representing, and knowing quantity.

240 As I was sketching final notes of students' work, Ms. Harding called all the children back to the rug. Once everyone was settled, she called children up in pairs and asked them to tell about their activities. The children said very little, and Ms. Harding paraphrased or summarized their very quiet comments such as, "they counted" or "they had pencils in

245 a bag." She did not engage them with questions or comments as much as she asked them to describe what they did and then asked for the next pair to come forward. The class time ended on this quiet note.

Debrief

As I walked from the classroom, I was struck by what I'd seen revealed in these counting activities, and I know there was much more to learn. I also

250 noted that there were students who needed the adults in the room to spend some portion of time redirecting them to the counting task itself many times. I was left thinking about the job of teaching students who are in so many places, working at such varied levels. But could this Kindergarten math class of so many stages, strategies, and understandings stand as an

255 example—obvious by virtue of the simplicity of the counting task—of what happens in every classroom, no matter how old the students are?

I raise this question when Ms. Harding, Ms. Bruggeman, and two of the three assistant teachers settle into our debrief meeting. Ms. Harding replied, "I wrestle with this every day. I tried a high-low student pairing

260 strategy, which worked in some ways but really didn't work at all in others. . . . I stopped doing that because I felt like I was asking too much of the more advanced students. It was too chaotic, they weren't able to manage the personalities and manage the math. I thought they would have been able to, but it didn't work."

265 The conversation now continued through discussions of pairings and responsibilities and input from the paraprofessional teachers about which students are better matched than others. It seemed, because the needs in the class are so varied—emotionally, physically, and intellectually—that we each had lots to offer to this conversation about personalities and

270 students we'd observed. We talked about individual students focusing mostly, it seemed, on the students who had trouble starting the counting or who counted but had no way to follow through with a representation related to the count. I described how methodical Catherine was, and Ms. Brown said how stumped she'd been in trying to help Nye "get what

275 she was doing." It was all so clear that the children and their needs and "styles of being in class" were intriguing and sometimes very puzzling; we had lots of energy for the conversation.

But as the bell rang and the group needed to disperse and gather their students, I realized that, as the coach facilitating this debrief, I'd missed my

280 chance. I knew that these discussions and this visit with Ms. Harding's students had so much more potential than what we covered in our debrief.

What does Ms. Harding do next? Surely, asking students to simply tell what they did is only an exercise in speaking and describing; it's not mathematical, and it doesn't further a math agenda. But what should she do? The children I observed illustrated a great range of coming to know aspects of counting. If we don't quite know what to do, the answer can't possibly be just doing more of it. What did we learn about what it takes to count, to keep track, and to make the connection between object and number? How do the students come to understand quantity? What do we expect of them? What is it we are really aiming to teach? We had fallen into the trap, enticing as it was, to discuss children individually, and we had missed the chance to talk about the math with which they were engaged. We had missed the chance to make sense of what we were witnessing or to put what we saw in a context of building our own knowledge about counting in Kindergarten. In reflection, I have so many math questions—and I know there will be more opportunities—but I need to figure out how to get these discussions going in the right direction.

Getting from novice to the next stage of my own practice is strewn with these kinds of meetings; I want to take this example of so many things going well in a class and see if I can discuss this in the coach group. Perhaps together, we can see the potential that was in the lesson, what coaching might have been activated, what moves I might make next time, and what we might have a chance to be learning in a more disciplined way. Ms. Harding and I, and all the teachers, are heading out on a journey, and I think that if I really look carefully, I can get this debrief meeting work on the right track.

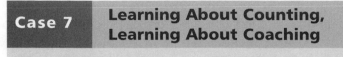

Case 7   **Learning About Counting, Learning About Coaching**

Focus Questions Activity

On Your Own

Spend some time writing about Rafael and Catherine:

1. Consider Rafael in lines 93–110 and again in lines 148–162. What logic does his work suggest? Capture on paper a brief description of the counting ideas he understands and note line numbers that support your thinking.

2. Catherine, a persistent and organized learner, is working at a different stage of counting. Write a brief articulation of the learning about counting work that Catherine is engaged in.

In Your Small Group

Reflect together about these written responses. Next, discuss the following:

3. Nye and others in the class are wrestling with other issues of learning to count. Articulate the learning ideas in Nye's counting work and consider the coach's list about other's in the class in lines 187–239.

4. List specific questions you would choose to ask of the students in this case during their ending whole-group discussion. As the coach or teacher, what do you want to learn from them? What might they learn from each other?

5. What ideas or beliefs might a teacher have about student learning as she shifts from facilitating *descriptive* sharing to an *inquisitive* sharing? How might a coach support this transition?

6. Highlight coaching decisions in the debrief discussion. What does Elaine mean when she comments, "I realized that, as the coach facilitating this debrief, I'd missed my chance?" After some time for reflection, with what question or comment might you begin a mathematically-focused discussion with this group of teachers?

Case 7 — Learning About Counting, Learning About Coaching

Planning Activity: Cultivating Collaborative Study

On Your Own

In Learning about Counting, Learning about Coaching, Elaine writes that she and the teachers missed the opportunity to learn more about young students' developing counting ideas and thinking revealed as these students, in particular, learn about counting. In this Planning Activity, you will have a chance to consider what might be accomplished by engaging with a single teacher, or a group of teachers, in activities that have a specific focus on studying *student learning.* Come to your small-group discussion prepared to listen to your colleague's thoughts and to articulate your own.

1. Consider the contexts of your coaching and the mathematics topics that are coming next in the school year. Choose a math topic or idea that students and teachers will be working on and for which student work and activities will provide rich data. Some examples of topics teachers and coaches might explore include models for subtraction, the relationship between multiplication and division, using models to explore problems, and analyzing angles; there are many options. Describe your ideas and write notes on your reflections.

2. Consider how you might propose a study of this aspect of mathematics and of students' mathematical thinking. Explore the possibility of developing a course of study or a *study project* with teachers, designed to highlight and examine students' thinking, as a vehicle for supporting teacher learning and collaborative work. As you think through what such a study or project might entail, spend time reflecting and writing notes on the following:

   - What is important or challenging about this particular math topic?
   - Who could be involved in such a study of how children engage in learning?
   - How might you prepare to facilitate and focus the study? How could you get the investigation off the ground?
   - What school structures might you take advantage of to activate the collaboration? What new structures might you consider?
   - If a teacher or a group of teachers are ready to choose a topic of study, what role could you play? How might you help shape a study that would be aligned with and support your overall coaching goals?

In Small Groups

In a group of three, take turns explaining your topic, the structures that support a study of this topic, or how you might create new ones that will.

- Articulate what you want teachers to learn.
- Describe the ways this type of work, or this specific study, will help support your overall coaching goals for this teacher or this school.
- Describe a next step.
- Explain what you might consider a tangible or measurable outcome of the study.

8

Cultivating Relationships With Administrators and Other Leadership Colleagues

Chapter Elements

✦ Case: Crafting an Invitation: Shifting From Isolation to Inclusion

✦ Focus Questions Activity

✦ Planning Activity: Considering Collaboration and Communication

CASE DESCRIPTION

Crafting an Invitation describes the draft of a letter that Seth, the coach-author, wants to share with his colleagues so that he can hear their feedback and ideas. Seth has written his letter for several reasons but, most importantly, as a way to bring his principal in as an effective partner toward the goal of developing a strong math program in the school. In addition, Seth uses his letter as a way to frame his coaching goals so that they will connect to the principal's point of view. He also includes two well-articulated lists of vital aspects of the school's math program and of his coaching work there. So that the principal might understand fully what he is asking, Seth meticulously describes the lenses he takes to the work he does, the teaching practices he observes, and his assessments of the student learning environment as it is enacted in the school. Finally, the letter stands as a strategically crafted professional development tool for the principal's learning and an example of inviting in collaborators to support one's well-defined goals.

NOTES TO THE READER

You may choose to read the Focus Questions (page 85) prior to reading this case as a way to orient yourself to the important issues the coach describes. As you read the case, write comments or questions in the margins and note line numbers of sentences or paragraphs that interest you or raise questions for you.

Case 8	Author: Seth

Crafting an Invitation: Shifting From Isolation to Inclusion

1   Dear Principal Moore,

As a precursor to our midyear discussion, I thought it might be helpful if I wrote some of my reflections of the work to this point, offer thoughts on math learning goals for the year, and ideas about next steps.

5   I look forward to our meeting and hope that this letter provides useful background for our discussion next week.

Your clarity of vision and the external structures you have put in place have supported the work I need to do with your teachers beautifully. I feel lucky to work at a place that is well organized and where the standards are

10   high. The overall picture of the school is clear, and important structures are in place, such as the following:

- The school has an engaged math team that meets regularly.
- The math team has worked on several professional development series.
- The math leader attends district meetings and regularly communi-

15   cates with teachers.
- The teachers follow the district guide and use many of the resources provided by the math department.

- Teachers regularly meet with the coach.
- Two of the teachers took university courses to learn how to facilitate professional development sessions for the district.   20

Teachers know that better understanding of the mathematics content is critical—they work hard at this. It is clear, through the opportunities for other teachers to come visit your school, that teachers who come here are impressed by the continuity of instruction and focused attention on the mathematics. Other schools can, and do, learn a lot by coming to see what   25
you all have done.

I know one of your goals for the school is to continue to have high state math scores. I would add that having high scores on the local district assessments would also be important. The students generally do well on these assessments—each year they do better, and that is a good thing! When I look   30
at assessments and visit classrooms I see a lot of good, strong work on both the teachers' and students' part; they all take learning seriously.

While there is much that is supporting the school's math agenda, there is a critical area of learning that I believe we have yet to tackle—and it is not a simple or straightforward agenda for teacher learning. *Mathematical*   35
reasoning is fundamental to learning mathematics deeply, and discourse, meaning classroom discussion, is directly in service of students' growing capacity for reasoning. Being able to reason mathematically is what ultimately carries students' learning forward and, too, will support them in performing well in the future. The foundation of this work can begin   40
early—even as early as Kindergarten.

I would like a chance to collaborate with you and with the teachers on the goal of strengthening student's mathematical reasoning by focusing on *increasing productive student dialogue* in classrooms. As a coach, this is the place where I see teachers needing opportunities for thoughtful discussion   45
and support. Although the teachers and I discuss, in teaching debriefs and in grade-level meetings, the lack of student voice in classrooms—or to the same point, the strong emphasis on "teacher talk"—learning how to cultivate student voice in a classroom is no small endeavor. In theory, the teachers have expressed a real desire to hear student voices and a devel-   50
oped habit of reasoning about mathematics, but in reality, it seems hard for the staff to figure out how exactly to make this happen.

For the most part, every classroom teacher is developing a classroom learning culture that fosters good problem-solving skills. As I said before, teachers know there is great benefit to hearing student voices—more   55
voices, more of the time. And as with most teachers who are taking on these new aspects of a math teaching practice, they are beginning to ask really good questions but appear still not quite sure what to do with the students' answers. At this stage, one asks the "right question" and then moves quickly to asking the next "right question." Integrating the student   60
response into the classroom activity and agenda is a complex task.

There are lots of things that support strong dialogue in classrooms. For one, it is essential that teachers have a belief in student thinking—that students have mathematical ideas—and that mathematics is a sense-making enterprise. This agenda is where I focus my work as a coach. But   65
I also think, and am coming to think this more strongly as I am coaching this year, that teachers would benefit from hearing you echo this goal of mathematical reasoning in classrooms. At first, I think that teachers can

feel that pacing is at risk if they stop to really have student discussions. "Will we get to the end of the activity by the end of the lesson if we stop and talk? How do I know which ideas to follow, which ones to veer off from? How do I know what to do with students' ideas when I don't understand what they're talking about?" These are legitimate questions and worries. Your support in pursuing the answers could give the teachers permission to keep at it!

Understanding the point of classroom math discussions *and* learning how to facilitate them is important inquiry for teachers whose goal is to provide a robust learning environment. Students need to have opportunities to present ideas that may or may not be fully formed. Questions, insights, and arguments of logic and reason are all aspects of good math discussion and highly valued as tools for learning deeply. Learning how to make these discussions work for each student—to ensure that the dialogue in the classroom is interesting, productive, and useful no matter where the student is in his or her learning—is a teaching skill that takes practice, support, and reflection. As a math coach, I think it's my job to get at the heart of what it means to facilitate a mathematics discussion well and then provide guidance and learning opportunities for teachers so that classrooms begin to thrive.

I wonder if you and I might think through, together, a plan for moving this idea forward. To that end, I have some thoughts about what we might do, and I would love to brainstorm with you and hear some of your own. We might visit some classrooms together and then have a discussion with the teacher as a team of three afterwards. We could collaborate on studying students' voices, students' ideas, and ways we understand what we are hearing in classrooms. This is the work that I am engaged in; I have come to understand that for teachers to see you invest in this same effort would also provide them with your support and guidance in taking the risks that new shifts in practice require.

It might be helpful for me to offer some background on how I, as a coach, position myself to facilitate the learning of teachers. If we could discuss this list together, I'd be very interested in the ways it intersects with what you think about as you are engaged in the same sort of classroom work. As a way of beginning, here are the lenses—the questions, the issues, and the ideas—that act as filters for the ways I think and respond, as a coach, to classroom work:

Are the foundations of the district math program in place? What's my evidence?

- *Morning math:* Teachers are moving from "question of the day" to using the resources from the math department. They know how to connect morning math to module work and understand the purpose and curriculum of morning math.
- *Curriculum calendar guide:* Teachers are within a couple of days to a week of the district guide for curriculum activities.
- *Review days:* Review days are planned out and thoughtfully executed. Teachers use these days for "looking at student work" sessions and to critique student work with an eye towards "next steps" both with colleagues and with students.

- *Homework:* Teachers are accessing and distributing homework, reviewing it daily, and responding to students.
- *Assessments:* Are teachers utilizing district and module assessments consistently? Analyzing them? Are teachers—and students—able to talk about what they are learning from the assessments?
- *Math team leader and math coach:* Do the teachers view us as useful resources? Are teachers asking questions and getting responses and support from each of us in a timely way? Does each teacher know who to go to for which supports?

Teacher Preparedness and Content Knowledge

- Is the teacher prepared for each lesson? Has she done the mathematics herself before working on an activity with the class? Does she have all the materials necessary to teach the lesson?
- Does the teacher have a clear vision for the goals of the class? How is his timing? Does he begin the lesson with the class all together and then move into small groups or pairs or individual work and come back all together to share, and do students continue to learn important mathematics during this sharing?
- Has the teacher read the lesson thoroughly? Has she read the curriculum background material for the lesson?
- In the coach and teacher debrief, is the teacher reflective about the lesson? Does he talk about student learning, student ideas, and confusions?
- In the debrief, does the teacher have questions about how to understand the module or lesson better—or how her students might? Is she using student work and student talk as evidence for their understanding and confusions?
- What evidence do we have of students' learning from the math class?
- Is there an exchange of ideas between teacher and coach? Are we learning from one another? Is there a give and take of information and ideas about the students' work and learning?

Classroom Culture

- *Equitable classrooms:* Is each child appreciated and heard? Is the teacher respectful of differences? Is she thoughtful about issues of race, gender, and class?
- *Voices:* Does each child have an opportunity to offer an idea or express a question? Does each child have an opportunity to have the teacher's ear, to be listened to? Do children listen to and respond to each other? Do students expect to defend their thinking? Do they expect to follow each other's thinking? Do students expect to be responsible for proving, constructing arguments, and listening to each other's ideas?
- *Structure of the lesson:* Is there a balance of whole group conversation and student-to-student conversation? Are students responding to other students' ideas in whole and small group work? Is the teacher the center of the "wagon wheel" in the discussion or is he the guide of a web of communication within the classroom community?

- *Mathematics:* Is there a clear direction of a mathematical agenda from the beginning of the class to the end? From day to day or week to week? Does the teacher measure the ideas that come up in class against an important mathematical agenda? Does she know how to forward the appropriate agenda with useful questions for students? Does she know how to respectfully listen to a child's idea that she may or may not understand or that may or may not fit into her mathematical agenda? Does she know how to respond to ideas in such a way that students' feel encouraged to persevere?

If you and I can come to an agreement that centering on mathematical reasoning in the classroom is a good place to focus on our work and collaborations with the teachers, then one thing we could do is talk with each other and think through what this means. We could look at a couple of excerpts of classroom dialogues and talk about what we are seeing—or what we think might be missing. It could be possible to use these excerpts as ways of thinking about what we might see in the classrooms we later visit.

Forwarding ideas means holding onto the important mathematics content and being able to listen for threads of those ideas in children's statements and queries. We want to see teachers pose questions, use mathematical vocabulary, and present new material for students to ponder. One of the things I do (because I believe it's true) is acknowledge how hard it is to shift one's stance as teacher to move from telling students the answers to giving them opportunities to develop the ideas themselves. This does not mean I'm sitting back waiting for them to discover the ideas. In fact, it is at this point when a teacher must be highly aware and listening for ideas that are connected and support the development of the math agenda.

I think it would be helpful for teachers to hear that you, too, position yourself as a learner and that you want to learn from the students also. If they can appreciate that you and I are intrigued by the possibilities mathematical reasoning and student discussion could offer for student learning, I think the teachers would soar.

Thanks so much. I'm looking forward to meeting with you.
Seth

Case 8	Crafting an Invitation

Focus Questions Activity

In your small group, discuss the following questions about Seth's letter to his principal. Keep in mind the goals he has for the students, the teachers, the principal, and for his own coaching.

1. In crafting this communication with Principal Moore, Seth lays out a coaching and learning agenda for the rest of the year. What are Seth's goals for the students? Throughout the case, there are very specific statements about Seth's vision for students' learning. Be prepared to move from a general "umbrella" description of a goal to discussing the specifics.

2. Explore the goals for the teachers. Specifically, Seth describes the complexity of meeting certain goals of practice. How does Seth describe these?

3. What is it that Seth wants Principal Moore to do?

4. Communicating with principals or other supervising administrators is an aspect of coaching that can utilized for both *updating* and *continuing* the conversation of work at the school and for professional development purposes. Consider the underlying structure of the letter and the messages in Seth's writing. In your group, determine different sections of the document and label them with a subtitle of your choice. In each of your sections, what is it that Seth is working on?

5. How might you describe Seth's image of coaching and of his role as a coach?

Case 8	Crafting an Invitation

Planning Activity: Considering Collaboration and Communication

In this Planning Activity, you will be trying out Seth's method of asking for help and for partnership toward a goal: Now it is your turn to write your version of a letter. You may or may not actually send this letter, yet the exercise of this writing experience will allow you a chance to reflect on and refine your articulation of your vision for a whole school or for the children, principal, or teacher(s) in the school. Developing a disposition of setting goals, strategically working in collaborative ways, and articulately framing or reframing a position are central ideas in coaching.

On Your Own

1. As you review the case, reflect on these two aspects of Seth's writing: Consider this coach's goals and reacquaint yourself with the structure of Seth's letter to his principal.

2. Choose a coaching goal that you believe would ultimately serve to improve students' opportunities for learning mathematics. Yours might be a goal for your school, one particular teacher, or one that pertains to a group of teachers—but it is a goal that could be more successfully reached through collaboration with a specific principal, administrator, or teacher with whom you work. Think carefully about your invitation into the work and who is in a position to make a difference.

3. Take some notes to clarify your coaching goal and why this goal is an important one. Include your thoughts on the ways your potential collaborator may or may not already be aligned with the goal you have in mind.

In Pairs

With a partner, take a few minutes to explain the goal you are choosing and why you are choosing this particular goal with this school, teacher, or principal at this time. Listen carefully to your partner's ideas. Use this sharing as an opportunity for each of you to have just a few minutes to practice refining the articulation of your goal.

On Your Own

Construct a letter—an invitation—to your collaborator. Use your jotted notes to complete an outline that offers structure. Be clear in the articulation of your goals and the reasoning or argument for this point of view. As you write, consider how you might acknowledge ways this person may already be contributing toward the goal and, too, how you will construct an invitation for collaboration that respects the authority you both hold.

In Pairs

Take just a few minutes each to explain your new thoughts on this developing collaboration. What plans do you have in mind that respond to the goal you chose?

9

Taking the Lead as a Teacher of Teachers

CASE DESCRIPTION

This longer case, written by an experienced math coach, describes a coaching context that unfolds over a series of days. It offers a poignant and intelligent example of a coach who is unafraid to teach a "willing, but far from novice" teacher by giving her homework assignments and setting up opportunities for the teacher to examine and reveal her practice. The case follows the thread of a story of developing collaboration by describing first the introductory meeting with Venus, a teacher of students with special needs, then a math interview with Venus' students, and, finally, debriefs with Venus and the coach. The dialogue between the coach and the teacher throughout the case is evidence of the link between strong coaching and strong teaching; both are grounded in firm beliefs about how others learn.

NOTES TO THE READER

Prior to reading the case, you will have an opportunity to work on the math activity in small groups. As you read the case, write questions or comments in the margins and note line numbers of sentences or paragraphs that interest you or raise questions for you. If you finish reading before the rest of the group, highlight line numbers related to the Focus Questions (page 99) as a way to prepare for small group discussion.

Case 9	Author: Gloria

Encountering Venus

Part 1

First Conversation

1   I met Venus in the first weeks of my new coaching job while finding my way around the K–8 school—as usual, I was lost inside the warren of hallways that seemed to go nowhere. I popped into the learning center so someone who knew better could point me toward the third and
5   fourth grade wing of the school. It was there that Venus and I introduced ourselves. Her response to my role as brand new math resource teacher was, "Boy, do we need one. None of the kids in this school can do math. Every year it seems to get worse. I'm the middle school special education (SPED) teacher, and since we've implemented this new math,
10   more and more kids are referred to me for learning problems around mathematics. And most of them have no other issues. Reading and writing are at grade level. I really don't get what's happening here." I made note of this person. Other teachers had reported that the new math program (actually implemented years ago) was causing problems, but
15   no one else had seemed to be puzzled by this or to find it a matter worth pondering.

    The next week, I stopped by her room to see if she needed anything—materials, a lesson plan, portfolio or assessment problems, an interview of a puzzling student, or simply a person to drink coffee with. Venus told me
20   that her seventh and eighth graders didn't know what operation to use when solving story problems. Some of them had language processing issues, so Venus wasn't sure if the kids didn't understand what they were reading or if their difficulties were math-based. She said she was teaching them to underline the question they needed to answer and to circle the key
25   words in each problem. I grinned and said, "I always include the wrong key words to throw kids off."

    She was surprised and laughed, then replied, "You're a mean one!"

    "Well, how about this problem: 'George bought 17 mushroom pizzas and ate 9 of them. All together, how many were there by the time he went
30   to sleep?'"

Venus pondered this. "Well, how are the kids supposed to know what to do when they read a story problem?"

I asked how she would know, given this particular pizza problem.

"Well, I'd realize that 9 of them disappeared so that's subtraction."

I agreed. She would analyze the structure of the situation to see what *action* the problem described. "I think of story problems as little movies. What's happening in the movie? Are things replicating, putting themselves in groups, disappearing, combining, being compared, getting built up or broken down?"

"Stop! My head is hurting!" It was her turn to grin at me.

I stopped.

"Can you bring some of these problems to my class next week? I want to see you do this with kids. They're going to think you're tough!"

"Do you have any manipulatives?"

"They're going to hate that too. They consider them babyish. No one will use them."

"Well, I'm going to try to make them useful. We'll just see what happens." I was really happy to have connected with Venus. The issue she'd raised about her students and her invitation to come to the class felt like the start of a real journey for both of us.

I came back a week later with a set of problems, and Venus asked me to work with two of her seventh grade boys. I gave her a copy of a page from the Facilitator's Guide for *Making Meaning for Operations* (Schifter, Bastable, & Rusell, 1999) one of a series of math professional development books. The page describes an adaptation of a chart called "Classification of Word Problems" from "Using Children's Mathematical Knowledge in Instruction" (Fennema, Franke, Carpeter, & Carey, 1993). (And since this meeting with Venus, I've learned to keep this "Classification of Word Problems" chart on my clip board at all times because I end up handing one to somebody so often.) I explained that I used the classification chart when I had my own classroom, and now as a math specialist, I use this as my guide whenever I make up story problems. I try to include problems of all different types so I know that children will have to wrestle with making sense of different problem structure situations.

"See?" I said. "Here's an *unknown start* problem: 'Patty had some beautiful shells. Lily gave her 48 more. Now she has 107. How many did she start with?' What do you think? Addition or subtraction?"

Venus thought about this. "Well, it's a *missing addend* problem, so we teach those as subtraction, but I see what you mean. I would probably add to solve that problem." She told me that she thought about it this way: "48 + 50 is 98, 9 more gets me to 107. So Patty had 59 shells to start with."

"I'd do something like that, too. What about this one? 'Dave had 213 donuts. He gave a bunch to Ericka. Now he has 186. How many did he give away?'"

"Well, you are definitely taking away, but the answer is part of the problem, it isn't the result. . . . That's pretty interesting. I have no idea what kids are going to do with that."

Venus was working hard. Really hard. She was sticking with me, and I know we were moving right along at a fast clip.

Part 2

You Mean You're Not Going to Tell Me?

The two seventh grade boys arrive and eye me suspiciously. Venus introduces us—I'm introduced as the math specialist—and the boys grown both groan. "We're doomed now," Phil quips. (Venus has explained that these two 12-year-olds can manage to pull the rest of the kids off task, and we talk briefly about this strategy students sometimes use to hide the fact that they don't know what to do with the math.)

Bruce goes ahead and reads the first problem out loud, the one about the shells. "'Patty had some beautiful shells. Lily gave her 48 more. Now she has 107. How many did she start with?'" He looks up and says, "That's easy. Add."

Phil agrees, "Yeah. 48 + 107 equals what?"

Venus begins to tell them they are wrong, and I signal her to wait. She falls silent. We study the boys. "What? Why are you looking at us? What's wrong? Did we get the answer wrong? That's impossible. 8 + 7 is 15. Put down the 1. Carry the 5. 5 + 4 = 9, put that down. Then just put down the 1, so the answer is 191."

"You carried wrong," Venus observes. The boys revisit their work. Phil figures out where Bruce made his mistake and fixes it, now presenting 155 as the correct answer. Venus looks at me; she's not sure what to do next.

"Is that a sensible answer?" I wonder aloud. In a nanosecond, both boys agree that it is.

"Who can tell me the story of the problem in their own words?" I ask. "If this were a movie, what would be happening?"

"Everyone in the theater would be dozing!" Phil snorts.

Bruce says, "The kid had some shells. The other kid gave her 48 more. Then she ended up with 107. Ohhh. She *ended up* with 107. 107 *is* the answer."

"Is it?" wonders Venus. "Is 107 the part you have to find out?"

Phil's face is a knot of concentration. "You have to find out how many she started with. We don't know how to do this. No one ever showed us how."

"When in doubt, act it out. Use these cubes. Pretend they are shells," I suggest.

The boys stare at the table awhile, uncertain. Then Bruce says, "It's impossible. You don't know what to put down." He continues, "She had some. Then she got 48 more. You don't know where to start. Is this a guess and check?"

"Would that work?" Venus asks. The boys are silent.

Bruce sputters, "I can't do this." Phil adds, "This is stupid. There aren't any shells here."

I can tell that the boys are worried. Their sarcasm and tone of voice are familiar to me. I know what it's like to be afraid of not knowing. "Whenever a problem seems too hard, give yourself exactly the same problem with much smaller numbers," I suggest. "So what if Lily had some shells and Patty gave her 9 more? Now she has 16. How many did she start with?"

Phil writes ____ + 9 = 16 on his paper. "That's easy," he says, filling in the blank. "It's 7."

"How did you get 7?" Venus asks.

Phil tells us he counted up on his fingers under the table. "Can we go now? It's time for gym." Venus nods and sends them off. Bruce taps a pencil like a drumstick on each table as he races across the room. They bump into each other as they wrestle with the doorknob on their way out.

Venus turns to me and says, "I think I talk too much."

"What do you mean?"

"I was all ready to just jump in and do it for them. I bet I always do that and have never noticed it before."

"What else did you notice?"

"Well they don't know how to do subtraction with borrowing. They've only been working on that since Grade 2, and we've been working on it all year."

"Why do you suppose they don't have that down yet?"

"I really don't know. Because I'm a lousy math teacher?"

Venus has said out loud what I know so many teachers feel. "You've only had them for six weeks. This is their eighth year in school and probably their sixth year of studying subtraction with regrouping. . . ." I point out. Venus is silent.

"I didn't know what to do. I didn't know what to say," she observes after a while.

"Does that feel new?"

"Yeah, it does. I think I must jump in with the lectures whenever they get stuck. No wonder they can't do math. . . . I always do it for them."

"Why do you think that is?"

"Because I don't know what else to do. I don't know how to teach math. I'm just doing what my teachers did with me. This is how I learned math so this is how I teach math."

"How well did you learn it?" I know that was a zinger, so I add quickly, "You are describing my math history, too, and probably the math history of most teachers here. I know I didn't learn math very well by having the teachers model it for me. 'First do this, then do that.' I couldn't do any of it. Actually, it's life's little joke that I'm a math teacher now. . . ." Venus is upset and I'm trying to defuse how angry she is at herself. I wait.

"How *do* you teach math?" Venus blurts out. "I mean how do you teach it so kids really get it?"

"Ah—you're asking one of those *major questions*. And I can say I'm pretty sure it's going to take time to find the answer."

"You mean you're not going to tell me?" Venus is deeply in earnest here.

"I can't, Venus. The answer is different for each one of us and for every class and every kid. It's different for every topic and each idea."

"What am I going to do?" She sounds panicky.

"How about one small thing at a time?"

"But I don't understand math to teach it well," Venus tells me.

"I can remember exactly where I was and what I was doing the day I realized that about myself. It was a Tuesday in October, ten years ago. I was sitting on the floor of my classroom while the kids were at music. I had a ring of textbooks around me—fourth, fifth, sixth, and seventh grade math; they were orange, purple, brown, and white—and all of them were pretty much the same. They even presented topics in the same order. That

180 was the day I picked up the phone and called the university about the math professional development program I'd heard about, where the unsuspecting innocent who answered heard me shout, 'Help! My kids are at risk in mathematics!'"

Venus laughs. "This isn't funny," she added.

"How about this?" I suggest. "Take home this Classification of Word Problems chart and act out each problem type with cubes. Figure out what
185 the action of each situation is and write a number sentence to match it, put in blanks to show the numbers you have to find in each case. We'll meet again after that and plan a lesson for your class."

Venus shakes her head. "I can't believe this is such a revelation to me. How could I not have known?"

Part 3

Investigating With Venus

190 The next time we met, Venus described a lesson where she constructed her own problems and had Bruce and Phil solve them. She made a point of not leading them. She did give each of them a highlighter and asked them to highlight the information they should pay attention to in order to solve the problems. "Bruce had no trouble, but Phil was lost," she reported.
195 Venus described that for the problem, "Jane has 27 marbles, how many more marbles does she need to have 42 altogether?" Phil added 42 and 27 and got 69 for his answer. In order to solve, "Mrs. Pew bought 34 pots of flowers. 15 of these pots have yellow flowers and the rest of the pots have red flowers. How many pots of red flowers did Mrs. Pew buy?" he had to
200 draw a picture. He only had 32 pots in his picture, but he did cross out 15 of them. Then he miscounted the leftovers, getting 16 for his first answer and changing it to 17 after he was told to check his math. Bruce had solved the flowerpot problem by crossing off the 3 and making it a 2, putting a 1 in front of the 4 and doing two separate subtraction problems to get 19.
205 Venus showed me the boys' work. "I knew Bruce was the stronger math student, but what are these? Second grade problems?"

I agreed that they were and said, "I wonder why Bruce had to borrow to solve 34 – 15?"

Venus looked sideways at me. "Wouldn't you?"
210 I shook my head. "No. I'd do it mentally. 15 + 15 is 30; add 4 more to get 34. You've added a total of 19, so that's your answer."

"Wait. Do that again." I did, while Venus wrote it down so she could look at it. "That's cool. I never would have done it like that."

"Well, you could also start with 30 and subtract 15 to get 15, then add in
215 the 4 you deleted from the original number to make it easier to deal with."

"Let me write that down." Venus did. "Wow. How did you learn that?"

"A second grader taught me that one. Here's one that will really be 'out of the box.'" I wrote the problem vertically:

$$\begin{array}{r} 34 \\ -\ 15 \\ \hline \end{array}$$

"This is something one of Connie Kamii's kids taught her. You do:
220 $4 - 5 = -1$. And then you do $30 - 10 = 20$. Then $20 - 1 = 19$."

"I can't believe it. A second grader came up with that? Who is Connie Kamii?" I told Venus that Connie Kamii is a teacher and university professor who lets her students solve problems any way they want to as long as they can explain what they are doing.

"How does a second grader know about negative numbers?" Venus asked. I told her that I didn't know what that student's experience was but that I have heard kids talking about putting an amount in the "save box" or dealing with "under numbers" (those under zero) or "left-handed and right-handed numbers" (those on either side of zero on a number line).

"We talk about six degrees below zero on a cold day or of owing other people money we don't have, so the topic does come up, even with little kids."

Venus nodded, and then exclaimed suddenly, "What's going on with Phil? He's been doing problems like these for a long time. He should know what to do."

"You're right. He should. What's he confused about?"

Venus stared at his paper for a while. "Well, Jane has 27 marbles. Phil looked at the key words, 'How many?' and knew the problem called for addition because that's what I taught him."

"Okay, so what's he missing?"

"He doesn't see that the 42 is the total, though I was careful to put the key word 'altogether' in there to signal that 42 is the answer. But of course, 42 isn't the answer because you are looking for the missing marbles you need to add to get from 27 to 42. I see. It's my fault that he's confused, but I'm not sure what to do about it."

I wonder out loud if some of her other students might have similar issues with subtraction problems that aren't conventional "take away," and she agrees that they will. We decide it would make sense for Venus to create a lesson based on the Classification of Word Problems chart. She will make up some problems with small numbers like the ones on the chart and have the kids analyze the structure or action of the problems in order to figure out what operation to use. If they can't tell what to do by simply reading the problem, they'll be directed to act it out with cubes. My job will be to jump in whenever Venus signals for help.

When I arrive, Venus has already written the first problem on the board:

Serena has 7 candies. Bruce has 2. How many more does Serena have?

The students file in and take their seats. Phil notices me in back. "Oh no! Not the mean lady!" I grin back at him in what I hope is a mean lady kind of way! Bruce is reading the problem from the board.

"Hey, that's not a seventh grade problem."

"You're right Bruce, it's a different kind of problem from what we've done before. Who can tell me how it's different?" Venus asks calmly.

Karen squints through her thick glasses. "Nothing's going away."

Venus wonders out loud, "Is it still subtraction?"

Karen says it is and Venus wants to know why. "Because you are comparing two things . . . two numbers . . . amounts."

"What makes that subtraction?" I ask from the back of the room.

Bruce rolls his eyes. "She *really* wants to know!"

"You're right. I do," I said. Bruce smiles.

Natalie says, "You are finding the difference between them." Using Karen's language, she adds, "One amount is bigger than the other, and you need to find out how much bigger, so that's subtraction."

"What's going on in this problem?" asks Venus as she writes it up on the board. "Serena has 2 candies but she wants 7. How many does she have to get?"

275   "That's the same. You have to find the difference between the ones she has and the ones she wants." Natalie sounds confident that she is right.

"But to me it feels different. Seems like a plus problem," notes Karen.

"Yeah, I'd go 2 + what equals 7. It is an addition problem," adds Bruce, almost in spite of himself.

280   "You telling us that subtraction is addition? Great. That's just what I need to know." Phil is getting agitated.

Venus sends me the jump-in signal.

"So what is subtraction anyway?" I ask.

"It's take away," fires back Phil.

285   "Always?" I wonder.

"No," say the girls together. "Jinx!"

Venus takes the reins. "So what is subtraction if it isn't take away? You've already given a couple of examples."

"Well it can be compare," says Karen.

290   "Or add up," says Bruce. There is a pause here. Venus signals me again.

I move to the side of the classroom and ask the class, "Well, if subtraction is sometimes take away and sometimes compare and sometimes add up, how can you tell a subtraction problem just by reading it? And are

295   there any more types of subtraction? What do all the different types have in common?" I realize I have just asked way too many questions. Venus picks up the important one and repeats it.

"What do all these different types of subtraction have in common?" She glides over to where I am sitting and whispers, "What *do* all these

300   types of subtraction have in common?"

I whisper back, "They are all about parts and wholes. When you know the whole and one of the parts and are looking for the missing parts it is *always* a subtraction problem. Comparison problems are tricky. Sometimes you are comparing two parts, sometimes a part and a whole, and some-

305   times two wholes. Let's leave those out for now . . ."

Phil snorts. "Can you talk a little louder?"

"For tonight's homework," Venus begins. The kids groan. "Make up some subtraction problems. Each one has to be a different kind. Write one that is take away, one that is compare, one that is add up, and see if you

310   can figure out some other kinds."

"How many different kinds are there?" Natalie wants to know.

"That's part of the assignment. Figure that piece out, and we'll talk about it some more tomorrow."

"Why can't we just do worksheets?" Bruce moans.

315   "Because this will make you smarter," I rejoin. He smiles just a little.

Part 4

Debriefing With Venus

After the students file out and are on to their next class, Venus turns to me and says, "I have only five minutes until the next class comes in, can we talk quickly about what I do next with that group?"

"Well, when they bring their homework in tomorrow, collect examples of take away, compare, and add up, and ask if anyone can talk about what's going on with parts and wholes in each of those problems." Venus is writing this down. "Then I'd see if anyone was able to come up with more problem types. If not, give them the ones you wrote based on the Classification Chart and have them talk about parts and wholes in them. Have them give each of the new problem types a name that will help them remember what the problems are." 320 325

"Give me an example."

"Okay, let say someone writes a missing change problem. 'Serena has 7 balloons. Some burst. Now she has 5. How many popped?' Ask the kids what each number in the problem represents. 7 is the whole, 5 is the part that is left after the others pop. The *part* that popped is missing. If you know the whole and one of the parts and are looking for the missing part, it's a subtraction problem, even if you choose to add to solve it." 330

"That's the thing that is confusing them, and me. How can it be subtraction if you add to solve it?" 335

"Get Natalie to explain that. She understands the idea of finding the difference really well. The question you are moving toward, I think, is whether or not there is such a thing as a pure subtraction problem, or if all subtraction problems can be solved by addition . . ."

Venus is staring at me. 340

"What?" I ask.

"You aren't telling me the answer." She seems both excited and perplexed by this.

"I can't. I don't know what your answers are," I tell her.

"You're playing with me," she exclaims. 345

"Well, it may feel that way, but I just gave you my answer—that all subtraction problems tell you the whole and one of the parts and you have to find the missing part—whether or not you actually use subtraction to solve it, and you are telling me that this answer isn't right for you, that it's confusing and unsatisfying. 'How can it be subtraction if you add to solve it?' you want to know. There's an implied comparison in every subtraction problem. I can sit here and tell you this, and it doesn't help, does it?" 350

Venus shakes her head, "No."

"You won't believe me for awhile maybe, but my answers probably aren't going to work for you, just as our adult answers haven't worked for our students. We've been telling them the answers all along and they still don't know what they are doing. They haven't found their own answers, ones they can use to make sense of the math for themselves." 355

"So if we aren't giving kids the answers, if we don't know the answers to give, what are our roles as teachers?" 360

"If you are like me, it's going to take a lifetime to answer that question, and your answer will change frequently. At this point in time, what do you think?"

"I don't know what to think," Venus admitted honestly.

"I think you do, at least a little. You were playing your role so well today, I guess without knowing what it should be. What did you do that felt different? Or is this what you do every day?" 365

"No, this isn't what I do every day, and it felt really different. Usually, I stand up there and tell the kids what to do, step by step. I'm really organized and clear. I number each move. 'First underline the question the 370 problem is asking you to answer. Second, circle the key words. . . . ' As I'm saying this, I'm realizing that I'm up there lecturing and there isn't any math in my lecture! I can't believe it! That's incredible."

"What would come next?"

375   "Well, next I'd say something like, 'Okay, in a subtraction problem you always put the bigger number on top and you line up the digits so that everything is in a column on the right.' Oh my gosh. There are no ideas in there at all. . . . Ugh, I'm giving them recipes without any food!"

"What a great way of putting it!" I laugh. "So what's the teacher's role

380   in all this?"

"Well, she has to go food shopping, right away!" Venus is chuckling now. "But I don't really know what that means. It means I have to learn math and that I don't have the ideas I need to teach. I need to be asking questions not giving answers, but if I don't know the subject I can't ask the

385   questions. What am I going to do?"

"You're going to do what all good teachers do. You're going to learn it as you teach it, and my job is to help."

"Okay, so tonight I have to figure out what subtraction *really* is, and I have to try to answer that question about whether or not there is such a

390   thing as a pure subtraction problem or if all subtraction problems can be solved by addition. Where did you get that question anyway, did you just make it up?"

"No, the fourth graders upstairs asked me that one on Monday. Isn't it great? We spent a whole class time discussion about it. Kids worked on it

395   in pairs, first, trying to come up with subtraction problems that couldn't be solved using addition. People jumped up and presented their arguments. Others rejoined with counter arguments. When lunch rolled around, we were in the thick of it, and nobody wanted to leave until the issue was resolved."

400   "What did you do?"

"I told them to think about it some more and we'd continue talking next time. They were mad. They said they were going to sit right there until I told them the answer. I said that I didn't need to tell them the answer, that some of them already knew it. Then I reminded them that it

405   was pizza day." Venus laughed. I looked at her and said, "Do you know that a month ago I was told by people in this building that these kids aren't intellectual and couldn't sustain an hour-long math discussion?"

Venus was thoughtful. "Until today, I probably would have agreed. What if I can't answer that question for myself? What if I come to school

410   tomorrow and I can't explain what subtraction is and don't know if there is such a thing as pure subtraction?"

"Well, there are a couple of things you could do. You could tell the kids that you've been thinking about the question and you have some ideas about it but haven't made up your mind yet and you would like to hear

415   their ideas, or you could borrow those fourth graders and let them duke it out in front of the seventh graders, then have the seventh graders do some writing about what they think and why."

"So do you learn a lot of math from the kids?" Venus asked.

"I've learned most of the math I know from kids."

420   "Isn't it kind of scary to not know what you're doing or where you're going?"

"It's totally scary, but it's also really exciting. The year I threw away the textbook and started trying to learn how to teach math, my classroom was the site for a National Science Foundation research project. One of the evaluators came in at the end of the year and interviewed   425
some of my students. The students said it was really good that the teacher learned the math along with them." Venus shook her head. "One student said it was really good because of the kind of math explorations we all got into together."

"I'll have to think about that," Venus told me. "It seems like knowing   430
less math couldn't possibly make you a good math teacher, but because that's where I am, I'm going to think about how that might be true."

Case 9   Encountering Venus

Math Activity: Exploring Story Problems

Use drawings and/or cubes to show how these problems can be solved. As you work in your small group, engage in a discussion of what you notice about your strategies. Write number sentences that model each problem.

1. Connie began her day with 17 sticks of butter. By the time the last meal was prepared, there were 8 sticks left. How many sticks of butter did she use?

2. Lily keeps chocolate kisses in her desk drawer for those chocolate emergencies. This week she had some *real* sugar cravings and ate a lot of kisses. If she ate 18 kisses during the week and by Friday afternoon ended up with 17, how many chocolate kisses did Lily start the week with?

3. The Movie Palace showed two movies. Last night, the big seller sold out at 215 tickets. The other movie was a bit of a dud and only sold 27. How many more tickets were sold for the big seller?

4. There was a flood in the math department. The staff needed to move 153 boxes of curriculum units to another room as fast as they could. Even with volunteer helpers, they had only moved 89 boxes by midday. How many more boxes were left to move?

Consider the set of problems and compare them to each other. Discuss what you notice about the operations, the actions embedded in the stories, and the way you approached solving each one?

Case 9　Encountering Venus
Focus Questions Activity

Part 1

First Conversation (lines 1–80)

1. Consider lines 1–16. We see from the start of the case that Gloria responds to Venus in a particular way. What choices *might* Gloria have made in this first and second encounter?

2. Why do think Gloria chose to respond the way she does?

Part 2

You Mean You're Not Going to Tell Me? (lines 80–189)

1. In Part 2, lines 80–133, we read about Phil and Bruce as they work to solve a subtraction problem. In capturing dialogue in her case, Gloria lets us in on all four people in this section. What is Venus working on? What is Gloria doing?

2. Reread the dialogue from lines 133–155. What do we learn about Venus in this conversation?

3. In Parts 1 and 2, what does Gloria do that matters?

Part 3

Investigating With Venus (lines 190–315)

1. Review lines 190–204 and 255–291 and consider students' ideas about subtraction. What does Phil's work suggest about conceptual understanding? What might you want him to investigate? Follow Karen and Natalie's line of thinking in this section. How do you make sense of the ideas the two girls offer?

2. Consider the coach and teacher interactions: What is Venus trying to accomplish in this classroom episode? In what ways does Gloria's coaching matter?

3. What is it Gloria wants the students and Venus to consider? Why do you think Gloria might be pushing in this direction? What are potential implications for teaching?

4. Consider lines 291–305. How do you resolve the question, "What do all these different types of subtraction have in common?"

Part 4

Debriefing With Venus (lines 315–432)

1. In Part 4, we see an evolving collaboration and more evidence of coaching. What's happening between Gloria and Venus?

2. At this point, if we can say that a coach makes moves based on her understanding of mathematics, the students' ideas, the teacher's ideas, and her beliefs about both learning and about her role, what do we learn from Gloria about coaching?

REFERENCES

Fennema, E., Franke, M. L., Carpenter, T. P., & Carey, D. A. (1993). Using children's mathematical knowledge in instruction. *American Education Research Journal, 30*(3) 558.

Schifter, D., Bastable, V., & Russell, S. (1999). *Developing mathematical ideas: Making meaning for operations—Facilitator's Guide.* Parsippany, NJ: Dale Seymour Publications.

10

Maintaining a Focus on Mathematics

CASE DESCRIPTION

The case Struggling to Keep Math at the Center describes a coach's efforts to facilitate productive and math-centered dialogue with teachers and with the principal. In her writing, the coach, Ivy, describes two different teacher team meetings; one she deems a failure, the other a success. Sorting out her reflections and ideas as she writes, Ivy uses case writing as a tool for analyzing and affirming the features of a successful classroom debrief. In addition, she explores strategies for maintaining an effective facilitation stance even in the face of potentially undermining distractions. This case reminds readers of the importance, and the complexities, of keeping the math in math coaching.

NOTES TO THE READER

In this session, you will begin with a whole-group mental-math activity and then respond to a series of reflective writing prompts offered by the facilitator. When it is time to read the case, write questions and comments in the margin and note line numbers of sentences or paragraphs that interest you or raise questions for you.

| Case 10 | Author: Ivy |

Struggling to Keep Math at the Center

1   It sounds weird, as I envision people reading this case, for me to say I'm having a hard time "staying with the math" when I do my work. After all, isn't math my job? But, as I see it, my effort to "stay with the math" continues to be so interwoven with relationships and trust and learning and
5   understanding politics that in meetings and discussions with teachers, in the moment of work, the math can be hard to find and to "stay with."

What I feel sure about is that *if*, in the moment, I can stay focused on the math, the quality of our discussion will be better. It will be more purposeful, and it will be centered on the more important issues of learning.
10   However, knowing to stay focused and learning *how* to stay focused— while in the moment of facilitating discussion—are two different things. So many other things come into play when I'm in schools that despite my determination to stay with the math, it's amazing how much has to be negotiated and figured out. Really, what I want to do is vent about what
15   my experiences are like in schools. I want to write about how I handle and mishandle interactions with teachers and principals. So here are the titles of the cases I wanted to write (but decided against!):

From Cold as Ice to Kisses: Building Relationships With Tricky Teachers

Leadership in Shambles: The Impossible and Complex Job of Being a
20   *Principal and How Coaches Learn to Navigate This Territory*

Math Coaching: It's Not About the Big Ideas; It's About Keeping Track of All the Details

Why Does His Math Class Never Change? Or What Am I Doing Wrong? After a Year and a Half of Coaching Classrooms That Are Stuck

25   The cases I could write! As I refrain from writing cases with these titles, I have written them out to give you some context for how difficult it is for me to stay focused on children's math ideas when all these other issues implied in these titles are so present for me in my work from day to day. Even my most enthusiastic teachers are just beginning to know how to
30   engage in the mathematical ideas beyond thinking solely about implementation of curriculum. I think it's critical to work on both sides of these issues of practice. This melding of curriculum, teacher moves, and student ideas takes time—I know—but we need to get closer than we are, and as a math coach, I need to get better at using every opportunity to focus us
35   all on what's essential to good practice. Thus, my effort to really press on staying with the math. I know that it's in *that* place where learning has an opportunity to unfold.

In the last couple of weeks, I've been trying to make a conscious effort to push on making *discussion about the mathematics* to be the focus of every meeting, with varying degrees of pushing and varying degrees of success, depending on the teacher and the relationship we have.

When I say, "pushing on the mathematics," I mean I know that I will be moving into territory that will be uncomfortable, where the teacher will have to make a decision about his or her practice. So far, teachers have found ways of avoiding actually talking about math and, instead, talking about the curriculum and what it lacks or other issues of practice that don't get at actually *improving it.* I have, in one way or another, let the teachers know I want the conversation, the math class, and the learning going on in this school to be different. Something—teacher practice, students' work—needs to change. My job, in part, is to find the moments when I can shake the accepted understandings about how children learn and about how to teach. I want to do that through focusing on the math, not on the peripheral details of everyday life in school.

In this writing, I describe two recent examples of interactions in meetings when I tried to stay with the math in the face of distraction. The first describes a scenario where the coaching felt unsuccessful, though the second felt a bit better. My question as a coach now is: How can I frame my work in my own mind so that I can more purposefully facilitate the kinds of math discussions that will matter, that will help teachers begin to examine students' learning in purposeful ways? I'm looking for your perspectives on this aspect of our work.

First Moment

Where: A meeting with two teachers, Maria and Leanne, who each teach combined second and third grades.
What: A discussion on the math classes I just visited. The two classrooms have focused on teaching about "doubling" in different ways.

The meeting began with Maria describing an interaction she had with a parent that morning. She feels as though there was a racist element to the conversation and has been preoccupied by it all day. She wants our feedback and thoughts. It is a complex story, and we listen carefully and take some time to sort through it.

At a certain point, I decide to move the conversation toward the math classes. The teachers discover they are working on the same math topic and are interested. (At that moment, another goal becomes clear to me—if they developed comradeship through our meetings together, they might actually begin to discuss their teaching in a day-to-day way. They would know that they were working on the very same topic because it would make sense to plan or debrief together.) I lay out, very generally, a description of both classrooms. Maria has used a lesson from the new curriculum, during which the teacher reads the students a story about a magic pot. The children, then, write riddles about a particular number of objects that go into a magic pot and double. It is a good lesson; although, when it came time in this classroom for students to write the riddles, they were confused, the paper had been folded in a way that made it difficult to write a

85 story on the lines, and the kids weren't clear about the expectations. This is a practice issue that we *could* talk about. But here's an example of when I want to choose the mathematics of the lesson instead.

Leanne's class worked in small groups. Four second graders worked on a sheet I assume is somewhat familiar to them. It looked like this:

2 doubles---4

90 3 doubles---

4 doubles---

10 doubles---

12 doubles---

95 Around the word, "doubles" is a box or, what Leanne has named, "a machine." After they complete the page, the students are to write their own machine problem with a number that goes in and the number that goes out after it's been through the doubling machine.

Both classes were rich with ideas—children's ideas about doubling and children's confusions about doubling. I knew I wanted to spend our

100 time discussing what the students did and what happened in class. What did each of us see students doing? What did the students say? How do we, the adults in the room, keep track of these ideas? What important math ideas are involved for a child thinking through doubling—what's the potential learning here?

105 When I was in class I took notes and planned to discuss students' work in our meeting. These are the notes I took.

- What was going on for Darlene, who wrote $2 + 2 = 4$, $3 + 3 = 6$, $4 + 4 = 8$, $10 + 10 = 20$, $12 + 12 = 14$, and $13 + 13 = 16$? Do we have any evidence that she understands the ideas? Does she understand doubling but can't add accurately? Is she adding 2 and then 3, or is her
110 recording just wrong?
- What about Kwame, who noticed a pattern and said, "I'm noticing why the answer is always 2 more. It's because to each double 1 is added, and since there are two in a double then there is always 2 more."
115 - What did Rachel notice when she said, "It's kind of like when we made 10s? $1 + 9$, $2 + 8$, $3 + 7$, $4 + 6$, and so on."
- What did Sandra understand when she took 3 squares and partnered each one to make an array of 2×3 and said the answer was six? When her teacher gave her 4 squares and asked her to find the
120 double and left her side momentarily, she made a box of 20-some squares. What would be useful questions to ask Sandra?
- Jose has written numbers all over his page. No machine, but lots of number sentences. All except one are expressions of doubles. His doubles range from $2 + 2 = 4$ to $100 + 100 = 200$, all accurate sentences.
125 The one other number sentence is $10 + 10 + 25 = 45$. When I ask him about the last one he says, "I did a triple machine, too."

We could learn so much from looking carefully at the ideas embedded in these. Wouldn't it help them both if they understood the power of

Kwame's thinking? Before I can bring these questions up, Maria derails the opportunity to talk about the math by announcing that she's decided to teach only with students in small groups. There will be no more whole-group math class, that is, no sharing or whole-group talking time. She suddenly begins a stream of complaints. She says the structure of the curriculum makes it so students sit too long and then explains that she can't get to half the students during the class time. She announces, grinning and pounding her fist on the table, "I quit." Both teachers laugh.

Okay, I'm so discouraged . . . and I'm mad. I want to talk about the children's ideas, some of which I listed above, and creating a community of mathematicians discussing ideas is a priority for me both as a teacher and a coach. In the moment, I can't decide whether to let this "I quit!" comment go.

Interestingly, I don't want the conversation to be about this teacher's decision. But I *do* want Maria to make a decision about this whole-group, small-group business, a different one than she came to the meeting with. Now, what do I do? Leanne, who, up to now, is really trying to work on facilitating whole-group conversations, strongly agrees with everything Maria has said, and while I'm hesitating, she launches in with how hard it was for her to get doubling riddle books from her whole class. Time is slipping from me, and there is little time left for this meeting and the discussion I had hoped to initiate.

So I go ahead and worry out loud about how students will get the chance to exchange ideas or build a classroom community of math talk without the opportunity to talk about the ideas together in the whole group. I say that I wonder how Maria will provide this essential of math learning, . . . and then . . . (what's key here is I don't leave time for her to respond, which I acknowledge by saying that time is scarce) I say that I want to discuss the ideas we heard in class. (Now, there are maybe only minutes left of the meeting.) Two thoughts are put on the table, one is something about counting by 2s and the other is about adding a number to itself. I end by giving a concrete suggestion to Leanne about how to allow students more time to delve into the ideas. She loves the idea and wishes I had suggested it during the class. Meanwhile, Maria is visibly frustrated that I didn't give more time for us to discuss her choice of having only small groups.

Second Moment

Where: A first grade team meeting.

What: A discussion of assessments with two first grade teachers and the principal.

At the last meeting with Annie and Willa and their principal, Annie cried because she felt so stretched with all the meetings she had. The principal had spoken disparagingly of Annie after the two teachers left the meeting. He doesn't understand how difficult the work is for teachers and regularly complains about teachers to the literacy support person. As the math specialist, I try to stay clear of these kinds of conversations with him, but it's tricky territory for me. By not getting into the discussions with him, I give him the message that I won't "go there," which could be interpreted as siding with the teachers—when I want to stay professionally neutral. Very tricky. (Do you see how sidetracked this whole coaching business can get? Remember, I'm the "math person"; I want people to talk about math!)

Today, the teachers say how hard it is to get their students to do the math work the way the curriculum describes in the Notes to Teachers section. Annie and Willa have chosen an assessment to give their students at the end of the chapter. The assessment has story problems that will require students to combine and separate quantities. The separating problem is about 13 children on a bus, 5 leave the bus, and the students find the remaining total.

Annie worries that her first graders will add the two numbers. She thinks they'll take two piles of cubes, one pile of 13 and one with 5, and then, they'll combine them. At this, the principal suggests that Annie do a demonstration of a similar problem and use just one pile of cubes, counting out the starting total of, say, 18 and then, very explicitly, removing the "leaving children," say, 7 cubes. The idea is that then there wouldn't be a second pile of cubes available for children to combine to the original total. It would, in essence he thinks, force the children to take away 5 cubes, instead of combining two piles.

Okay, once again, I feel like I'm in delicate territory. I have to think while I'm in the middle of facilitating this discussion, and there are so many options to choose from. For one thing, I'm thrilled the principal is trying to discuss the mathematics. He's really trying to find the moment when a child gets confused. I like how closely he is looking at this problem. His emphasis on the teacher move is interesting to me. I could let it go. But I am trying to press on talking about the math in this school, and his suggestion to just demonstrate "how you do it" is not exactly what I would call useful math instruction.

I also know these teachers, who complain about the curriculum regularly but are trying to implement it the way it's "supposed" to be done. They laugh at the new materials because it's crazy to think children can actually do what the book describes; yet at the same time, they want to be successful. Here are the complexities for me to sort out *in the moment:*

- For starters, the teachers don't know what to do with the 13 − 5 problem in their own classroom teaching. They are right to think the students might solve the problem by adding the two piles. I would have envisioned this happening during the work of this chapter while students are working on the content, but by the time of the assessment, I don't want my students to be solving a subtraction problem by mistakenly adding two piles of cubes.
- They don't like the principal telling them what they could do. We have such a long way to go before these meetings have a collegial flavor to them.
- The principal is trying hard but it isn't clear he respects these teachers, and there may be a familiar tone in his manner of . . . slight condescension? I don't know what it is but it's not "encouragement."

So here I am, the coach. I don't let it go. I'm going to take this ship and grab the tiller. Does this sound scary? Well, it is to me. Not the terrifying kind of scary or even the kind where you feel all flushed, but the kind that you know you can make or break relationships you've been working on. 225

I acknowledge the principal's idea about looking closely at the children and trying to find the teachable moment. I quickly move on to say that teachers do this throughout the day. The thing is, it's okay for kids to be confused. In fact, this is often the time when teachers can learn more about how a student is thinking. In this case, as with all mathematics, it's important for teacher moves to be about working with children to understand the context of the problem so children are making sense of the work. We don't want our moves to be about making sure the children don't have to confront the ideas, in this case, by removing the cubes. 230 235

In that moment, the principal was silent. The teachers were silent. Do I let it sit for a minute or do I run with it in case my silence provides an opportunity for someone to sink the ship? I stay the course and keep going. I ask them to think with me about what a student might be doing when they attend to a problem such as 13 – 5 by setting up two piles. I want us to consider the logic in it. I get up immediately and get a bucket of cubes. "So let's do the problem together," I say. "Is there a way to solve this using two piles? Is that an effective strategy?" 240

For the next ten minutes, we talked about 13 – 5. It was amazing. Something fell away, and we *stayed on the math* and kept it front and center. I'm working on this idea. Now, I need to keep thinking about what will help me stay focused on it "in the moment." 245

Case 10   Struggling to Keep Math at the Center

Focus Questions Activity

First Moment

1. The coach has taken notes on the students' talk from her observations. What logic do you find in the students' work? What ideas do you see emerging from the two classrooms?

2. In lines 112–114, Ivy describes Kwame's idea—what is he working on?

3. Review the case and locate three places (note line numbers) where the coach articulates her own beliefs that support her decision-making process. What do we learn about Ivy's intentions?

Second Moment

4. In solving 13 – 5, a student might put out two piles of cubes. What might be going on when a student approaches subtraction this way? What's logical about the approach? How does it help us think about students' ways of encountering work with subtraction?

5. In the Second Moment, Ivy describes a meeting that includes the principal. In lines 168–179, she raises an issue math specialists deal with in one form or another. On what basis might a coach make choices in these situations?

6. Anne raises a concern about strategies her students might use to solve the assessment problem (lines 187–195). What ideas about learning may underlie the principal's contributions to this discussion? Describe the conflict this raises for Ivy.

7. Discuss the coaching moves Ivy chooses to make in this second moment meeting. What might be lost and what might be gained when the coach, in such a scenario, claims the authority to press forward?

11

Framing the Connection Between Coach and Teacher Goals

CASE DESCRIPTION

The coach-author, Bonita, describes her efforts to facilitate meaningful and challenging math professional development for teachers. She describes her struggles in reaching two resistant teachers and in connecting the seminar to their beliefs and concerns. Bonita includes specific examples of her correspondence between the teachers and her efforts to reframe the professional development goals in order to meet the teachers' perceived needs and so that the teachers can appreciate—and connect to—the purpose and direction of the seminar. In this way, Bonita's case also highlights the use of written correspondence as a useful coaching strategy.

NOTES TO THE READER

You may choose to read the Focus Questions (page 118) prior to reading this case as a way to orient yourself to the important issues the coach describes. As you read the case, write comments or questions in the margins and note line numbers of sentences or paragraphs that interest you or raise questions for you.

| Case 11 | Author: Bonita |

Unsatisfied in the Seminar

1   With the implementation of a new curriculum, math has moved to center stage in our district. It is a direction that is taking a lot of us—teachers, administrators, and coaches—out of our comfort zones. The math is a leap (as are the assessments), issues of pedagogy are new for many, and these

5   things are "heated up" by resistance and opposing viewpoints on what's "best for our children." There are pockets of enthusiasm, mostly coming from the math department and some teachers; it seems that, for some of us, this is a long overdue and much appreciated shift. On the other hand, it's a bit of an upheaval for administrators who have not been directly

10   involved in math teaching for years and for many teachers who have not been exposed to learning in new ways. And I find myself in the thick of it as a math coach early in my second year of coaching.

Coaches are responsible for professional development in mathematics for all the elementary school teachers in the district, and every teacher is

15   required to participate at some level. Sylvia and I, both elementary math coaches, have just facilitated the first of many math seminars to come. This experience has left me with questions I'm still trying to sort out.

Ours is not the typical "make it-take it" sort of workshop teachers are used to. It's not a course where lessons in teacher behavior is the valued

20   idea, nor is this seminar presented as a chance to learn new models of "how to do it" or "how to fix it"—and this is disconcerting to some. A goal of this seminar is to give teachers opportunities to work with material and activities so that they experience math as a reasoning enterprise. We want teachers to get in touch with their own mathematical thinking, examine

25   the concepts of early mathematics, and come to appreciate their students' ideas. We want to help teachers learn to analyze students' thinking and to focus their teaching decisions not only on the new curricular activities but also on how their own students are learning in the classroom. I know from my own experience as a participant in the seminar that it can move

30   teachers into analyzing and studying children's thinking in deeply reflective ways. I know, too, that the math activities in the seminar—ones that really push on and strengthen math content knowledge—can upend one's perception of teaching practice.

The seminar requires a different level of engagement and responsibility

35   on the part of the teachers than workshops we've all attended in the past. There are readings and written reflections to do for homework. The writings are turned in to facilitators who read and write responses. The seminar can

be taken for credit, and so it is a new idea (complication!?) to be "graded" by a facilitator who may also be your coach. As the one responsible for offering professional development, I have been thinking about how I manage this transition from one way of adult learning in this district to another. I have my own insecurities about facilitating this new type of professional development with my teacher colleagues even as I firmly believe the seminar is about the *right stuff*. How do I stay centered when the going gets tough? What do I rely on as the facilitator that will help me stay the course and push through resistance to a place where people want to "come to the table"?

I am forging new territory with this seminar, and I am on a steep learning curve knowing how to manage and prepare for the bushwhacking and leadership it requires!

I was a participant in this same seminar at a university last summer, and in many ways, it was similar to the best of my classes in graduate school. I realize now that before offering our math seminar to colleagues, I hadn't thought enough about what it might mean for others who haven't had similar, or recent, positive learning experiences. It might take time to figure out how to shift gears from the more standard math workshop to one that requires as much from the participant as it does from the facilitator. I knew Sylvia, and I would spend a ton of time preparing for each of the eight sessions—reading the material, doing the math, and thinking about the goals and the connections between each session. *But I hadn't realized how much time I would spend thinking about the learners' experience, about what it means to engage someone—and engage people coming from lots of different traditions and beliefs.* I know this is at the heart of professional development and working with adults (and seems obvious when I think about teaching), but it's one thing to know it intellectually and it's another to face some of the challenges in the moment! One thing I know is that it wasn't until we were actually into the seminar that I realized how hard I was going to be thinking about *this* aspect of my work.

In the Seminar

The second of the eight sessions was difficult for me to facilitate for all the reasons I've written about so far. It seems that people brought into the second class their fears of change, their anxieties about "knowing math," or their general frustrations about how they feel they are treated in the system. There were some who were eager to return from the last session and who had really prepared well by reading and doing their reflective writing. This was exciting but by no means the norm. Several people voiced their discontent by saying in the whole group that the seminar wasn't meeting their needs in trying to use the new curriculum with their students. In my head, I know that, in the short view, it could be true. The seminar isn't geared to support, in specific ways, the day-to-day use of the new curriculum. In a longer view, it absolutely will serve their math teaching practice and the ideas of the seminar—and the math content of it—are tightly aligned with the district curriculum. While this is not a "curriculum workshop"—which the teachers can also attend—a better description would be that it provides an opportunity to learn how to think about elementary school mathematics and both the teacher's and the students' learning of it in new and deeper ways.

90

I struggled in responding to concerns from those who felt, for instance, that the students in the session video did not represent authentic struggles teachers are having in their classrooms. A few said the material and the video weren't connected to the frustration that "our students are just not coming up with any *strategies* to solve problems." Yet another complaint raised during the evening was that we (the district) "don't give students enough of what they need to succeed on high-stakes tests in third, fourth and fifth grades."

95

100

105

In the moment, I felt like I was offering a lot of nodding of my head and sounds of sympathy, but I didn't respond directly to what they were raising. As I fielded the discussion, I wrestled with how to get deeply into the content of the seminar—follow the purpose and agenda of seminar—while at the same time try to let some of the ideas and questions of the participants guide us in our facilitation. How do Sylvia and I gauge if this is just that the participants simply do not yet understand the purpose of the work we are doing in the seminar, and yet in response, when do we need to adjust and expand what we are doing to follow the participant voice? Some of their needs will be addressed in a curriculum-specific workshop— but the work they can do with this material is equally important and, perhaps, will be the thing that allows the learning of the mathematics in the new curriculum to really take hold.

Participants' Reflective Writing

110

115

Thoughts of how to address all this for the third session followed me as I went home that night and read through the participants' homework writing. They had been asked to describe their expectations for the seminar after the first session and in what ways these expectations were being met. I discovered that at least three or four of the participants specifically wrote that the seminar did not measure up to their expectations. I thought about what they wrote, and I knew I wanted—and needed—to respond by bringing the teachers closer to the important ideas of the seminar. I could begin to address some of their concerns in my written responses, while at the same time, trying to reframe for them the purpose of the seminar.

This is an excerpt from Nerissa's homework written after Session 1:

120

125

130

I am a first-year teacher, currently in the middle of the fourth grade curriculum. I was a paraprofessional last year and at that time taught a full year of this new fourth grade material. Prior to that, I was in Winston College where I learned a lot about this mathematics.

One of my hopes for this particular seminar is to find more practical ways of taking kids through these mathematical ideas. I came into teaching with the current theories in mind, but once I was thrown into a difficult teaching situation, my good intentions went to the wayside.

I have found that when I ask kids to tell me how they came up with a particular answer, be it mentally or on paper, most of them use the traditional algorithms, or they use inefficient strategies they are making up to please me. I find that I can show these other approaches to kids, but I am not sure the value they have for them.

I would like this seminar to help me know how to take kids through these ideas, and I want to get past the beginning stages of just showing all the ways you can solve a problem.

After the first session, I felt that the work we did, did not meet my expectations. I have already had experience with the various ways children (on videos and in books) and adults in class can come up with ways to solve problem. (I do understand that this is new for a lot of teachers who have not been in school as recently as I have, so I may be unrealistic in my expectations; perhaps, we will get more in depth as the course goes on.) Although I know the methods are important, I am finding very few of my students doing this sort of thing. I am confused with how to help children gain a deep understanding of the operations and problems solving. I feel like I need more practical things to do with the students.

Also, how do we move along through such a rigorous curriculum when we are supposed to be spending so much time letting kids come up with different ways to solve problems? The lessons in our curriculum, which are similar to the work we did in our seminar, can take hours to complete, and there is so much to cover. It is just so hard when you are in a class of 25 kids who have behavior problems, and are at so many different levels, to really get in depth with anything.

I know this course is not designed to solve the problems of the school system, but I just feel like I need practical ideas—actual lessons, even—that I can try with my students. I also want a discussion of where to take students after that point of discovering the way they think about problems. Is the goal to move them to a certain kind of approach or algorithm? When you can see how a child is thinking about a certain problem, what do you do next?

The following is an excerpt from Marta, a fifth grade teacher. Because the district's math curriculum is new, among one of the concerns she raises is that her fifth graders come to her grade level unprepared to take new approaches to learning math:

I came to this training in hopes of something different. When I was first informed about it, I felt I didn't want to go to yet another training, but I was told that these sessions would be quite different from curriculum workshops I'd attended before. They would give me insight into the ways children come to understand and develop mathematical thinking. Because the stories we read in the seminar were written by teachers about their own classrooms, I hoped I'd be able to hear about problems similar to the ones I've been experiencing and how they had tackled them. I then would be able to help my children. I cannot say that this happened in my first class. From the assigned reading, I understood that teachers had these perfect classrooms, where even students who had never been taught the new way, were coming up with all these wonderful strategies the very first time they were asked to do so. What have I been doing wrong? And what about all the teachers I've been

180 talking to? What are *they* doing wrong? I cannot deny that it is good to come together with other teachers, to hold discussions in groups about what goes on in our classrooms and talk about our successes and frustrations. It is good to work together on problems and discuss each other's strategies. It is even better to bring our-

185 selves to our children's positions because this will help us help them. But I would also like to hear about children like ours. Rather than hear about all these wonderful students who are doing so well with this new way of math, I want to hear about the ones who aren't doing so well. I know I'm not the only one with students like

190 this in my class. I want to read, hear, and watch videos about how other teachers tackle these problems. What can I do to make a child understand a concept? What did this or that teacher do to help that child? Where did he or she go from there?

In trying to write articulate responses to these two participants, I struggled

195 to find the right balance in what I should say. I thought about my intentions. To acknowledge their questions and frustrations. To give them concrete answers. To help them get more out of the seminar. What *did* I want them to understand and get out of this? What *would* make their experience more worthwhile? Could I help them find something useful in this seminar? After

200 talking and e-mailing with a few people about responding to these teachers, I'll include, here, the response I wrote to Marta and handed back to her at our third session:

Dear Marta,

Thank you for sharing your honest reflections on your expectations

205 for this seminar and how they were met during the first session. It sounds as though your work over the past few years with the math curriculum has included many frustrations—and some exciting moments.

As I stated in the seminar, I know that as an upper grade teacher

210 you are taking on an extra challenge in working with students who have not been asked to think this way about numbers and mathe- matics in previous grades. I can imagine that your students have more often been asked to follow specific procedures for solving problems and it's a new idea to be responsible for developing an

215 understanding of the relationships between numbers. It seems pretty reasonable that many students want to go back to "the old way"! On the other hand, I have also seen students invigorated by this new approach—it can be exciting to discover a way to multiply numbers when you never understood it before and are suddenly

220 feeling much more powerful in math. Yet I also know that for many fifth grade students this is a new and difficult process.

You may be in a different place than some of the participants in the seminar; for some, it is a brand new idea that there is a "different way" to solve a subtraction problem besides using the traditional

225 algorithm. I know we can learn a lot in reading these teachers' stories in the seminar book, watching the videos, and doing math— no matter what stage of practice we're in. For me, I've read these

stories and watched these videos any number of times and every time, I feel like I gain new insight into how students understand mathematics. I experience again that process of developing an understanding of a math idea and what that's like for a student— and I feel like I am continually gaining a deeper understanding of the mathematics we are all teaching. My growing sense of the mathematics and students' ideas about the mathematics has really helped me when I am working in classrooms. I have a better way of seeing where students might be conceptually as they are working through a problem, and I have a better sense of the math they need to know to solve it successfully. I am coming to understand better what students are struggling with when they make mistakes or when they feel stuck, and I am clearer about where I want students to go. This allows me to construct more purposeful and effective next steps for individual students.

It was never our intention to have the videotapes and case discussions make participants feel badly about what their own students are doing in class, nor did we mean to suggest that students are able to come up with complex strategies from the first time they're asked to work with mathematical ideas in these ways. If we consider the student voices, we do see a range of how deeply students understand the mathematics and how they are developing their own strategies. We have seen some of this range in the teacher stories of their students and in the video clips (a fourth grader who is solving double digit addition problems by counting by ones, a third grader subtracting 2 – 3 in the ones place of a double digit subtraction problem and coming up with the answer of zero). I think it's important that we highlight this range in the seminar.

I hope you will find it interesting to peer in closely at what your students are doing and what they are thinking about in the coming weeks: What ideas are they struggling with? What do they need to consider or understand in order to solve the problems in this new curriculum? What ideas might have come before this? What do they not yet understand? What helps them make sense of the problems? What's logical about their approach? What work is next for a student? These are important questions for us to consider. Our hope is that we can use this seminar as a way of learning how to attend to these kinds of questions and that by analyzing the teacher episodes of students' thinking, we will come to better understand what our own students are learning—as well as our teacher role in that learning.

My expectations for students as they are just beginning this work, first and foremost, is that they make sense of the problems and that they are using mathematically reasonable strategies. They might begin by choosing what looks like (and might well be) rather inefficient strategies to solve problems, but I think what matters most is that they are striving to make sense. Once I feel they are on the right track, I want to support them in deepening their understanding and developing more strategic approaches. This is going to be a process of helping them to build on what they already understand and know.

280 You wrote about students struggling to find strategies to solve problems, and I am curious to learn more about your class and their work. I wonder what ideas students are bringing to solving problems. What ideas do you think their approaches are based on? What do you think they understand about the composition of numbers and the meanings of operations that can help them? It
285 will be interesting to hear more as we move ahead in the seminar.

I hope you continue to look for ways that this seminar can be useful to you, and I look forward to reading more of your reflections.

See you soon,

Bonita

Reflecting on the Seminar

290 The third session of the seminar felt better to me. I made efforts to make sure we talked about what students would need to understand in order to employ the strategies they used. I worked to relate what was going on in the readings more to what I knew was going on in the class-rooms of these teachers. I asked more specific questions when participants
295 brought up frustrations about their own classrooms or their students' work. And when questions came up about what to do about a struggling student in one of the readings, I opened it up to the whole group to offer answers so that I wasn't the one fielding all the answers. In the following sessions, I worked to make specific connections between the seminar math
300 activities and activities in the new curriculum. This back and forth between responding to the teachers' beliefs and staying the course and maintaining the goals of the seminar became a continuous and conscious effort. I had to really stretch in my own facilitation learning—and in my written responses—to make sense of what teachers were really question-
305 ing or puzzling over and to make important connections visible.

Looking over their homework portfolios and my written responses to them, now I wonder, did these participants go on to find the seminar more useful because of our written exchanges? What part did this writing play in facilitating teachers' learning? I can't tell you for sure. However, Nerissa
310 thanked me at the end of the seminar for my responses to her homework.

In the last reflection she wrote,

For me, this course has not so much changed my thinking but redirected my thinking. I came to my first year of teaching with a lot of "ideals." However, when I got into the challenges of first-year
315 teaching, these ideas went to the wayside. I feel that this course has been like a retreat, a place to remember what my goals are. A place to refresh the ideas I discussed in college and think about how I am going to use them in my classroom, particularly next year when I get to start over with more experience under my belt.
320 I hope to set up a system from the beginning of the school next year where kids spend more time explaining their own thinking to the class, rather than me explaining my thinking. This means that I am going to have to work on listening skills with the students as well as public-speaking skills.

I am going to try to let kids have more time and encouragement to play with and explore numbers, in the breaking apart of numbers, and so on. I want to do this prior to showing them "cluster problems."   325

As far as algorithms, I need to think of a way to show them different algorithms, give them enough time to learn these algorithms, let them play around with the algorithms to make them their own, and fit this into a time outside of regular math classes.   330

These are a few of the ideas that I am playing with at the moment. There is obviously a lot more I need to work on, although this is a lot on its own. The most important thing for me is that I feel refreshed in my thinking, understanding, and approach to mathematics in the classroom.   335

This is a good outcome for Nerissa. I'm glad to hear about what's on her mind now and what she might do with what's she's learned—and I hope for her that the seminar has also achieved the goal to cultivate a sense of ongoing inquiry about her students as she also continues to develop her teaching practice.   340

I do, still, think about the intersection of the beliefs the participants come in with and the facilitator's role in making the seminar a compelling experience. In future seminars, I want the participants to develop a taste for the seminar, *and* I also respect that their initial expectations about wanting answers and validation come from a place of need and a hunger for learning more. I made progress, I think, in doing some facilitation around these issues not only in class but also in helpful ways, through the homework response exchanges. How to use my written responses as an avenue for connecting ideas and responding to questions is something I would love to have a chance to talk about with other coaches. How do we think about and manage the balance between staying the course and keeping everyone on board?   345   350

Case 11 Unsatisfied in the Seminar

Focus Questions Activity

1. In your small group, consider the goals of Sylvia and Bonita's seminar. What are the two facilitators working to accomplish with this professional development experience?

2. What ideas and beliefs does Nerissa communicate in her first homework assignment? What do you learn from Marta's writing?

3. How do you describe the dilemma Bonita sorts through as she decides how to respond to Marta? What is she aiming to accomplish in her written response?

4. What actions does Bonita take in response to the challenges participants raise in the seminar? On what resources does she rely? What connections is she trying to make?

5. At the close of the seminar, Nerissa writes, "This course has been a "like a retreat, a place to remember what my goals are." What new ideas or new ways of thinking are evident in this writing since the first session?

6. Consider the difference between Nerissa's request to learn "practical ideas—actual lessons even" and the goals of Bonita's seminar. What activities might contribute to the development of the type of plans and/or goals Nerissa now has for her classroom?

7. Bonita wrote her case as a way to describe and explore her experience of facilitating this eight-week math seminar. You may find that teachers raise related issues in a range of coaching scenarios where your goals might seem in conflict with theirs. In your own coaching work, how do you respond to the facilitation issue Bonita frames as "staying the course" and supporting a fruitful agenda?

Case 11 Unsatisfied in the Seminar

Planning Activity: Meeting the Challenge

Small-Group Discussion

Each participant takes a few minutes for self-reflection before a discussion begins. Focus on a challenging coaching collaboration or a working relationship you have been trying to establish. The context might be a seminar such as Bonita described. It might be in a grade-level meeting or a one-on-one meeting with a teacher or with a principal. You might describe the tension or dissonance the challenge presents as a feeling of resistance or a sense of "push back." It may be that the two of you have different expectations for coaching. The root of the conflict may be that your current beliefs about learning math are in quite different places.

Whatever the coaching context, focus on a challenge that needs to be sorted out in order to be able to coach most productively. Take a few minutes (but no more than five) for each person in the group to talk through *one* of these challenges and a goal as a preface to the reflective writing activity that follows.

On Your Own

In a written reflection, respond to the following prompts:

1. Describe a challenging scenario. Include hypotheses about what may be beneath the surface—from the teacher's point of view and from your own. What are your expectations? How would you describe the other's expectations? If you find yourself unsure, what questions might you raise and discuss that could illuminate the ideas?

2. How might you explain or convey the purpose of your goal for this aspect of your coaching work?

3. How could you thoughtfully and strategically respond to the other's objections or concerns?

4. What specifically could you do that will convey that you are working to address his or her needs but still maintain an important mathematical focus?

Small-Group Discussion

Return to your group of three. Discuss what comes up as you reflect on coaching with these issues in mind.

1. What new ways of working come to the foreground for you?

2. What questions or challenges are clearer? Which ones persist?

3. What new ideas or plans might you pursue?

12

Examining the Role of Authority in Coaching

Chapter Elements

✦ Case: Claiming Authority

✦ Focus Questions Activity

✦ Planning Activity: Two Posters Activity

CASE DESCRIPTION

Claiming Authority, written by a math coach in her third year of coaching, provides readers with a view of the trajectory of one coach's developing practice. The author describes connections between her developing coaching practice to the early developing years of her classroom teaching. The author tackles the issues of authority in coaching, an important theme that will have resonance for all coaches and teacher leaders. She considers ways she might have moved more quickly toward a stronger practice, including taking advantage of the wisdom of coach colleagues.

NOTES TO THE READER

Prior to reading the case, review the Focus Questions (page 129). As you read the case, highlight passages that resonate for you. Note line numbers of sentences or paragraphs that interest you or raise questions for you.

Case 12 Author: Carina

Claiming Authority

1   Last Friday when we met in our coach meeting, Estelle said this word "authority" and reflected out loud, "You all move with such authority in this coaching work." Or maybe she said, "You all need to call on your own authority so much in this work. Where do you find it?"

5   Either way, what stuck with me was the word *authority* and feeling strongly how different this third year of coaching feels than my first two years.

In fact, this year is *so* very different. I've been reflecting on a way to express what I mean. Estelle's word, "authority," has given me a diving-in

10   place to think about and describe how my practice is changing and how I understand the choices I make as a coach. In this writing, I want to explore the idea of "moving with authority." Do I? Me?

Here I am beginning my third year of this job. And how is what I do now seem as if I actually am moving and acting with authority quite

15   often? Somehow, Estelle's naming that—place/space/state of being—has really captured me because I hadn't had a way of expressing what, in reality, has very much evolved in my practice. So I'm going to use this writing as a way to reflect on how and what's different for me from my first year as a coach (what I've learned to do or how I've come to understand the

20   essence of my work).

I would like to use this writing also to describe how I find myself assessing schools and adjusting my suggestions for their work and negotiating with them for what their work might be as we collaborate this year. You (and I) might wonder: On what do I base my suggestions? What is on

25   my checklist that I definitely have in my head (right or wrong), and in reflecting, what's my sense of how I do these things—how I know how to do these things?

First, let me describe a bit about my initial year as a coach, only two years ago now. The word, that year, was handed to me by Lily. She said,

30   "Establish credibility." Gee thanks, Lily! How do I go out and do that?! Yet, it was a focus of my dynamic in schools. "Establish credibility" turned into something like: "Go establish connections and begin relationships with all the people with whom you interact, Carina."

For me, this act of establishing credibility also meant establishing a

35   significant list of *don'ts:*

- Don't advertise that you've only been a teacher for 13 years (many with whom you will work have been at it much longer).
- Don't advertise that in all those 13 years, you only taught Kindergarten and second grade because many of the teachers with

40   whom you work will need you to know fourth and fifth graders, or even sixth, seventh, and eighth graders just as well.
- Don't advertise that you taught in a different district—wealthy, suburban, and privileged. The validity of your experience will duly be challenged.

- Oh, yes, and don't advertise that you probably never actually imple-   45
  mented this district's curriculum in total ever because you taught in
  a district that used a different math program.
- Don't advertise that you taught the seminars you are responsible for
  facilitating only once before this.
- Don't advertise that you can't believe *you* have to start meetings,   50
  when just yesterday you were at those very same kinds of meetings
  and someone else was starting them.
- And don't advertise that you only left the classroom a short two
  months ago, which often feels too close to yesterday.

So how did I begin? I found myself trying to let teachers know that   55
I was truly interested in how they each think and in who they are as
learners. I could genuinely share with them that I had been thinking
about mathematics in elementary school for a long time and that I believed
that teachers are decision makers in their classrooms. Gradually, I brought
up ideas that might be something teachers would find useful to chew   60
on. I also learned to call on others' anecdotes about students or teaching
rather than needing to have my own to share. I found myself, in that
first year, sometimes talking about kitchen renovations and vacation
plans of my teachers rather than too much head-on mathematics.
I found myself offering rather than asserting. I also struggled with   65
feeling too personally attached to the new district curriculum and the
math department. The whole department was new, and the vision was
an emerging one. The math department was my lifeline, and we were in
this big new enterprise with all sincerity together. It was painful to hear
teachers' criticisms of either the new work or the people I worked with,   70
and this, sometimes, got in my way in facilitating discussions. In making partnerships in schools, I drew on my deep respect and admiration
for children's thinking.

I did my best through that first year and worked hard, although
establishing relationships can be difficult to actually document as a piece   75
of work. I was agonizingly aware that if I had more experience, I would
be doing a better job. I felt like a first year teacher and I *was*—of adults.
I had a hard time embracing the fact that I was the one in the guiding role.
But I *was*, and I felt too often that I was faking; inwardly, I wasn't so sure
I deserved the privilege.   80

I kept my hair gray (and I still do). I wore only dresses (and still do).
I took a lot of notes about whatever was being said. I yearned for being
able to move with the confidence that I was used to having as a teacher in
my own classroom. I yearned for my old school and the sense of belong-
ing I felt there: of being someone who is known, someone who is chatted   85
with, someone who pretty much knows what she's doing but with normal
doubts and questions. Someone, who in hindsight I now see, *moved with
authority.*

So now, here I am in this third year of coaching. And I am saying that
I feel so much more able to be totally present, to move with a real measure   90
of confidence, to assert, with a higher degree of clarity, the agendas that
I believe are useful for schools and teachers within them. I can see, now,
the parallels to my own past classroom work.

First Year

Teaching

As a first-year teacher, in math class for instance, I needed to be quite centered on immediate issues, such as how to teach this particular lesson, how to be in moments with students to collect ideas from them that I could begin, *just* begin, to sort out. I had confidence that there was a continuum of ideas into which my students' ideas could fit, but I had not yet experienced, or built knowledge of, the trajectory of ideas. Even though I had some notions about how ideas develop, I had no experience with watching them appear, no experience in really knowing which particular ideas to amplify so all of us could think about them more, and no experience with how ideas relate to other ideas. My perspective, although I was cognizant of a much wider one, was necessarily focused on me and on my particular students.

Coaching

For a while, the immediate issues were questions like, "How do I *get* to a particular school? Where do I park? How do I get into a building? How do I ask people if I can come into their class? What do I do with my stuff? What do I need to bring with me to schools each time? What does LASW (Looking at Student Work) stand for anyway?"

I knew there were bigger issues to tackle, yet dealing with the immediacy of these surface-level details took a significant amount of energy. I knew that supporting the development of stronger math-content knowledge was central to the big picture and that to get anywhere near anyone's math-content knowledge, I would have to establish credibility!

I wrestled with how I could connect with teachers and principals as quickly as possible and learn about the status of their knowledge. I had the coach title, but how would I suggest questions and activities that may or may not be welcome? And then, how could I be sure these questions or strategies would help or not?

I wondered, just how *do* I push this whole-district math program forward. . . . And what exactly are the requirements of the new math initiative again, anyway? Alone in a school meeting, I would be gripped with wondering just what *were* those exact details of it. And hey, what exactly *are* the relationships between factors and multiples? And does anyone *have* to meet with me anyway? Suffice to say, I am thankful to have lived to tell the tale.

We all, the whole coach cadre and the whole staff of the math department, were so new, so earnest, so flying by the seat of our collective pants. Thank goodness we had each other to meet with at the end of the week. And our cell phones to call each other at the end of the day (or in a stolen moment in the middle of the day). And a math department that stood firmly behind us—even as the department was charged with being as suddenly authoritative in this new initiative as we were. Despite this sense of camaraderie, learning to navigate the expected and the unexpected *alone* each day was a totally new orientation to functioning—to being—in a school.

Second Year

Teaching

Continuing with the parallels, in my second year of first grade class-room teaching, I now had a reference class—last year's. I was able to redo some of the lessons. I was able to recall how a group of students had already worked with these ideas and searched to see if my new group of students would share any similarities in the construction of their own. I was able to recall how one student in particular had made sense of a math idea, and I listened carefully to see if any student, in front of me this year, might think in a similar way. I began to be able to hypothesize about general ways students would engage with the math activities, but cautiously, as maybe my particular cohort the first year had been unusual. I could let my view enlarge. I was able to plan ahead a bit more. I could imagine where we might be, in terms of making sense of a particular math concept, in a few weeks. I could imagine how one student or another might move through some activities and emerge with new math sense. I felt more settled or knowingly purposeful, no longer flying by the seat of my pants, and yet the big picture was still elusive. I had many extremely focused questions. And at times, I had a sense that I was creating a working knowledge base of a continuum of math development for first graders that would help guide my decision making as their teacher.

Coaching

In comparison, in my second year of coaching, it was delightful to revisit some schools. To have people at least remember me. Often, I was greeted that fall with, "Oh, are you back this year?" which was certainly better than no one noticing! I knew how to get to most places. I knew that it was unlikely that I would have a spot offered to me where I could put my stuff, and I learned to carve out corners in teacher's rooms or find tables in hallways. I also knew that content knowledge would be an important focus and that ideas I had for different entry points into teachers' learning were more evolved. . . . I knew some things that were gleaned from a year's experience. I knew that LASW sessions could increase teacher content knowledge, that the student thinking seminars I taught would serve the same goal. I knew that classroom visits and debriefing afterward could increase teacher interest while focusing on mathematics at the same time, that curriculum module overviews with grade levels could make a difference in the way teachers approached their lessons, that doing model lessons and debriefing with the teacher could center on the math of the classroom and not only on teaching moves.

I discovered that sometimes even a quick check-in with a teacher was so helpful just because she could then ask me even one question. Looking at and analyzing assessments and using rubrics became an activity that I learned how to do with teachers and to make relevant and useful. I began to know more deeply the curriculum over the whole K–5 grade span and, thus, became a more knowledgeable resource. I knew relationships between particular grade-level activities that helped

140

145

150

155

160

165

170

175

180

185 teachers learn more about the math and how to support the connections to particular students' ideas. Yes, I was experiencing connections between and among ideas. I began to be able to think about the system, rather than just my teachers. I began to be able to generalize my experiences with a few teachers to what it might mean for a group of teachers. Just as in my classroom teaching.

Third Year

Teaching

190 In my third year as a classroom teacher, I really began to feel like I knew what I was doing. What a blast! (Short lived though it was; in later years, I learned how much I still didn't know!) It was thrilling to feel like I could bring some finesse to my teaching. I could focus on individual children and still keep group needs in mind. I could see how this idea one

195 child was working on was really a particular and familiar place in a continuum of math ideas. I had real notions about what the child needed to grapple with in order to learn more. My work with parents of my students got better. I could consider parents much more than I could in my first two years. My views, now based on experience about how the whole year

200 might look were at least an outline to follow. My work with my colleagues improved dramatically as I felt like I could listen better and felt less constantly challenged and naive. I think this feeling of confidence, or competence, is what "moving with authority" captures for me.

Coaching

Here I am in my third year of coaching. I do feel so much more

205 competent. I am more aware of what I know and I do know more than I knew two years ago. I can keep much more in my head because it isn't all so new. I have gotten used to (almost) being the one who has to start most of the meetings I attend! I have gotten better at suggesting specific agendas and being willing to adjust them, but *asserting agendas* . . . what an

210 idea! And I do it with *goals* in mind! I've become more comfortable with what it means to move in very close to someone's learning place and moving back, as well. I've felt confident enough to be able to ask people, more and more, about what they think they need and to offer suggestions (and make judgments) about whether I think those supports are possible, rea-

215 sonable, and aligned with the appropriate goals.

I find myself speaking for myself with a clear idea of where the math department stands; I can represent the department. I can feel aligned with the vision of the math department and, yet I am also able to differentiate my ideas for individual teachers and, sometimes, whole schools. By saying

220 this, I should describe what I have learned to look for—based on experience, vision, and goals—when I go to a school.

One of the first things I look for is the "stage" of curriculum implementation a school is exhibiting. I think strategically about whether one-on-one classroom support is the place to put my energy or whether common

225 planning time with more teachers is the place where I might more successfully support the whole school with their implementation. I think

about whether LASW sessions might be a best entry for teachers resisting or struggling with implementation as opposed to visits to their class-rooms. I consider these things. I weigh them. I make decisions.

I take a "pulse" on teacher or grade-level resistance and try to uncover where this energy is coming from. Does it stem from one very experienced teacher who feels ownership of her math program and experiences change as a power struggle? And, actually, are we locked in one that I might do the work of untangling? Might a teacher or principal be resistant because she is afraid of uncovering her math "weakness"? Is it because the teacher is quite competent in math, but doesn't yet see the complexities the children engage in when learning math for themselves? I feel now that I also have the courage to just simply ask, "What's going on?"

Once I have a sense of where the school is with implementation, I think about what the principal needs from me. Meeting with principals is far less scary; I know now that more often than not, I am a resource to them. I know that they need the information that I have, that there is the poten-tial for colleagueship. Maybe part of my coaching for principals is in help-ing them decide which of all the myriad things that vie for their attention will reap the greatest rewards.

I focus on leadership potential. I seek out individuals in the school viewed by colleagues as thoughtful and respected. I sometimes purposely suggest that colleagues hook up together and coach each other. I let prin-cipals know if a teacher seems open to taking on leadership. I ask prin-cipals which teachers she knows who might take on leadership. I also encourage teachers to let other teachers come visit. I have started to support some teachers in presenting at conferences. I couldn't imagine having this vantage point or doing this work in my first year.

So my word for this year might be "authority," and I might learn lots more about ways I take it when it isn't really mine. What I think now, though, is that there are ways I might have collapsed some of the lessons learned that are spread across these three years; by that I mean that knowing what I know now, I might have pressed more deeply in year one. I might have remembered—and trusted—that staying on mathe-matics and learning with my own classroom students was accomplished *at the same time* that I was "making relationships and building trust," the same would be true of working with teachers and principals. Starting in a new school now, I don't spend a year focusing mostly on building rela-tionships and stepping lightly. Three years ago, all of us were new. There weren't any "wiser and more experienced" coaches to teach us the lessons they'd learned.

In my second year, I might have pressed harder for accountability on the part of principals and teachers—and on students. I had been given that authority, but I struggled in believing I deserved to take that leadership role. As I look back on it, I made myself accountable to a coaching practice that I believed in. I worked really, really hard to do my work well and with good spirit and as a teacher of teachers. If teachers were falling behind, or making excuses, or their students weren't taking responsibility in their own classrooms, I could have insisted more directly that we are on a journey and that it requires commitment and cooperation and, yes, faith in each other. And I would have pressed more.

I see what I have been accomplishing in Year 3 is, in many ways, where I wish I could have been some time ago. And I don't mind that Year 3 comes with challenges or questions or some doubts. I have new ways of
280 seeing or appreciating the complexities of what we are all engaged in. We have more data to help us see where we are *and* to provide us with new puzzles, joys, and disappointments. As we move forward with our work, go deeper into it, there is—of course—so much more to learn. What was subtle in Year 1 feels obvious to me now. And yet, I think what's so dear
285 to me is that we are good questioners. We are unsettled, we are not complacent, and by the way, the math is amazingly elastic—my curiosity keeps stretching further. Every time I hear a child who understands something differently than I have ever heard before, it is such a joy; it is still a thrill!
290 And next year, when I am a fourth year coach, I suspect I will look back on this year and recognize the refinement another year brings.

Case 12 Claiming Authority

Focus Questions Activity

In your small group, consider Carina's reflections on the trajectory of "claiming her own authority" and the connections she draws between her first years of teaching and her early coaching practices. What can we learn from Carina that helps sort out "exploring the idea of 'moving with authority'"?

1. Examine Carina's reflections about how she initiated relationships (lines 55–73). What principles guided her line of thinking at the time?

2. Carina lays out the new teacher issues she struggled with in lines 94–105. How do you understand these, and how are they related to the new coach issues she wrestled with in her first year of coaching?

3. In lines 139–158, the coach claims a sense of authority in her classroom. In what ways had her teaching practice evolved from Year 1? What supported her developed sense of confidence?

4. In lines 159–189, Carina portrays coaching from a new vantage point. What comes into focus for her? How might you characterize the difference between her lens on coaching in the first year with her lens on the second?

5. As described in lines 190–204, Year 3 of classroom teaching appears to have coalesced a new level of practice and authority in Carina's work. How is this portrayal directly related to what she is learning in her third year of coaching?

6. At this stage in your own coaching, what gives you a sense of your own authority?

Case 12   Claiming Authority

Planning Activity: Two Posters Activity

Poster 1

On your own, reflect again on the trajectory of Carina's ideas about coaching. Now, take some time and write notes about your own trajectory of ideas. It makes no difference how long you have been coaching—three months, one year, or six years. Create a poster for sharing with the whole group that captures your own developing ideas about coaching.

Use headings such as

Beginning	Midway	Today
•	•	•
•	•	•
•	•	•

Poster 2

Poster 2 has three new categories: Guiding Principles, Next Questions, Ways to Continuing Learning. Brainstorm several guiding principles of your work—the very premises upon which you make successful coaching moves. In the Next Questions category, describe the next areas of your practice you want to strengthen, examine, or refine. And, finally, add a list of ways that you will continue *learning* about coaching and coaching practice.

Facilitation Guide

Dear Facilitator,

The Facilitation Guide is designed to support you as you lead these professional development sessions. In each chapter of the guide, Session Goals, Case Description, and Session Overview sections provide images of what the session is about and how it unfolds. In addition, the Facilitation Notes include in-depth descriptions of each agenda activity for each session and comments about materials to prepare. The Facilitation Guide was written as a companion document; in this way, it describes comments participants might make in whole-group discussions, details of math ideas participants might offer in a session, and effective responses from facilitators. The notes also include insights about trajectories of coaching practice, important ideas to emphasize, and commentary about coaching that should provide useful background for making facilitation decisions in the session.

Successful facilitation of the cases and related activities is predicated on the idea that facilitators carefully prepare for each session by reading the case, doing the math activity or planning activity, and by considering your own responses to each of the focus questions. Some facilitators have found that investing the time to actually write out responses to focus questions, taking notes on the math activities, and, then, keeping a journal of what participants say and do in the session, provides a detailed and personal resource.

At some point, you might ask the coaches in your group to consider writing their own cases for group discussion. In a structured professional development setting, coaches often take turns offering cases; individual coaches might share two cases during a school year. One way to begin is to ask the group to reflect on cases from these materials that have been influential and to talk together about what makes a case effective. It is helpful to work with the coaches to compare a variety of types of cases, for instance Case 1, Case 2, Case 5, and Case 10. Ask coaches to consider the similarities between the cases, the particulars that make these cases opportunities for learning, and the specifics of what makes a case readable and clear. Coaches will discover that recording specific dialogue, considering and representing the mathematics of students' ideas, and writing honestly about puzzles of practice and considerations for next steps are elements of productive cases. It is important to respect those who are written about and to protect these stories of teaching and coaching practice. For this reason, make a habit of using pseudonyms for teacher, school, and student names—*even in your own coaching group*. A noteworthy feature (and reward) of case writing and sharing in a group is the high value the group puts on confidentiality and trusting relationships that allow for open discussion. Discussing these norms before sharing matters. Facilitators are in a position to protect writers by doing two things: One is to ask for their cases ahead of the meeting so that you can create focus questions that will center discussion on the most salient features of the case and the second is to collect the copies of shared cases before the close of the session. And remember that, for many, writing and exposing one's practice takes courage.

I continue to be fascinated by stories of coaching and am deeply connected to issues of facilitation. I welcome the opportunity to hear from you if you have questions, ideas, or advice—or a case to share about your own experiences!

Amy Morse

amorse@edc.org

Chapter 1
Facilitation Notes

Observing, Studying, Analyzing, and Planning: Preparing to Coach

2.5-Hour Session

Session Goals

- Examine representations of rational numbers
- Explore relationships between fractions and percents
- Consider what it means to prepare to coach—examining classroom mathematics and students' ideas to build content knowledge
- Strategize about using school structures, or pressing for structures, that provide opportunities for coaching and for teacher learning

Case Description: Moving Between Models

The Moving Between Models case offers an example of a reflective practitioner who studies the curriculum, the central mathematical idea in the classroom, the students' work as they engage in a new concept, and the implications for her coaching. Lila, the author, wrote the case midway into her second year as an elementary school coach. Specifically, she raises questions, both mathematical and pedagogical, about the relationship between fractions and percents and the issues that influence children's reasoning as they begin to work with ways to represent rational numbers.

The coach uses her case writing to help her learn more about the mathematics she encounters in the classroom and, at the same time, to help her analyze her next coaching moves and supports for the teacher.

The case offers an interesting perspective on the role of coaching. All coaching does not happen in the moment; certainly, there is a significant amount of preparation coaches undertake for individual classroom visits and meetings or workshops. The case raises a question for discussion: What is the nature of preparing to coach?

Session Overview

Participants begin the session by reading the case. Before a case discussion, they next engage in small-group work on a series of math problems designed to highlight the complex thinking involved in establishing relationships between fractions and percents. The activity is followed by a facilitator-led, whole-group discussion, during which participants share their models for comparing fractional amounts and for describing percents. The discussion is an interactive one with participants and the facilitator both asking questions and exploring the variety of models created in small groups. At this point, the participants rejoin their small groups to work on a Focus Questions Activity designed to highlight both the student thinking and the coach's perspectives on the classroom visits. During the ensuing whole-group discussion, participants will have an opportunity to discuss the coach's role through the eyes of the coach-author and to think together about the implications for their own coaching and developing practices.

Materials Needed for the Session

- Create a chart of the agenda and the Session Goals
- Provide graph paper, plain paper, colored pencils, and counters or small cubes
- Provide chart paper and colored markers for displaying math work and participant ideas

Session Agenda

1. Introduction: 5 minutes

2. Case Reading: 20 minutes

3. Math Activity in Small Groups and Whole-Group Discussion: 70 minutes

4. Focus Questions Activity and Whole-Group Discussion: 55 minutes

Introduction

Introduce the session by describing the agenda, briefly reviewing the Session Goals and the context for the Moving Between Models case. Explain that this case is an example of journal type of case where the coach-author uses writing as a way of analyzing her work and considering next steps.

Case Reading

Reading the case is the first activity in the session. Encourage participants to write questions or comments in the margins and note sentences or paragraphs that resonate for or confuse them. A participant once remarked, "A case is a piece of work *to do,* not just a story to read!" This is a helpful analogy to offer the group.

Math Activity and Whole-Group Discussion

Before a case discussion, participants work in small groups to solve a series of math problems designed to highlight relationships between fractions and percents.

The facilitation of the math discussion is an opportunity to support coaches' consideration of expressing parts of a whole, in a variety of ways, and the models that represent these amounts. The focus of the discussion is also aimed at developing an appreciation for the trajectory of these ideas and for the complex thinking that elementary students—and teachers—engage in when challenged to express fraction amounts as related to 100. Questions participants will consider include:

- How does one's understanding and visual images of $\frac{3}{16}$ map onto a percent model? How are these models related?
- What sort of thinking do children need to do in order to ground themselves in this new form of expressing an amount?

These issues are central to the discussions of both the small and whole groups.

The math activity consists of three word problems. The directions ask individual participants to "think through these problems and draw models on paper," thus encouraging coaches to consider the representations and visual models that help support their understanding of the problems. It is important for the facilitator to circulate and encourage individuals to draw and share their thinking in these small-group discussions.

Note: You may find it useful to ask participants to solve only Question 1, discuss it for a brief moment in their groups, and then have the whole-group discussion with models displayed before you move on to Question 2. The first math problem gives coaches an entry place, and their resulting drawings will serve as the markers of the *conceptual distance* between the representations and ideas of early fraction work and the math ideas embedded in the final problem. Prepare for the whole-group discussion by moving from group to group during the math activity and noting the range of participants' models for "$\frac{5}{8}$ of the horses" described in the first problem. You will likely find a variety of models ranging from a randomly arranged set of 8 symbols with 5 looped into a collection to a rectangle or circle representing a unit of 8 with 5 sections shaded. In the whole group, when you discuss the participants' responses to Problem 1, scribe or ask participants to come up and draw the range of models for $\frac{5}{8}$. Keep these drawings posted so that you can refer back to them as you are bringing the math discussion to a close. It is useful to raise the idea that the model that makes use of a single unit where 5 portions are shaded requires a developed sense of organization than the one that shows 8 horses drawn with 5 crossed off. We begin here to appreciate a child's developing sense of number and reasoning. Question 2 steps up the inquiry for the group. If we now have a sense of how to describe the fraction $\frac{5}{8}$, how do we express $\frac{5}{8}$ as a percent? What does it *look* like? Participants who are less experienced with array or number line models may find it challenging to tackle creating the drawings and visual models for this activity. As the participants

Figure FG1.1

work through this problem, again make note of models and drawings that display a variety of approaches for the whole-group discussion. Participants are likely to create grids of 10 × 10 and shade in $\frac{5}{8}$ in several different ways.

The coach who drew this representation (Figure FG1.1) described the way she used her model to help her solve the problem.

> I used 50 as a landmark for $\frac{1}{2}$. So here I filled in the 50 squares and knew that took care of $\frac{4}{8}$. If I filled in 25 more squares that would be $\frac{6}{8}$, so I divided 25 by 2 and got 12 squares and one more half of a square. That makes $\frac{5}{8}$ equal to 62 and $\frac{1}{2}$ percent.

Another participant drew an array of 100 but thought about it area differently (Figure FG1.2).

> I had to make this arrangement of 100 squares equal to 8 horses. I cut the last two columns (with the shaded Xs) off and redistributed them evenly across the first 8. That meant that in each of the new 8 columns there are now $12\frac{1}{2}$ rows. Then, I could calculate that 5 columns contain a total of $62\frac{1}{2}$ squares or $62\frac{1}{2}$%!

One participant simply cut the array of 100 into 4 quadrants, shaded 2 quadrants and $\frac{1}{2}$ of another, thus illustrating 25% + 25% = 50% or $\frac{4}{8}$ and adding another $12\frac{1}{2}$ squares brings the total to 62.5%.

Figure FG1.2

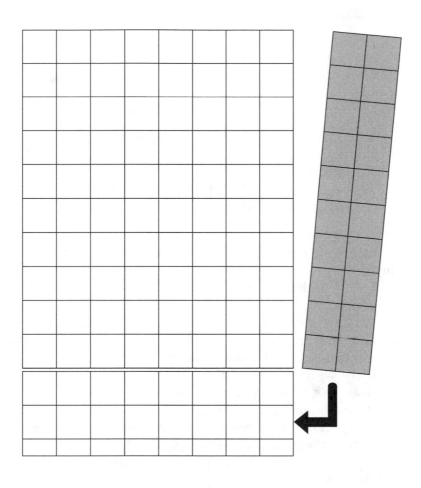

Another participant drew a circle, divided it into quarters, and then marked 8 even sections. She shaded one quarter ($\frac{2}{8}$) and labeled it 25% with a J, another quarter with a J, and one more $\frac{1}{8}$. She then added all the J sections to equal 62.5%.

You will likely see number line models illustrating 0 to 100 and use of 25 and 50 as landmarks again relating to $\frac{1}{4}$ and $\frac{1}{2}$ as a way of illustrating a comparison between $\frac{5}{8}$ and $62\frac{1}{2}$%. Another is a line labeled 0 through $\frac{8}{8}$. A participant created a chart below this model that read: 100% = $\frac{8}{8}$, 50% = $\frac{4}{8}$, 25% = $\frac{2}{8}$ and 12.5% = $\frac{1}{8}$. She wrote, "If $\frac{4}{8}$ = 4 jumpers, then $\frac{5}{8}$ = 5 jumpers which means 50% + 12.5% = 62.5%. If line number models are not explored in participants' work, it may be useful to suggest that participants try one.

One participant created a table representing ratios of horses to jumpers. She explained,

> I kept doubling to a certain point, and then I knew I would be over 100 so I just added what I knew about 32 horses to the 64 horses, and then divided by 2 what I knew about 8 horses.

She wrote: 8:5

16:10

32:10

64:40

96:60

4:2.5

so, 100: 62.25%

These models are all valuable for exploring the group's ideas. A selection of the different models that come out of the group's work should be displayed one at a time so that the whole group has a chance to consider the ideas inherent in each model, where the $\frac{1}{8}$ is, where the $\frac{5}{8}$ are, and how the coach who worked with the model used it as a tool for solving the problem.

Note: It is important to not only discuss the relationship between $\frac{5}{8}$ to 62.5% but also to have participants see the relationships between the models themselves.

As you bring this discussion to a close, refer back to the original drawings of $\frac{5}{8}$ and ask people to comment on the distance between students' working knowledge at the stage where describing "a part of one whole" is perceived using fractions and to where the discussion rests now with regard to the translation of this same fraction into percents. You will want coaches to leave with an appreciation for this complex work as well as with new ideas about the significant value of using—and discussing— visual models and representations. Participants should now have multiple representations to reflect on, more content knowledge to consider, and be ready to engage in the inquiry about the potential for student learning.

Question 3 is for a coach or small group of coaches to consider on their own. Inevitably, the time allotted and the focus of attention is on the first two problems so Question 3 gives individual participants and chance to further an investigation. The coaches' math work in Questions 1 and 2, and the ensuing discussion, is sufficient for the purpose of this case set activity.

Focus Questions Activity and Case Discussion

The focus questions are designed to help coaches engage in discussion both about the mathematics children wrestle with and the pedagogical implications for teaching. Because participants have had a chance to work through the related math activities for their own content learning, they are situated now to have considered discussion about the analytical questions and insights Lila raises in her case. In small groups, coaches discuss a series of questions with focused attention on young students' development of fraction and percent models and ideas with a more fine-tuned lens on the issues.

Have participants reference line numbers in the small- and whole-group discussions. Referring to line numbers and then waiting until everyone locates the passage, helps keep participants accountable to what is actually in the case and not slip into a discussion that can become overly general. As you circulate among small groups, encourage coaches to take the time to consider each student's response in Question 1. You might suggest that each participant write out her response to Question 2 before discussing it openly in the small group. Ask individuals to sketch a list of ideas in response to

Question 4 and to take time to write down their questions and ideas with regard to future work for Amari and her classmates in Question 5. It is important that coaches learn to, and are encouraged to, give themselves time to articulate their thoughts and bring words to their confusions or questions.

Considering the logic and reasoning beneath student responses helps coaches to focus on where students are in their thinking, as opposed to dismissing "wrong" ideas or underappreciating potentially robust ones. In the whole-group discussion, as participants are talking about the ideas present at the beginning of this classroom episode, remind them that these are ideas likely to be present in any fifth grade class. Not only is this discussion an opportunity to consider carefully the students Lila writes about, it is also an opening for coaches to enrich their understanding, in each of their own coaching contexts, of how students, naïve about these ideas, will likely respond.

Following the thread of Amari's thinking offers insights into the mathematical issues. On one hand, Amari has quite sturdy ideas about factors of 42 and how they are related to each other. In fact, her statement that generalizes this notion is not only appropriate; it is also an indicator of how Amari thinks. One might interpret her remarks throughout the case as based on the premise that mathematics is ultimately about ideas and about making sense of them. Asking coaches to comment on the generalizable nature of Amari's idea—even applying algebraic notation—illustrates the type of important reasoning work that Amari can do.

But we read on to find Amari in a perplexed state. Teddy, Amari, and their classmates offer images of students sorting through ideas. At this stage, Lila leaves off from writing about the classroom and begins to puzzle out how models influence children's ideas of fractions and of percents. From line 82 on, Lila considers what it means to understand and apply the model of "6 people out of 10 people wearing stripes" to a model of "60 shaded squares in an array of 100." Reading her question as, "What does it take to really see the link between the two?" we see she is asking what students need to understand, what models are useful images, and how students work with the ideas to come to reason and successfully apply these ideas.

While coaches may not yet (as Lila herself has not) come to conclusions, the point of the case discussion is to open up these questions to the whole group and to consider hypotheses and possible next steps based on this session experience and the opportunity for coaches to share and consider multiple perspectives.

Participants need an opportunity to talk about the implications of this case for their coaching. They have had a chance to discuss the mathematics of the case and to puzzle through the questions the author has raised; now, it is appropriate for the facilitator to help the group consider their new insights and what these mean to their own practices. Support this consideration by asking the group to note the ways the coach author considers her own next steps. Ask the participants to consider structures and opportunities afforded in their own schools. Ask, "If you have ideas and questions about how children come to learn and engage in the mathematical ideas we've discussed, how does this get incorporated into your own coaching?"

Save a few minutes at the end of the session for participants to respond to exit card questions. You might ask, "How was it to do math with colleagues? What did you learn about the way you work and the ideas you have?" Ask coaches to describe one way the case and case discussions have influenced their thinking.

Chapter 2
Facilitation Notes

Discerning and Responding: Coaching in Real Time

2-Hour Session

Session Goals

- Analyze multiplication and using numbers of groups to compare amounts
- Consider the use of grade-level meetings to support teachers' content knowledge
- Explore coach decision making and improvisational moves in the role
- Examine the role of coach and what it means to navigate a "teacher of teachers" role

Case Description:
Analyzing Multiplication

Lisa, the coach-author, first encounters a fourth grade classroom where the students are no longer working on the school curriculum; rather, they spend the math class hour working on drill and practice. She listens carefully to the teacher who expresses her dismay at her students' work and the tensions she feels about the upcoming state test. Her concerns drive her to revert to work that focuses on solving many problems with little, if any, emphasis on explaining or exploring reasoning and development of strategies for solving problems. Rather than intervene, Lisa takes it all in as she weighs her coaching choices. Lisa presents an image of a coach who sees her role in multiple dimensions. She describes a teachers' meeting that, through skillful coaching, responds to multiple issues. The case sheds light on how a coach perceives her role with respect to teachers' learning.

Session Overview

The session begins with a math activity, "How Do I Know?" Participants work through the same ideas that both students and teachers investigate in the case. The activity and ensuing discussion help prepare coaches to focus on the strategies described in the case as the coach navigates a single coaching day.

Participants read the case and discuss focus questions in small groups. Next, in the whole group, coaches explore such concepts as preparation for coaching, drawing on resources for teacher professional development, using school structures to enact coaching goals, and examining the role of the coach.

In discussing how Lisa considers her authority and her responsibilities, the coaches have a chance to consider why she makes particular choices and to analyze her decision making for the way it supports teacher learning. In this way, coaches are afforded opportunities to enrich their own ideas about ways to move in coaching and, too, to hear multiple interpretations from their coach colleagues. It is important for participants to explore these images of coach work; it is through analyzing and discussing these coaching stories that participants are able to reflect on and enrich their own images of their role.

Materials for the Session

- Create a chart of the agenda and the Session Goals
- Provide graph paper, plain paper, and colored pencils for exploring the math problems
- Obtain chart paper and different colored markers to display participants' math work

Session Agenda

1. Math Activity in Small Groups: 15 minutes

2. Whole-Group Math Discussion: 20 minutes

3. Case Reading: 20 minutes

4. Focus Questions Activity and Whole-Group Discussion: 65 minutes

Math Activity

Before coming together to discuss the case, participants work in small groups to solve a series of math problems designed to highlight important ideas the case writer raises. In addition to writing descriptive sentences, encourage participants to draw models that illustrate their reasoning. Explain that the purpose of the activity is for participants to analyze these problems and to consider the mathematical logic of their answers. There are several ways groups might work on problems. For participants with little experience working on adult math content, it can be useful for participants to work on one problem on their own and then discuss their ideas in small groups before they move to the next problem. This way, they bring new ideas and approaches to each of the successive problems. For more experienced participants, working on the problems alone before discussing them is one way they might challenge themselves to consider solving the problems in more than one way. Encourage discussion and collaboration in the small groups.

This collection of problems give participants an opportunity to consider the way the size of groups and the numbers of groups affect the total amount. As they work through the problems, make note of models and drawings that display a variety of approaches in preparation for facilitating the whole-group discussion. Participants might use multiples of 10 to approximate total amounts. They may draw arrays such as 312×10 versus 300×9 to compare two different amounts. If coaches have not explored diagrams (models or story problems) for these problems, encourage them to find the size of the total based on an array model. You might encourage a participant to draw a model that shows the solution such that no calculation is necessary. While some participants might use arrays to compare size, one might draw arrays of just the "missing" or "extra" amounts and compare these. If participants are not aware of open arrays, the whole-group discussion might be an opportunity to explore that idea. Some participants might use a chart or a graph to describe how amounts grow based on the number and size of groups. These models are all valuable for exploring the participants' ideas.

As you observe the groups working, listen for ideas or questions you can choose to highlight in the whole-group discussion. While these problems lend themselves to considering groups and numbers in a group, models participants use to describe the operation may lead to a broader discussion of how students' understand—and come to understand—multiplication. Some examples of participants' thinking that hold promise for discussion may be similar to the following:

> I enjoyed using my ideas to address multiplication concepts. My big "aha" came when I could see how these activities might help kids explore number sense (distributing, decomposing, landmarks.) For Question 2, I explored using representations a bit differently:
>
> $40 \times 22 = / + 22$ (/ = product for 39×22)
>
> $20 \times 39 = / - 78$
>
> 40×22 is closer since $+ 22$ is closer than $- 78$
>
> I didn't really care about the answer, just the numerical relationships. Looks a bit algebraic too, don't you think?

Another participant offered:

> Considering the 13×62 problem, I thought about building towers of 13. I first knew that 13×3 is 39. So then 13×30 would be 390. That meant that double that many (or 60 towers) would be over 700 already. I solved the others in different ways, but this was my way into to the first one.

Whole-Group Discussion

The whole-group discussion is an opportunity to support participants' investigations into multiplication and the relationships between groups and sizes of groups. The purpose of the discussion is also aimed at helping participants develop an appreciation for the power of arrays as expressions of multiplication and to examine models and other drawings by their colleagues.

Ask participants to describe the logic used to solve the first two problems. It will be evident that participants use what they know to decide on the approximate size of 13×62 and 39×22. Ask what ideas students would rely on to solve the problems. If participants understand that the numbers can be broken into separate problems and added together such as $(10 \times 62) + (3 \times 62)$, they might use this approach to help them appreciate the size of 13×62. If no one has used array models to compare sizes of, perhaps, 40×22, 39×20, and 39×22 in Question 2, it would be important to ask the group to take a moment and try using an array model to "see" the closer amount. Bringing to the discussion the logic and the strategy behind participants' responses for Questions 3 and 4 will round out the whole-group sharing.

The small-group and whole-group discussions should leave participants with an appreciation for the power of models and representations of multiplication, as well as, new ideas about how to compare sizes of factor pairs. Participants should now have multiple representations to reflect on and more content knowledge with which to consider the potential for student and teacher learning. Questions participants will consider in the following small and whole groups include "What sort of thinking do coaches, teachers, and students need to do to ground themselves in multiplication and how it operates?" and "What models make sense as ways to express multiplication?"

Case Reading

Reading the case is the second activity in this session. Encourage participants to write questions or comments in the margins and note sentences or paragraphs that resonate for or confuse them. Sometimes participants appreciate reading the focus questions ahead of reading the case. Explain that this is an option.

*Focus Questions Activity
and Whole-Group Discussion*

The case discussion focuses on two aspects of the writing, the mathematical ideas of the students' and the teachers' and the implications for coaching. In small groups, coaches discuss a series of questions designed to further explore multiplication and ways students understand the ideas of groups. Reference to line numbers in both the small-group and whole-group support discussions that are grounded in the case and issues particular to the work at hand. As you circulate among the groups, listen for ways the participants discuss Tyrone's reasoning in lines 53–59. Appreciating his thinking and considering the mathematical ideas his logic rests on is an important type of discussion for participants to engage in.

In addition, the coaches focus on the teachers' work. They consider Ms. Birt's hypothesis that "the estimate will be closer if the factor changes by a smaller number." Lisa, the coach in the case, gives the teachers an assignment to sort through Ms. Birt's hypothesis; now, the coaches have an opportunity to do this together in their small groups. The discussion in the whole group should also include reference to why Lisa was pleased with Ms. Birt's statement even though it doesn't prove to be true in all cases.

Finally, coaches are asked to work together to relate the mathematics of the students' work to future learning and to consider the kinds of work young students have done to be able to explore problems such as these. Listening to the participants ideas about this will offer you a window on how well articulated the connections are for your group.

The second part of the focus questions draws attention to the coach decisions and moves throughout the day. The exercise of exploring Lisa's ideas about Mrs. Martin's shift in pedagogy and content in her classroom both highlights ways coaches can think about what's beneath resistance or lack of confidence and ways one might attend to Mrs. Martin's needs. It also provides an opportunity to highlight the importance of careful consideration for teachers' behavior and concerns. Moving on to discuss the moves Lisa makes, in particular, will give participants an important chance to imagine a coach day and appreciate the judgments a coach makes in the moment. The discussion of how Lisa might characterize her role and how her perception of her responsibilities is likely to drive the decisions she makes is a most important conversation for participants and a big idea in coming to understand what coaches do and on what basis they choose the next steps in their work. It is in this conversation that participants have yet one more opportunity to examine the coaching role and the ways to leverage that role for teacher learning.

Chapter 3
Facilitation Notes

Strategic Coaching:
Goal-Centered Modeling
in the Classroom

2-Hour Session

Session Goals

- Investigate defining "angle" and measuring angles in polygonal shapes
- Explore reframing coaching goals and strategies to align with new insights about teachers' beliefs about teaching and learning
- Analyze variations of "modeling" as a coaching strategy
- Analyze students' mathematical thinking from a fourth grade geometry class
- Learn about the design of collaborative coach-teacher study with the math class as the primary site

Case Description: "It's 30 Less and 90 More": A Case About Listening to Children's Ideas

The case, written by an experienced elementary and middle school coach, describes teacher and coach interactions based on fourth grade geometry ideas and students' work in class. The coach negotiates the teacher's requests and expectations and considers her own goals for the teacher's learning. As she works to frame a coaching experience that will get at the heart of important ideas of teaching practice, in the case, she lays out her own beliefs about guiding principles of teaching and learning. It is from these beliefs that she devises a structure for her collaboration with the teacher in the geometry class. The case presents an opportunity to "peer in" closely at student work and to analyze the logic of students' ideas as they explore angles and measurement. The case also stands as an example of strategic coaching, by capturing an image of core elements of the role as they are enacted in a single math class.

Session Overview

Participants will begin the session with a small-group math activity exploring the central geometry themes of the case. Followed by a discussion about angles and measurement, the group reads the case and engages in a small-group Focus Questions Activity. The focus questions are designed so that coaches explore the same math ideas as they emerge in a classroom setting, examine the teacher's practice, and consider the implications for Tina's coaching. A whole-group discussion then centers on two things: the student's ideas that may still need to be explored and more clearly understood and the ways the coach negotiates her role in this context. This whole-group discussion also offers coaches a chance to air their own thoughts about modeling in classrooms. This common coaching strategy is portrayed in a new way in this case and the coach's skillful use provides a learning opportunity for novice and experienced coaches.

Materials for the Session

- Create a poster of the Session Goals
- Provide sets of plastic polygonal shapes or prepare sets of paper polygon shapes (see Figure 3.12 in the book)
- Supply plain paper, colored pencils, and graph paper
- Use chart paper and different colored markers to scribe participants' ideas

Session Agenda

1. Introduction: 5 minutes

2. Small-Group Math Activity: 15 minutes

3. Whole-Group Math Discussion: 20 minutes

4. Case Reading: 20 minutes

5. Small-Group Focus Questions Activity: 30 minutes

6. Whole-Group Case Discussion: 30 minutes

Introduction

Begin the session by offering a brief description of the agenda and the learning goals for the session. Set the stage for the math activity by explaining that these same ideas will be addressed in the students' work explored in this case about a fourth grade geometry class.

Mathematics Activity

Participants work in pairs or small groups to explore 90-degree angles. Next, they choose two shapes and determine the exterior angles of each of the shapes based on information and measuring ideas from their work on the first problem. For the final problem, participants will determine the sums of both the interior and exterior angles of shapes and make summative comments about what they discover. As always, giving yourself time to explore with the shapes and, too, anticipating participants' responses to the activity ahead of the session will enhance your facilitation of the math activity.

Whole-Group Math Discussion

In almost every group, there will be participants with very little experience investigating angles and angle measures. Some will only have a memorized definition of what constitutes an angle, unable to rely on hands-on experience. A participant might offer, "When two lines meet each other, they form an angle" or "An angle is a measure of a turn." While these definitions can be further refined (the figure formed by two line segments sharing the same endpoint is one version of a fleshed out definition), asking a participant to demonstrate "a turn" can be illuminating for many. It is useful for this whole-group discussion to be a very visual one, supported by participants' drawings on the board so that the whole group is focused on the very same space. In one group, a facilitator asked a coach to draw an angle on the board. She next asked the group, "Where is the angle?" What appeared to be a simple question brought up confusions about the relationship of the lines, the site of actual measure, and others that were a part of that groups' new learning about angles. It is reassuring to participants to honor and sort through these confusions as they are directly related to the issue the coach brings to light for the teacher with whom she's working in this case. Having conversations about the way we perceive, or have to adjust our perceptions, of angles and measurement is the point of this math discussion. Some terms may come up such as "reflex angle" or "interior" and "exterior angle." For the purposes of this discussion, a reflex angle is an angle greater than 180 degrees but less than 360 degrees. An interior angle is one on the inside a shape; these polygon shapes have one interior angle per vertex. If you add the measure of an interior angle and the contrasting exterior angle formed by one side of the polygon and a line extended from the adjacent side, together these two angles measure 180 degrees.

Reading the Case and Focus Questions

Participants will need at least 20 minutes to read the case carefully. Let the group know that the case discussion will focus on ideas from these three points of view. Remind them to separate three different lines of thinking: the coach's, the teacher's, and the students'. Ask participants, explicitly, to focus on sorting out the thinking of individual students and to underline or note sections where their own or the students' confusions surface.

Focus Questions Activity

The focus questions are designed to offer participants four lenses: understanding the students, understanding the teacher, coaching goals, and, finally, strategic opportunities for learning. The focus questions, discussed in small groups, provide time for participants to practice listening to and discerning early geometric ideas and to consider how to approach a debriefing discussion with the teacher after the lesson.

Case Discussion

Begin by asking participants to focus in on the students in the case. Ask how the small groups sorted out Bobby's confusion by looking at Figures 3.7 and 3.8 in the book. What hypotheses do they have about his question, "Aren't they both the same?"

In this discussion, participants will likely note that it took some time to make sense of the two sets of shapes. Some participants consider the triangles similar enough that Bobby cannot discern a difference between the two. Others offer that Bobby cannot distinguish a 90-degree angle formed by the rhombus and the triangle in Figure 3.8 or that he is looking in the exterior angle formed to the left of the rhombus between the rhombus and the triangle, which indeed, are the same. One participant pointed out, "Just looking at the shapes and comparing Figures 3.7 and 3.8 so carefully makes me think of the kids who I don't pay close enough attention to. Because it says in lines 190–196 that Bobby "hadn't touched the shapes much," I would have assumed that that's why Bobby says they're the same and not because he's genuinely engaged in this as a question."

You might ask what tools the students are using to make decisions about the measurement of angles. Kelan, for instance, uses arithmetic by adding two 45-degree angles and justifies by saying that each is half of 90. At the same time, some children (line 200) decide that the slim brown rhombus is 30 degrees because three same shapes create a 90-degree angle. Others are using horizontal lines as a tool. In the case of Chloe and Emerald, the horizontal line becomes an essential tool for discerning that "it's 30 less and 90 more."

After a discussion of the students' ideas, ask the group to consider, "What are the decisions that Tina is making in this case? Where are the decision points for the coach?" In sorting out these questions, participants can follow the ways the coach continues to evaluate the opportunities she has for coaching.

It is important to make the point that Tina is gathering information about the teacher with whom she's working, discerning learning goals for the teacher, and evaluating the scenarios and the resources she has to make progress. In this case, the coach suggests up front that the teacher spends more time on his math "teaching" and less on his students' "learning." The coach uses this insight to highlight a tenet of her coaching—that she could spend more time on coaching strategies and behaviors but if they are not linked to the teacher's beliefs and ideas and knowledge, then what's the effect of the coaching? This case provides an example of a coach bringing the teacher's attention to the mathematics his students are working on and the ways they are engaging with it.

Ask the group how the coach chooses to respond based on what she's hearing from Mr. Gallagher. Ask them to use line numbers to point out the coach's moves and to discuss why she's making them. Participants often raise the issue of modeling; the teacher has asked the coach to model teaching. It is useful for coaches to have an opportunity to discuss this strategy for coaching. How does the coach in this case work with this idea? In what ways do the participants in the group understand the benefits of modeling? Do they use modeling for a particular focus? Under what circumstances is modeling helpful and when it is it, perhaps, detrimental? How do individuals in the group make choices about modeling? As the coach in this case explains, she steps through every window of opportunity to align her goals with the situation at hand and the developing interest on the part of the teacher. What does it mean to "step through windows of opportunity" in coaching?

Ask participants to talk about what Mr. Gallagher learned through the experience in his classroom. What would they have hoped for? Some participants might talk about individual students by noting, for instance, that Mr. Gallagher has a new appreciation for Chloe and how important it is that coaches bring to light students who might otherwise recede from the teacher's view. Others may point out lines 242–252, where Mr. Gallagher raises a new insight about moving about the class from student to student but not making mathematical connections between students' ideas, nor using this as information gathering to support a plan for a whole-group discussion. This insight is an important one to cover in a discussion. If a participant doesn't raise it, you might ask how participants think about the issues Mr. Gallagher raises in this section. Ask, "What work would Mr. Gallagher have to do to make the connections between students' mathematical ideas?" Or ask, "What work would he have to do to conceive of a purposeful whole-group discussion?" and, "If we agree that these are of high value in a teacher's math practice, what are the implications for coaching with these ideas in mind?"

Save time for exit card writing at the end of this session. Ask participants to reflect on what it was like to sort out these students' ideas; one thing they learned, in particular, from the coach-author; and to describe how this insight will affect their coaching practice.

Chapter 4
Facilitation Notes

Reaching a New Teacher:
Math as the Conduit

2-Hour Session

Session Goals

- Investigate ideas about division and explore related story problems
- Examine the logic in student thinking
- Consider coaching implications for engaging a hesitant teacher in the study of her students' ideas and a reexamination of the grade-level mathematics
- Explore written communication as a tool for coaching

Case Description: A Case of Coaching:
Multiplication and Division Journal Entries

A Case of Coaching is a set of journal entries written by a second-year coach as she works to cultivate a successful coach-teacher relationship with a new teacher. During her visit to the fourth grade math class, the coach, Ellie, is surprised to discover that her own ideas about division are less than solid. In preparation to coach well, the author sets about studying types of division and sorting through related story problems. She decides to use this example of a self-directed investigation as an entrée to a collaborative study with the classroom teacher and, thus, begins a series of written communications that help form the basis for their working relationship.

Session Overview

The session begins with a small group math activity focused on division and multiplication problems similar to the ones the case writer poses for her own investigation. Participants next work to uncover the logic in a fourth grader's response to a daily number routine, the same response that stumps the coach as she describes in her journal. A whole-group discussion of the math follows during which the point is made that as a coach one has a new vantage point from which to study classroom mathematics and that continuing to learn math from this perspective is a facet of preparing to coach well. Participants read the case and work together in small groups on a Focus Questions Activity designed to highlight mathematical issues, coaching issues, and considerations of beliefs and attitudes of hesitant or resistant teachers. The session ends with a whole-group discussion.

Materials for the Session

- Create a chart of session goals
- Provide about 150 connecting cubes per pair for the focus questions and math activities
- Obtain chart paper and different colored markers for displaying coaches' math work

Session Agenda

1. Introduction: 5 minutes

2. Math Activity in Small Groups: 15 minutes

3. Whole-Group Math Discussion: 20 minutes

4. Case Reading: 20 minutes

5. Focus Questions Activity in Small Groups: 30 minutes

6. Whole-Group Case Discussion: 30 minutes

Introduction

Begin the session by briefly describing the session goals and the agenda. Set the stage for the case reading by describing, in just a few words, the context for the coach-authored case. Let the participants know that before anything else happens, they will have a chance to dig into a math activity designed to surface ideas directly related to those described in the case.

Math Activity

Participants begin the session by working to solve a series of math problems. Remind the participants to talk for a few minutes about ways they most successfully work on math in group settings. Remind them to listen for each other's ideas and questions.

This math activity provides an opportunity for participants to work through the logic of three division and multiplication problems. In small groups, participants consider the reasons why the answers are correct or incorrect. In this way, the coaches considers students' ideas about breaking numbers apart in hundreds, tens, and ones to multiply and divide, just as students have learned to do with addition and subtraction. The first two problems are different versions of 48 ÷ 4. In one case, 48 is separated by 10s and 1s into 40 and 8. Then, 40 and 8 are each divided by 4. The results, 10 and 2, are then added together for a total of 12.

A participant might think of it this way: I want to put 48 cookies in bags of 4. First, I take 40 cookies and find that I can fill 10 bags with 4 cookies. Then I take the other 8 cookies and fill 2 more bags. I know that 10 bags and 2 bags gives me 12 bags with 4 cookies in each.

Another might act out the problem with cubes. She takes 40 cubes and 8 cubes and arranges them in two arrays each with one dimension of 4. She counts off 10 sets of 4 and 2 more sets of 4 and adds them for 12 sets of 4. For Part B, the coach follows the problem by separating 48 into two amounts, and this time, separates the divisor as well. 48 becomes $24 + 24$, and each 24 is divided by 2. For the total, the next step is described as $12 + 12 = 24$.

In working to figure out why the first strategy works and the second doesn't, the participants meet up against solutions that fourth grade students might offer while, at the same time, investigating both physical models and story contexts.

Next, participants examine a fourth grade student's idea that $17 \times 17 = 149$. In considering the student's logic—and this theme of breaking numbers apart and operating on them—participants again run into typical confusions about multiplying. In both cases, ask participants to draw pictures, use the cubes, and to consider story problems to illustrate their thinking. In the whole group, use several models to support the discussion. Ask the participants to consider Martina's response. Her comment highlights the idea that examining the operations and the similarities and differences between them is particularly useful work for students, just as it is for adults.

Case Reading

Encourage participants to write questions or comments in the margins and note sentences or paragraphs that are confusing or that resonate for them. This case carefully takes the reader through a thorough examination of the coach's ideas about division. More than just underlining or noting important sections of the case, press readers to get out paper and pencil and work the mathematics alongside the author.

Focus Questions Activity

The focus questions help participants dig into issues regarding; developing trusting and productive relationships for coaching; explorations of division and multiplication through the eyes of the students, the teacher, and the coach; and ways to consider the next steps for the teacher's learning.

Remind participants to reference line numbers for clarity in building their discussions. As you circulate among the groups, listen for ways the participants engage in this deliberate exploration of multiplication and division. These explorations will help you get a picture of how your participants understand these math issues for themselves. Listen for ways participants are responding to the coach's considerations of building trusting relationships, "telling," and resistance to change. The coach in this case makes an interesting and somewhat unusual decision to share her math exploration quite explicitly with the teacher. Participants will have a variety of opinions about this move.

There is a tendency for people to react and respond to the math issues too quickly; for this reason, you might need to press people to take their thinking to a deeper level. One way to do this is to be explicit about this as you introduce the activity. You can say that sometimes we just don't press ourselves to investigate questions as thoroughly as we might, and in this way, we miss going beyond what we already know. Then ask the group to pay explicit attention to whether their own group has fully investigated each of the focus questions. You might hear participants say, "Division means groups of 17 and this isn't groups of 17," and then move on or "I'd do multiplication arrays with this student so he can see 17×17 isn't 149." These responses are along the lines of solutions and are not yet representative of investigations into the mathematical issues. Suggestions, such as to write a story with a descriptive context for the math problem, draw arrays to explore multiplication, and to apply the same strategies using different sets of numbers, can offer participants different ways to work through the math of the case.

Whole-Group Discussion

Begin your discussion by asking participants to take a few moments to consider lines 214–246 where the coach describes her work on the idea of sharing. She concludes, "So what I know about division and sharing tells me that this is not sharing the cards evenly between 17 friends." Ask the group to sort this out. What has the coach figured out?

Next, explore the coach's reasoning behind the lines 247–261. Ask participants to demonstrate this line of thinking with cubes. How does the visual image shift in playing out the coach's work in lines 262–274?

In a discussion of these math explorations, one small group of participants shared the following problem context to illustrate their ideas: "Imagine 149 baseball cards in one room, and you send in 17 kids to share them. You could have 100 cards on one table and 49 cards on another. That shows you can break up the number you are dividing into. But if you think of 100 cards in one room and 49 in another, and then you send 10 kids to one room and 7 into another. Then 10 kids get 10 cards and 7 kids get 7 cards; that's not the same."

The forays into *sharing* and *partitioning* explored in the case and focus questions open up useful ways of examining what Ellie, the teacher, and the students are wrestling with in learning about division. The coach's work is accessible and thought provoking. She has taken just a few student ideas from class and played them out in depth, both for her own learning and, also, so that she can join this teacher in an exploration of her students' thinking. You will want to step aside of the math at this point and explicitly make note that this work Ellie is doing represents one interesting and purposeful image of *preparing to coach*. As we also see in the chapter Moving Between Models, coaches prepare for their workday by examining the mathematics for themselves. It may be supportive, as the facilitator of the group, to acknowledge that learning how to prepare as a coach takes some time, but in many respects, it is not so different from the fundamentals of preparing for classroom teaching. Doing the math ahead of working in class—or with teachers—is a norm of good teaching. Coaches learn that seeing math activities and listening carefully to classroom discussions, coupled with paying close attention to students' and teachers' ideas from this new vantage point of a coach, often raises new questions, new insights, and new ways of thinking that are worthy of exploration.

The second aspect of Ellie's case deals with sorting out the pathways toward a relationship built on trust and a mathematical focus. Participants have a chance to talk about the issues of resistance the coach describes and to consider the choices Ellie makes in establishing a relationship with a teacher who might otherwise have remained isolated.

Sometimes, participants disagree with Ellie's choice to offer the teacher her letter. They ask, "Why would she want to *tell* all she knows about division?" or "Why not let the teacher figure it out for herself?" and "Hasn't she done just what we ask teachers not to do with their students?" And yet others might find Ellie's exploration helpful; one participant said, "The way Ellie laid out her thinking was helpful to me. She did things I never would have thought of doing. I still needed to do my own thinking and work alongside hers."

After discussing the mathematics of the case, this can be a useful debate. Not only will the conversation afford you insights into your participants' ideas, but it also gives the group a chance to try on different versions of the case and to make decisions based on thoughtful dialogue. There is, of course, no one right move, and Ellie's choices are not meant to showcase "the way to do it." The more important questions are, "How do you nurture teachers' curiosity about their students?" and "How do Ellie's coaching moves relate to her earlier reflections on 'cracking open' one's practice?" In the final portion of the group discussion, turn the group's attention to their own considerations of practice. Ask, "Given this scenario, what are the implications for coaching?" "What is it that you would want this teacher to learn?" and "Consider some ways of working with this teacher; in what ways are your next steps related to your goals for her learning?"

One facilitator of this case wrote, "The next-steps question can be difficult for participants to answer, especially when you are asking the coaches to make connections between the next steps they suggest and the goals they have for the teacher—in light of what the teacher does or doesn't yet understand. Even though we talk about using student work to figure out what to do next, it isn't that easy or that commonly done. We do not have routines to follow that help us determine next steps."

While participants may have some difficulty articulating appropriate next steps, you will likely also sense that it is agreed among the group that these are important questions to consider as a rule in coaching. They are questions that help coaches consider their own work with goals in mind. At the time, as the facilitator, it may feel less than satisfying that participants struggle with these issues and responses. The power of the questions is in the consideration of them rather than in participants' answers conjured up in the moment. Pressing on questions such as these establishes a habit of appropriate norms for coaching, new ways of thinking that can be incorporated in a coach repertoire over time.

Chapter 5
Facilitation Notes

Preparing for
Thoughtful Dialogue

2-Hour Session

Session Goals

- Consider implications for coaching, collaborative relationships, and teacher-learning based on ideas about *considered* versus *reactive* coaching
- Examine a classroom transcript for mathematical ideas and teacher-student interaction
- Explore number sense and addition strategies in the primary grades

Case Description: Considered Coaching

The Considered Coaching case examines one coach's responses to a math exchange between the teacher and her students in a second grade classroom. Rosa, the coach, has set out to more fully understand ideas about number sense. As a way of capturing these ideas as they play out in math class, Rosa, with permission from the teacher, brings her laptop to class and transcribes a brief round of mental math. As she types the students' and the teacher's dialogue in one column on the screen, she also records her reactions to what's happening in class in a second column. The title word "considered" becomes central in discussions about the transcript and the implications for coaching. Rosa, herself, explores the difference between her immediate take on the students' ideas about number sense and the teacher's facilitation and the later, more reflective and substantially more useful exploration of the transcript as she prepares for a thoughtful dialogue with the classroom teacher.

Session Overview

The session begins with a mental-math activity where coaches engage in a mental-math routine similar to the one described in Rosa's transcripts. The deliberate facilitation of this routine is participant-focused with opportunities for the facilitator to draw out coaches' math ideas. Participants then work with Transcript 1 to read the teacher and student dialogue from the second grade classroom Rosa observed. Coaches write their own responses, questions, and insights about the classroom discourse on the right hand column of the transcript. The transcript activity is followed by a whole-group discussion exploring the math ideas and student thinking in the class. Next, participants read and reflect on the coach's considered commentary as she writes out her responses later that night. This, too, is followed by a whole-group conversation. Next, coaches read about the way Rosa first responded to the classroom discourse as she scribed in real time. This in-the-moment commentary leads to an important whole-group discussion of the difference between reactive coaching and considered coaching—the main theme of the session.

Materials for the Session

- Obtain chart paper to scribe coaches' strategies and ideas during the mental-math activity

Session Agenda

1. Introduction: 5 minutes

2. Mental-Math Activity: 10 minutes

3. Read Transcript 1, Respond to Steps 1 and 2: 30 minutes

4. Whole-Group Discussion: 15 minutes

5. Read Transcript 2, Respond to Step 3, and Whole-Group Discussion: 40 minutes

6. Read Transcript 3: 5 minutes

7. Final Whole-Group Discussion: 15 minutes

Introduction

Begin this two-hour session by describing the agenda. Explain to participants that this case presents a unique version of case writing in that the coach, Rosa, with permission from the teacher, brought her laptop to school and transcribed the mental-math portion of a second grade math activity early in the school year.

Before class started, Rosa had set up a template with a grid on the left where she would type in the teacher and student dialogue and a grid on the right where she would record her reactions, in the moment, as the discussion ensued (such as participants will find in Transcript 1). Rosa had explained that this would help her capture what happened in the class and that the two of them could use the notes in their subsequent discussion.

After school, Rosa took the transcript home to review in preparation for a teacher debrief the next day (and, too, as a way to consider more carefully her own in-the-moment interpretation of the dialogue). That evening, Rosa carefully studied the classroom dialogue and replaced her own initial in-class reactions with more reflective responses and questions (see Transcript 2).

Let participants know that they will first be working with a transcript of just the teacher and student dialogue so that they might have the same opportunity as Rosa did in interpreting the math ideas and the ensuing discussion as it plays out in class (Transcript 1). Later in the session, participants will have opportunities to consider the implications of the other transcript versions. But first, this session begins with a brief mental-math activity.

Math Activity

Through this math activity, participants will familiarize themselves with the mental-math routine, referred to as Math of the Day in the Considered Coaching case. As the case describes, the second grade students are asked to suggest a variety of arithmetic problems resulting in the same total, 17. Another function of this first activity is that, as the facilitator, you can model seminar discourse that focuses on the mathematical sense of participants' choices of numbers and operations to create the total and that highlights relationships between these math ideas.

Ask participants to create number sentences that equal 67. Then give the group a few minutes to consider the possibilities that you will scribe for everyone to examine. In the following snippet from a Considered Coaching session, we follow a facilitator as she capitalizes on the number sense and relationship ideas that arise in the mental-math routine:

Participant 1: $20 + 20 + 20 + 7 = 67$.

Facilitator: Can you say tell us something about the way you were thinking about 67?

Participant 1: Well, for some reason, 60 always conjures up three 20s for me. I never see it as 40 and 20 more. It might be because of the way I interpret an hour; I think in 20-minute increments. So I made the problem into three 20s and just added on the 7 to make 67.

Participant 2: I said, $50 + 10 + 7$.

Facilitator: And so were you thinking along the lines of Participant 1? I mean, first thinking about how you know 60?

Participant 2: In a way I was, but my first thought was that double-digit numbers are always either below 50 or above 50—well unless it's 50, so I added the amount on to 50.

Facilitator: Okay, let's see if we have other ideas out there.

Participant 3: I used subtraction. $100 - 40 + 7$.

Facilitator: It is interesting how, so far, in thinking about 67, the 7 doesn't get much play.

Participant 3: Yes, I was thinking about how to make 60 and, sort of, who cares about the 7! I was thinking more like Participant 2 though, than Participant 1. I was thinking about how far away 60 was from 100.

Facilitator: Oh, you mean that Participant 2 was considering the distance between 60 and 50, and you were using 100 as a landmark?

The dialogue goes on for just a bit more, including a point where the facilitator asks the rest of the participants to comment on how the ideas of the next two participants' are related either to each other or to the previous problems. This facilitation strategy is markedly different from scribing a simple list of responses and sorting out each one distinct from the others; it is clear that the facilitator is working to highlight the ways the participants are considering the number system, operating on numbers, and for the sense of the number 67 as in distance from 50 or 100, equal groups that add to 60, and considering 67 as a group of 10s and 1s. Mental math can be mined for a variety of uses including as practice in flexible thinking and for solidifying number facts. It is usually a brief, ten-minute exploration. The point here is that it can also, even in just a few short minutes, reinforce for students that sharing their thinking and articulating their ideas is of high value to their teacher and to their classmates' learning and that there is something to be gleaned from even a quick dissection of relationships between numbers and operations.

While you will want to move on to the exploration of the transcripts without further debrief of this mental-math exchange, it may be that the facilitation of it will serve as a marker for later whole-group discussion. For that reason, post the scribed equations so that they are available for reference later in the session.

Case Reading

Participants should now refer to Transcript 1 and Step 1. Ask participants to read through this transcript twice before writing comments in the blank grid. Let them know that there are two streams of thought that they will want to keep in mind but follow separately. The first is to consider just the students' math talk. The second is to pay attention to the student-teacher dialogue. Some participants may find it hard to toggle between the two; it is more effective to consider one line of thinking and record one's comments about the students' ideas and then go back and work on the interactions between the teacher and the students. Participants should work on this activity on their own before coming together in groups of three for small-group discussion of the Step 2 questions.

Whole-Group Discussion

The case discussion focuses on two aspects of the writing: (1) the mathematical ideas of the students' and (2) the teacher and the implications for coaching. In this first pass at the transcript, participants will have recorded a range of questions, assumptions, and hypotheses about the students' use of numbers and operation. Most often, the participants will make note of the different ways students use addition to make 10 and the use of doubles. The subtraction problems offer similar ideas, starting with using 10s and + x, − x. Encourage participants to first discuss the students' work. Ask them to look at and discuss the students' math as a series of ideas. Suggest that they consider the relationships between one student's idea and another's. Ask, "What do participants notice about the student work in this first month of second grade?"

The discussion then shifts to the teacher-student dialogue. Before you begin, remind the participants that it is important to assume the teacher is working on new skills in her practice; the author has written about this. It is sometimes difficult for participants new to this kind of investigation to focus on what analyzing the case can offer their own practice. Thinking carefully about what the teacher is working to do in this student-teacher exchange is one way to learn more about what can be gained by asking students to participate in mental-math activities. The considered look at the dialogue is meant to be a way of pinpointing places that will ultimately prompt useful conversation between the teacher and the coach. In other words, you may need to actively steer the conversation toward factual commentary about what participants see happening and help them refrain from negative judging talk about the teacher's responses to students. The point of the discussion is to simply read and note what's going on in the snippet of a classroom activity. Next, they will have a chance to view the same from the coach's perspective.

Read Transcript 2 and Small-Group Discussion

Now, the small group has a chance to read the transcript that includes the coach's reflective thinking. In Transcript 2, the coach writes down ideas and questions that will inform her coaching. She knows that carefully examining the transcript will help her to prepare in thoughtful ways for a debrief discussion with the teacher. This reflection activity is mean to help Rosa make decisions about her own coaching moves.

Give the participants about 30 minutes to read and discuss the focus questions related to Transcript 2. It is helpful to be explicit that participants reread the classroom transcript for Transcript 2, not just the coach's reflections. Remind them to note particular places in the dialogue and in the coach's reflective writing they would like to raise with in their small groups. Circulate as the participants are discussing the focus questions related to Rosa's reflective thinking.

Whole-Group Discussion

The small-group work is followed by a brief, 10-minute whole-group discussion. You might jumpstart a group discussion by simply asking participants what stood out for them in Rosa's commentary or by asking what they are learning from the coach's reflections.

Read Transcript 3 and Small-Group Discussion

Participants will find, again in Transcript 3, the full transcript from the classroom, yet this time the transcript is accompanied by the coach's initial reactions recorded as she was in class observing the Math of the Day activity. You will likely hear some laughter as participants are reading and recognizing the increasingly exasperated tone of the coach's commentary in this very reactive mode. Because we know the coach later went home and reflected carefully about the class and saved herself from responding to the teacher with her initial reactions, we can find some relief in this reading. What is exasperating to Rosa in class becomes data to study with respectful consideration after class.

Final Whole-Group Discussion

Rosa has generously contributed this very honest collection of writing as a way of supporting a critical idea in coaching. The final whole-group discussion can reiterate the importance of considered versus reactive coaching. In a considered approach, the coach responds to the teacher with learning goals at the forefront of the conversation. In reactive mode, the emotions are at the forefront, and often the coach's own immediate reactions blur the line between coaching and criticism. It is important to assure participants that considered coaching is cultivated over time, that the goal for coaching practice is that a considered mode is the norm even when there is little time for reflection. Going into classrooms with a framework of goals already in mind supports a considered coaching response. These transcripts offer one powerful way of highlighting for math specialists and administrators the importance of both exposing one's practice—even in diary form—as a way of critically examining the ways one might develop a considered and thoughtful, mathematically focused stance. So often the coaching role is held as that of the judging, critical expert. Without a focus on teaching and learning on the part of both the coach and the teacher, we risk falling into the trap of simply reacting. Again, it seems that cultivating a norm of sharing issues of practice, sharing new mathematical insights and questions, and collaborating to refine and strengthen both areas of knowledge are important features of learning to coach.

Chapter 6
Facilitation Notes

Purposeful Planning and Facilitation

2.5-Hour Session

Session Goals

- Explore the purposes and potential for grade-level or teacher-team meetings
- Strategize about creating meaningful agendas for group meetings
- Analyze coaching strategies for responding to teachers' needs and issues while facilitating focused discussion on issues of mathematics
- Sort out factors that help determine an appropriate balance of sharing responsibility for the agenda and facilitation of teacher meetings

Case Description: Coaching in a Group: Moving From 1:1 to 1:?

In the case, Coaching in a Group: Moving From 1:1 to 1:?, the coach-author describes her struggles as she branches out from one-to-one coaching to coaching groups of teachers in team meeting structures. This novice and yet deeply self-reflective coach describes her attempts to design agendas that matter and facilitation that captivates groups of teachers at a meaningful level. Chloe's case moves between descriptions of two group meetings, the planning and preparation for each meeting, and her reflections on her coaching. As she struggles, she also gains new insights that help her develop a stronger coaching practice. Novice coaches and experienced coaches will easily relate to the complexities of planning and purposefully facilitating group meetings described in Chloe's case.

Session Overview

The session begins with a brief introduction to the agenda and the session's goals. The participants read the case and focus questions before engaging in small group discussions. Responding to these questions helps participants follow Chloe's story and analyze the dilemmas she poses. The Focus Questions Activity also calls on coaches to articulate questions for Chloe that would help her consider coaching strategies—just as they would pose questions for teachers that would help teachers uncover new ideas for themselves. Through a Planning Activity and group discussions, both novice and experienced coaches sort out goals, agendas, and issues regarding the engagement of groups of teachers with whom they work.

Materials for the Session

- Create a poster of the Session Goals.
- Participants will need chart paper and markers for the Planning Activity

Session Agenda

1. Introduction: 5 minutes

2. Reading the Case and the Focus Questions: 10 minutes

3. Small-Group Focus Questions Activity: 35 minutes

4. Whole-Group Discussion: 30 minutes

5. Small-Group Planning Activity: 40 minutes

6. Whole-Group Discussion: 30 minutes

Introduction

Begin the session by offering a brief description of the agenda and the learning goals of the session. Set the stage for the case by describing, in just a few words, the context of the case written by Chloe.

Reading the Case and the Focus Questions

Let participants know they have the choice to read the Focus Questions before reading the case. For some, acquainting themselves with the questions helps center their attention on issues that will be discussed in small groups. Others may still choose to read the case first and then peruse the focus questions quietly while they wait for their group to begin discussion. Reading both should take about 10 minutes.

Focus Questions Activity

As participants are discussing the focus questions, it is important to move around the room and listen carefully to the small groups talk. Joining by pulling up a chair and simply listening for a few minutes to individual's responses to these questions may offer insights into the degree of comfort your own group has in planning for and facilitating group meetings at their own schools. You may hear some disdain for

Chloe's efforts, so it may help to remind participants that Chloe is a beginner and is clearly working hard to improve her practice. You may also hear many sympathetic or "I've been there" kinds of responses to the frank descriptions of her struggles. It is not uncommon that coaches have more confidence in their one-on-one work with teachers than in their ability to plan for and facilitate the discussions of teachers in a group. For many, these meetings may be the first time they are responsible for a whole group's learning—that is, for a group of adults. And, indeed, for many, these same adults were only recently their role-alike colleagues. It is not a trivial matter to take responsibility for moving a whole group forward, nor for juggling the issues that arise simply because of past—or current—relationships with members of the group.

With regard to Question 4, some might find themselves stuck on the assessment issue Angela raises in the case. While you, or the coaches in the group, may agree or disagree with Angela's point of view, Chloe decides not to move the teachers in this direction. For the purpose of this session, participants might have to agree or disagree with Angela (and Chloe) and move on to discussing Jolene's work.

Listen for the way participants attend to Question 5. There are two separate parts to this question. One part is to craft questions for Chloe that will help her come to her own conclusions. The other is to consider what one might hope for Chloe to be learning. It's a good coaching skill to know how to ask questions that will help the other person uncover their own intentions or directions. And it is useful for each participant to consider how she might refine her thinking if she were in Chloe's position.

Whole-Group Discussion

As you facilitate the discussion, keep in mind that you will have another group discussion to end this session after the Planning Activity. In fielding participants' responses and questions at this point, you can make decisions about whether to follow through with an idea or ask participants to "hold on to that thought" for the final whole-group discussion. Start off this discussion by asking participants to make explicit what happens in the case, how they understand Chloe's questions, and to analyze how she goes about planning and facilitating the teacher meetings. This time provides an opportunity to stay centered on the ways Chloe chooses to move in her coaching. Asking participants to share the questions they articulated for Chloe (Question 5) will let the whole group hear alternative ways of asking questions meant to support another's learning. Ask the group to keep refining the questions they've crafted until they feel satisfied that these will help reveal *for Chloe* what has gone well and what her next steps are—questions that help her reflect and refine her thinking. Assure the group that the final discussion will provide time for coaches to talk about their own experiences and how they intend to prepare, or refine their preparation, for coaching responsibilities that move beyond 1:1.

The Planning Activity

The first section of this activity is a reflective writing assignment. The task is for each participant to explore two different points of view—their own and the teachers.' Keep in mind the goal is that, in the end, everyone should be clear about the overall purpose and goal of group meetings. This goal-oriented planning, designed with the teachers' beliefs and ideas as well as the coach's agenda in mind, is not a straightforward aspect of coaching practice. If the facilitator of a group meeting is the only one with a clear idea of the agenda, such as we see unfolding in Chloe's case, the participants in that group are left responding to each move she makes. If the participants have a point of view that is out of synch with the facilitator, or if the facilitator is unaware of the participants' beliefs and points of view, this can lead to meetings cloudy with mixed messages and little substance.

Take stock of the level of experience your group has in facilitating group meetings. If your group is very new to, or naïve about, coaching, they may find it more difficult to think about appropriate agendas for group meetings that will help teachers learn or reflect in meaningful ways. If your group includes experienced coaches, provide opportunities for these coaches to share what they have learned about designing and facilitating successful group meetings. And yet we see that even experienced coaches may still struggle with defining the purpose of meetings, designing useful activities or explorations, and helping teachers think more deeply about the mathematics they teach, or the students' ideas in the classroom.

The goal of this planning activity is for participants to have the opportunity to work with colleagues to sort out issues regarding designing agendas for groups and ways of considering the implications for facilitating with teachers' beliefs and expectations in mind—*before* the group meeting. In addition, it is important to press the idea that taking into consideration long- and short-term goals for the school in every opportunity where math specialists', or coaches, have a group's attention is a strategic aspect of coaching. One goal of this session is to help participants come to appreciate the complexity of negotiating teachers' expectations, designing appropriate agendas, and determining coaching goals for teachers' learning in whole-group meetings.

In considering the work of Question 4, think ahead about whether you want to assign each small group a specific question to chart (so that you are assured a poster about each) or whether you want small groups to choose the question from the bulleted list. The second option offers groups the chance to create a poster about what they have the most confidence, the most questions, or that has generated the most discussion in their small group. Ask participants to hang their posters so that the whole group can do a gallery walk and move around the room to read each one.

Whole-Group Discussion

After everyone has reviewed the charts, begin the discussion by asking those who charted the same question, or bullet, to talk to the whole group about the ideas—and questions—their small group discussions raised. Then ask the rest of the participants to add new ideas or perspectives from their own planning activity conversations. In turn, continue to move the discussion back and forth between the ideas offered by those who created the posters and the perspectives and ideas offered by the rest of the participants.

After the posters have been discussed, ask participants to take five minutes to write about the ideas raised in this case and in this session's activities. Ask them to describe at least one specific way the discussions today will influence the planning and facilitation of their school group meetings coming up. If you have time, ask for volunteers to share from their writing.

Chapter 7
Facilitation Notes

Refining and Reimagining One's Coaching Practice

2-Hour Session

Session Goals

- Analyze young students' work and math talk as they analyze young students' work and math talk as they engage in counting
- Examine stages of making sense of counting and representing "a count"
- Consider coaching strategies for helping all grade-level teachers develop a fine-grained picture and a big picture of their students' mathematical learning
- Explore effective coaching preparation for the facilitation of prebrief and debrief meetings with teachers
- Consider purposes for whole-group student discussions

Case Description: Learning About Counting, Learning About Coaching

In Learning About Counting, Learning About Coaching, the coach-author describes a Kindergarten classroom observation, interviews with several students as they engage in counting activities, and her subsequent questions about effective coaching debriefs. Elaine, a coach with past experience as a high school math teacher, becomes intrigued with the varied strategies for counting in Kindergarten and, over the course of one classroom visit, she is bursting with new questions and a real appreciation for the children's effort involved in sorting out counting as an idea. She describes the ensuing teacher debrief, which she soon realizes falls far short its potential. As she reflects on the classroom experience and her facilitation of the teacher debrief meeting, she gains new insights about the questions she might have asked and about the teacher and coach learning she is aiming for.

Session Overview

The central focus of this session is a case that, on the surface, is about young children's counting strategies and what is involved in learning about counting. And yet, it is most assuredly a case about coaching dilemmas and strategies applicable to any grade level. Participants begin the session by reading the case and analyzing the children's ideas and to make sense of counting. Through focus question discussions in small groups, coaches also work through the dilemma of facilitation the author poses in her case. In the Planning Activity, coaches spend time planning teacher study groups focused on student learning of specific mathematical topics. They work together to help each other refine their ideas, get clear about the structures available to support such studies, and to discuss ways of measuring the outcomes, or evaluation, of the work. The session ends with a whole-group discussion, during which coaches share and elaborate on coaching plans and insights from the session.

Materials for the Session

- Create a chart of the session goals
- Coaches will need coach journals or writing materials for the Planning Activity

Session Agenda

1. Introduction: 5 minutes

2. Case and Focus Questions Reading: 15 minutes

3. Small-Group Focus Questions Activity: 25 minutes

4. Whole-Group Discussion: 25 minutes

5. Small-Group Planning Activity: 30 minutes

6. Whole-Group Discussion: 20 minutes

Introduction

Briefly review the goals of the session and the agenda. Describe, in just a few words, the context for this case of young children's thinking about counting. Be sure to tell participants that while they may or may not coach teachers of Kindergarten children, this case serves as an example of what it means to take a very close look at student thinking and, also, that the facilitation issues that emerge relate to coaching in any grade-level classroom. As such, this case is less about the specific math content and more about the implications for teaching and coaching.

Case Reading

Sometimes, participants find that reading the focus questions offers a preview and a lens with which to focus their attention on a new case. For coaches who have less experience with very young children, such as those described in the case, it may be particularly helpful to have them preview focus questions and the various ways of orienting oneself to the topics that will be discussed in this session. Participants will need about 10 minutes to read the case.

Focus Questions Activity—Small Groups

In this Focus Questions Activity, participants are asked to write brief responses to Questions 1 and 2 on their own before engaging in group discussion. This will give each coach a chance to practice looking at the "fine grain" of the Rafael and Catherine's math talk and engagement with the counting tasks. *Peering in closely* is a stance coaches develop with practice and is a central idea in highlighting and understanding students' ideas. As we develop strong images of how students engage with specific math ideas, we also develop a keen attention to important work and talk that is all around us in the classroom.

By the time participants have moved to Question 4, they should have a list of their own ideas about young children's counting ideas and strategies and will have added those Elaine noted in her case. Some participants might talk in terms of developmental or more or less sophisticated ideas. While there are many ways to make sense of children's counting processes, it is important to remember that this is, indeed, simply what learning to count looks like. You might find yourself reminding participants that while it is useful to see a trajectory of ideas, it is much less useful to jump to conclusions about students or categorize those who get it and those who don't.

Question 4 asks participants to suggest ways to facilitate the children's group meeting at the end of the counting activity time. Listen for the types of ideas the participants offer. What do your participants want to learn from the students? What do they want the students to hear from each other? What might they ask or how might they begin the classroom discussion? Listening carefully and reflecting on your participants' responses may give you some insights into the ways coaches are supporting the teachers with whom they work. Elaine's writing about the *descriptive* version of a sharing session is certainly not unique to the case of this teacher's classroom. This is a common issue in math teaching practice and coaches encounter sharing meetings that are quite similar in nature, not just in Kindergarten but in all grade levels. Understanding your own participants' notions of how to run an end-of-class math discussion will help you press for analysis of these ideas in the whole-group discussion.

Question 6 comes full circle from the teacher's approach to an end-of-class discussion to the coach, Elaine's, approach to her own meeting. These are very important parallel issues to be examined. Just as the teacher must learn how to use the whole-group time as an extension of the class *learning* time so must the coach learn to use teacher debrief discussions as opportunities to extend the teachers' learning. Just as the teacher needs to carefully plan for the final discussion—and participants might discuss how—the coach also needs to think in terms of a learning agenda for debrief meetings.

Whole-Group Discussion

The whole-group discussion will cover a number of topics. It will be useful to explore and analyze the students' actions and ideas in class. Another topic to raise is the issue of whole-group sharing in a class of very young children, and yet another is to explore the coach's moves and how these moves might be refined so that the teachers in this scenario could learn more.

Begin the whole-group discussion by asking participants to contribute to a list of how the students were thinking about and attending to the task of counting and recording a total. You might ask one participant from the small group to record a group's response on chart paper as you accumulate a list. Do not hesitate to step in and ask for clarification if a charted idea has not been fully articulated or to ask a question that helps the participant elaborate on her point. Having a participant chart the responses gives you the opportunity to step back and ask for these clarifications.

When the group has a final list that captures a collection of young children's counting ideas, strategies, and approaches to the task, check it to see that the "naïve" approaches are included. It's common to see a range of counting—disorganized and inaccurate, physically organized and inaccurate or accurate, a miscount total represented by drawings of an even different number objects, deliberate one-to-one correspondence, and repeat counting of even a small number of objects. You might see tally marks accurately representing the number of objects counted and papers that reveal little about what they child knows. These can all be represented as ways that children approach counting. Ask participants what they learn from the list. Ask what questions the list raises. Spend time listening to the ways the participants discuss the list; listen for a sense of curiosity, for an energy about wanting to know more. In creating this list, the participants have acted out one portion of what might have been a more satisfying teacher meeting for the case writer and coach, Elaine. As she has written in her reflection, she missed the opportunity; this list creating and discussion is one image of what got lost.

What does a coach raise with a teacher to help her move from whole-group discussions from *descriptive* sharing to *inquisitive* sharing? Ask the participants to consider how the description of the students' sharing circle compares to the teachers' experience of the debrief discussion. You might ask the participants to turn to a partner and talk about the similarities and differences and then come back to the whole group so that these ideas can become part of the larger discussion. Consider the small group discussions you listened to; now is the time to raise questions about what you heard.

Ask participants to suggest what might be a productive agenda for this debrief meeting. What might the coach want teachers to learn, to think about, to become curious about? Ask the participants to suggest, very specifically, how they might begin the debrief meeting with an agenda in mind.

Planning Activity—Small Groups

The point of this Planning Activity is to press participants to take their coaching out of the solo arena and into a context of group work. In this way, coaches are not working entirely in the background, surfacing to coach, and then retreating to a place of self-reflection. Instead, they are helping to build a community of teachers learning together. In fact, the coach may appear more overtly a learner when working with a study group, and this is a useful perspective for teachers to have about coaching and what it entails. It may be that teachers will more readily see that they are able to contribute both individually and as a group toward a collective understanding about a math topic and the ways children come to learn the math ideas.

The Planning Activity has two parts: one that participants do on their own and one that is a small-group sharing of new ideas about working with teachers. Each portion should take about 15 minutes, though you can make adjustments if the group finishes writing earlier. In that case, you might want to have them move to the small-group listening and sharing portion. If you have time, ask the participants to spend just a few more minutes going back to their writing and adding new ideas or writing notes that reflect refinement of their earlier written responses.

Whole-Group Discussion

The whole group discussion also has two parts; the first is a sharing about the Planning Activity, and the second is a wrap-up discussion of the entire session.

The talk generated by the Planning Activity small-group discussions can be shared for the whole group. Given what you have been hearing as you moved from group to group and the amount of time before the session closes, you might choose different versions of facilitation. You might want the whole group to hear just briefly from each small group and then move directly to a session wrap-up. Asking each small group to share two ideas of value that came from their activity work and from listening carefully to each other will give every one a chance to hear new ideas. You might find that this is enough for now; let participants know that continuing to refine their plans—or move right into them at school—is something the whole group can revisit when you come together at the next session. Or, if you have time, you might chart some of the ideas generated by the planning activity and ask the participants to share more details. This is particularly helpful if a group came up with an idea or plan for collaborative work with teachers that is closely aligned with your own goals for the coach group. It would be strategic for all participants to consider the plan together. Participants might express a concern about strategies for organizing collaborative work. This may merit attention in the whole-group discussion. Ask participants who are strong strategic thinkers to contribute. It is important for the group not to get bogged down in complaints or discouragement about "having enough time," but rather help participants accept that structures may not yet be in place (or that they may yet have discovered how to take advantage of what is in place) and that part of coaching is learning how to build these possibilities.

The whole-group time is also an opportunity to discuss how a collaborative study of students' ideas might further one's coaching goals. Ask participants to think carefully about what steps each *coach* will need to take to get such a collaborative study off the ground, what it might take to maintain the focus of the work, and to support a specific and important coaching goal. These questions are important to ask; they press on the participants' sense of responsibility and authority in creating goals and agendas for work with teachers.

It is not the case that even with a great plan a coach can turn around and execute the plan with immediate success. But it is important to understand that one aspect of coaching is learning how to reframe existing structures, building relationships with those who can influence how structures for learning could play out, and cultivating partnerships that will actively promote math study and learning in the school. In each of these areas, we can imagine that effective coaching is not always possible if the coach perceives his or her role as a sole interventionist. Thinking long term, considering collaboration, creating opportunities, and determining and maintaining an important focus are all complex aspects of the coaching role.

Take a few minutes to end with exit card writing. Ask participants to describe one new idea and one next step generated by the session.

Chapter 8
Facilitation Notes

Cultivating Relationships
With Administrators and
Other Leadership Colleagues

2-Hour Session

Session Goals

- Explore ideas of *mathematical reasoning* and *mathematical discourse*
- Counter the notion that the coach is on his or her own in creating a vision for schoolwide success in math and in facilitating teacher learning
- Discern learning agendas for teachers and for school communities
- Explore strategies for, and the design of, principal professional development
- Craft an invitation to a principal or other school or district leaders to collaborate with an eye toward moving math education agendas forward

Case Description: Crafting an Invitation: Shifting From Isolation to Inclusion

Crafting an Invitation is composed of a draft of a letter the coach-author, Seth, wants to share with his colleagues for their feedback. Seth has written the letter for several reasons, most importantly to invite the principal in as an effective partner toward the goal of developing a strong math program in the school. Seth also uses this letter as a way of framing his coaching goals such that they connect through the lens of the principal. Finally, the letter stands as a strategically crafted professional development tool for the principal's learning. In the case, Seth lays out two masterfully articulate lists of vital aspects of the math program and coaching. First, he describes, in bulleted form, the successes of the current math program. Next, he meticulously describes the lenses he takes to the work he does, the teaching practices he observes, and the student learning environment as it is enacted in the school.

Session Overview

The session begins with a brief introduction of the goals and the context for the case, Crafting an Invitation: Shifting From Isolation to Inclusion. Participants will read the case and, in small groups, respond to focus questions that surface the knowledge for coaching Seth articulates in his case. The Focus Questions Activity is followed by a whole-group discussion aimed at highlighting the goals Seth has for his own practice as well as the goals he has for teachers and students. Coaches will analyze Seth's letter for the coaching strategies he describes and the ways he carefully structured his "invitation" to the principal. After a whole-group discussion of the letter, coaches will work, individually and in pairs, on a Planning Activity designed to help them articulate their own goals and craft an invitation to a collaborator. The session ends with a whole-group discussion of the insights and next steps brought to light through the activity.

Materials for the Session

- Create a chart of the goals for the session and have extra chart paper and markers for the session
- Participants will need coach journals or other writing materials for the Planning Activity

Session Agenda

1. Introduction: 5 minutes

2. Case Reading: 15 minutes

3. Focus Questions Activity: 20 minutes

4. Whole-Group Case Discussion: 20 minutes

5. Planning Activity and Whole-Group Discussion: 60 minutes

Introduction

Begin the session by offering a brief description of the agenda and the learning goals of the session. Describe, in just a few words, the context for this case of a letter to a principal written by the school coach, Seth.

Reading the Case and Focus Questions

Participants will spend about 30 minutes reading the case, exploring the focus questions, and discussing their reflections in small groups. While Questions 1 and 2 ask participants to describe the goals Seth has for students and teachers, you can help participants avoid overgeneralizing by letting them know, upfront, that this might seem to be a simplistic question to answer. (Some might simply say Seth wants students to talk in class and to think that they have fully answered the first focus question.) Press on this point by saying that you want each participant to really dig through the case for the many places where Seth lays out an agenda or a goal for teachers and students. Examples of these are sprinkled throughout the case and are worth looking carefully to uncover.

Participants will spend time going through this well-crafted letter to highlight the structure within it. The coach has strategically used this letter as a professional development tool for his principal; Seth has not only determined a learning goal for the teaching staff but learning goals for the principal too. Zeroing in on the structure of the letter will help participants see just how strategic and thoughtful Seth has been in crafting this invitation. And also, as participants discuss their ideas about Seth's image of coaching, it is the intention that they see Seth as moving beyond carrying the charge of change and shifting practice as the definition of a role he plays out on his own. Rather, in this case, one sees Seth moving to bring everyone—coach, principal, and teachers—together in meeting the math-learning goals for the students in the school.

As you circulate in the small groups, you will likely note that participants have reactions about a variety of ideas raised through this case. It might be that this is the first opportunity these math leaders have to discuss the necessary support of the school principal.

Whole-Group Discussion

Participants are often quite taken by the lists Seth describes and the way his ideas compare to ones they might have listed. (Many participants, both new and experienced coaches, express admiration for how clear Seth is about his coaching work.) Some participants remark that they are seldom asked to articulate their goals. They might also add that if they were asked, they would not be able to describe them as articulately as Seth does in his letter. As the facilitator, you may know the very contexts in which the participants are coaching—in fact you may know the principals and school leaders with whom the participants work. This may effect what you want participants to gain from the discussion. You could ask groups to talk together for just two minutes and decide the most important issue that came up in their small group; these ideas, by table group, can then become the list of topics to discuss.

It may require some effort for the whole group to stick with discussing the specifics of Seth's case instead of veering off into issues that pertain only to their local district contexts (the curriculum pacing guide or district assessments, for instance, might be a point of tension and the group wants to talk about this instead of what it means to set goals for a community, how one determines the goals, and how one articulates these ideas). To that end, to fully explore issues of mathematical reasoning, you might ask specifically what Seth feels teachers need to work through or engage in. It is useful to bring participants attention to Seth's idea of mathematical reasoning as the central goal, with math discourse in classrooms in service of that goal. Ask participants to reflect on the purpose of classroom discourse and the difference between *dialogue* (or student talk in classrooms) and *discourse*. As some participants have noted, there is more to discourse than simply assuring that students "have a voice" or that students are heard in classrooms. Mathematical discourse, as Seth is describing it, is about building ideas by listening to each other and analyzing what one hears and measuring that against what one already knows, by learning in the context of listening, contributing, and making sense.

Planning Activity: Considering
Collaboration and Communication

This thinking, writing, and planning activity consists of a series of structured tasks to take on alone and in pair discussions. The back-and-forth structure provides time for the participants' ideas and writing to develop—and with each interaction, become more clearly articulated—and the invitation to a colleague more effectively laid out.

Let the participants know that the Planning Activity is equally focused on all three elements: thinking, planning, and the actual writing of a letter of invitation. In introducing the Planning Activity, tell participants that this is an opportunity to think both about their coaching goals and potential collaborations with those goals in mind—at a school level, or a personal level, as goals for a specific teacher, or for a principal. To construct or discern goals to ground this activity, coaches should consider questions such as the following:

- What's complex about what the teachers are learning or struggling with and how might coaching support that learning?
- What do the students need that is not yet a part of the norm of teaching practice in the school?
- How refined are specific aspects of math teaching (such as facilitating classroom discourse, initiating important math tasks, and the like)?
- What mathematics content needs to be addressed with teachers that will support more robust teaching and learning in classrooms?

As the facilitator, you may have a sense of other questions you would like participants to consider as they work to define appropriate goals for their coaching work. It might be helpful to participants to post a chart of these reflection questions before participants begin the writing activity.

Activity Description

On Your Own

Participants will spend 10 minutes on the first portion of the Planning Activity reviewing the case and thinking about the coach's goals and the structure of the letter. These issues will have also have been addressed during the focus question portion of session. The idea is that by reacquainting with the case, the participants will have one structure (Seth's) to work from as they write. Their task now is to think through a coaching goal for themselves that might be more successfully reached with the collaborative help of another. Make it clear that a participant does not need to choose a principal as the collaborator for this activity. It may be that a teacher leader's support would enhance the coach's work. Or it may be that a coach would want to choose another coach who could form a collaborative effort across schools.

Participants should be encouraged to work on their own and to aim to write as clear an articulation of their goal as possible. An important aspect of the participants' thinking in this activity is exploring a justification that will support the *appropriateness of the chosen goal for their particular site.* Another is to choose a collaborator whose strategic participation will make a difference in achieving the goal.

In Pairs

At this juncture, participants meet with a partner. Each person has several minutes to—as clearly as they can—describe their coaching goal, why it's important, and whom they have chosen to *invite in.* The idea is for each person to simply describe these things as carefully as they can to the other. Each person will listen with real care without discussion. Tell the group this is a time to "have the ear of a partner who cares that you are becoming more comfortable with the articulation of your ideas."

On Your Own

Next, participants spend 10 minutes writing *an invitation to collaborate* to a carefully selected teacher, administrator, or other whose role, authority, or knowledge will lend the work some heft. In some sessions, there will be participants who are reluctant to actually sit and write a letter. They might complain that they are too tired late in the day (if you have a session late in the afternoon, there is some empathy for weariness!) or that the task seems too burdensome. Stay the course, and specifically press these participants to push through their resistance and see what comes of writing. If you insist, you will find that in almost every instance, the participant is surprised at the depth of what they write and the way the writing lends a measure of reality to actually extending an invitation and opening up the coaching arena to a larger group.

In Pairs

Partners take turns describing new ideas about collaboration that were brought to light through this writing activity. Plans may have unfolded, challenges may have emerged, or goals may have been further refined. Give participants 10 minutes to take turns talking to each other about these new ideas. If you have time in your session, at this point, you might choose to have participants write one sentence on chart paper that describes the goal, one sentence that articulates the importance of that goal, and the person they are choosing to invite in. Again, if there is time, you could also ask for a sentence that captures the next steps. These chart papers can be viewed by everyone during a brief break, and then discussed in the whole group.

Whole-Group Discussion

The Planning Activity is followed by a whole-group discussion of articulated goals and of next steps for how coaches will initiate and follow-through on these collaborations. You might start the discussion by asking participants what they learned by working on the activity. Ask how their goal shifted in their thinking as they worked toward articulating it and in writing an invitation for someone to join them in it. It might be useful to explore the reason for participants' goals. (Why that one? What importance does it hold?) As the facilitator, you may find that there is a range of purposeful thinking regarding the "why." Are the participants thinking strategically about important issues in schools? Ask how the goal ultimately supports overall goals for the learning community.

Another aspect of the group discussion is to explore the next steps. Ask participants to describe the plans generated by this activity and to specifically name some next steps they have in mind. Ask coaches to describe which aspects of their work will be affected by the work and thinking that they have done today. Ask participants to think back to the ways the group discussions and the talking in small groups and with a partner supported the deeper-level thinking they were able to experience. In that sense, you will reinforce the *collaborative nature* of the session.

End the session by reserving a few minutes for exit card writing. You might ask participants to describe a new and important idea heard from a colleague during the session. Ask participants to describe one next step for the coming week or month.

Chapter 9
Facilitation Notes

*Taking the Lead as
a Teacher of Teachers*

4-Hour Session or Two 2-Hour Sessions

Session Goals

- Analyze models for subtraction and students' ideas about the operation
- Learn about gathering data on teacher beliefs and math knowledge to design appropriately challenging assignments and "study opportunities" for teachers
- Analyze coaching questions that support teachers' construction of new ideas about teaching and student learning
- Examine teacher, coach, and student exchanges in a classroom for students with special needs
- Explore images of the coach role as a one who actively *teaches teachers*

Case Description: Encountering Venus

This longer case, written by an experienced math coach, describes a coaching context that unfolds over a series of days. It offers a poignant and intelligent example of a coach who is unafraid to teach a "willing, but far from novice" teacher by giving her homework assignments and setting up opportunities for the teacher to examine and reveal her practice. The case follows the story of the introductory meeting with Venus (a teacher of students with special needs), a subsequent math interview with her students, debriefs with the teacher and the coach, and the collaboration that develops between the two.

Session Overview

Because Encountering Venus is the longest case in the series, giving participants ample time to read the case, participate in math activities, and discussions of focus questions will require four hours. However, because of the way the case is structured, it is possible to separate this session into two separate two-hour sessions. The agenda describes the two-hour sessions and notes for a single four-hour session. (If using the Encountering Venus chapter in a full-day professional development session with coaches, separate the two two-hour sessions with a lunch or other break.)

The two-hour periods are described as Session 1 and Session 2. Session 1 begins with a math activity exploring story problems and specific types of word problems. The math content of the case centers on subtraction, and this operation is explored in ways that may be new for teachers and for coaches. Ample time is allotted for the math exploration before participants read Part 1 of the case and discuss it. A whole-group discussion follows before the group reads Part 2 of the case. Next, coaches work on a Focus Questions Activity, again meeting in their small groups to analyze the next section of the case. The whole group will convene again to explore these first interactions between the coach and the teacher.

When used for two separate professional development sessions, begin Session 2 with a brief review of the previous readings. Otherwise, the session starts with participants reading Part 3 of the case, Investigating With Venus, followed by small-group discussions and a whole-group discussion. Next, participants read Part 4 of the case, Debriefing With Venus and, again, move into the small-group discussions focused on the final teacher and coach meeting described in the case. A whole-group conversation wraps up the session.

Materials for the Session

- Create a chart of the Session Goals
- Provide counting cubes for exploring math problems and chart paper and colored markers for displaying participants' math work for group discussion.

Session Agendas
Session 1: 120 minutes

1. Math Activity in Small Groups: 25 minutes

2. Whole-Group Discussion: 20 minutes

3. Case Reading—Part 1, First Conversation, and Small-Group Discussion: 20 minutes

4. Whole-Group Discussion: 15 minutes

5. Case Reading—Part 2, You Mean You're Not Going to Tell Me? and Focus Questions Activity in Small Groups: 25 minutes

6. Whole-Group Discussion: 15 minutes

Mathematics Activity

Session 1 begins with a math activity. Participants, in groups of three, work through a set of story problems designed to highlight a collection of math ideas such as relationships between subtraction and addition, the role sets and subsets play in reasoning through the stories and influence solution processes, and models of subtraction-type problems.

These four story problems represent a variety of *problem types*. To explore this notion fully, the directions ask participants to use manipulatives and/or drawings to model each story context and then to create a number sentence that matches the problem. As you circulate among the groups, encourage individuals to actually draw sketches and use objects to show the ways they are thinking about the situations and to share their ideas in the small group. Sometimes participants, new to working alongside other adults on elementary arithmetic problems, will work to expand their thinking when they hear you validate their developing ideas about problems that appear so easily solved. Simply listening in, asking clarifying questions, or helping participants compare their models are ways to help participants go deeper with confidence. Keep an eye out for a variety of models, questions, and insights raised in the groups.

Whole-Group Discussion

Once participants have had a chance to work on the story problems and to discuss their ideas, begin a whole-group discussion by asking for volunteers to come up to the board and share their models for individual problems. For each, ask participants for alternative ideas or models. Overall, aim to help participants compare the problems and the operations used to solve the problem.

Some participants will draw number lines; some will use pictures or model the problem with linking cubes. Some will cross off (or separate) cubes starting at the end of the line of cubes and some will start at the beginning. Some will add up, and some will subtract chunks of numbers. Ask participants to comment and make note of the similarities and differences between these approaches to the problems.

Ask the whole group to share visual images for what's happening in the problems that are not yet represented in the shared drawings. Some participants welcome explicit directions to practice constructing mental images. One participant offered, "I just don't think that way. My math is cut and dried—I'm not a visual thinker." The facilitator then suggested that conjuring up mental images of how the numbers operate as a useful way to engage with problems may simply be a *new* idea and that practicing this way of thinking can be help develop new insights. The facilitator's comment left open the possibility that one can develop skills of visualization that have been previously untapped and helped dispel the notion that we are necessarily limited to our usual ways of thinking.

Some participants have difficulty making sense of the operation used to solve the second problem:

> Ella keeps candies in her desk drawer for those chocolate emergencies! This week she had a real craving for sugar and ate a lot of candies. If she ate 18 candies during the week and by Friday afternoon ended up with 17, how many candies had Ella started with?

Most participants will view this collection of problems as subtraction types whether they solve the problems with addition or subtraction. "This candy problem feels different. It's just pure adding. There's no subtraction in here," claimed one participant. Another countered that she had set up her number sentence as ___ − 17 = 18. Comments such as these will generate discussion that, again, seem to unsettle the group; this time with regard to a previously held notion of subtraction.

At some point, it will be clear that many people used addition to solve the same problems they perceive as subtraction problems. This poses a challenge to the group—just what is subtraction if one uses addition? Let participants know that the teacher and the students in the case pose the same question and that as they read and discuss the case, they should keep this question in mind.

Case Reading and Related Focus Questions

Let participants know they have about 10 minutes to read Part 1 of the case and to respond in small groups to the accompanying focus questions. Reading Part 1 of Encountering Venus is the second activity in the session. Encourage participants to write questions or comments in the margins and note sentences or paragraphs that resonate for or confuse them. If a participant finishes reading before the rest of the group, suggest that they highlight line numbers related to the focus questions as a way to prepare for the small-group discussion.

In groups of three or four, participants briefly discuss the questions designed to orient the readers to the issues in the case. In reading Part 1, we see a relationship being established between the coach and the teacher. Participants take a few moments to discuss how the dialogue unfolds and how Gloria and Venus are setting up a collaboration.

Whole-Group Discussion

The whole-group discussion turns the reader's attention to the coach and teacher interactions. Ask the group, "What's going on between the coach and the teacher so far in this case?" The group might consider variations of, "What is the teacher saying?" "How is the coach interacting?" and, "What seems to be contributing to the developing collaboration?" Remind participants that referencing line numbers in both small- and whole-group helps ground discussions in the details of the case.

In a discussion about Part 1, one participant offered, "Gloria is really direct. Look at line 38; she just goes right for it! I'm not sure I zero in so quickly." Another participant concurred, noting that Gloria did go right to the mathematics by offering a math problem for the teacher to solve in just the first minutes of their first sit-down discussion. The facilitator recognized these observations as an opportunity to press on what Gloria was doing—and aiming for—in this first substantive discussion with Venus. The facilitator asked, "So what happens as a result of Gloria's direct approach? What do we learn about Gloria and about Venus?"

It is true that Venus is forthcoming, and we know that not all teachers are, especially at the first teacher and coach meeting. Gloria does, however, say that Venus is working hard; participants might need to hear that again. It is especially important to note that Venus might have just said, "My students can't really solve these really simple problems" and Gloria *could* have chosen to empathize and express friendly acknowledgment that Venus has challenging students. Instead, as we see consistently throughout the case, Gloria takes statements like these as entry places for coaching work that supports a learning agenda for Venus—a learning agenda based on math content for student understanding, developing an ear for student thinking, and considering students' ideas—while at the same time, working to deepen Venus' understanding of the content. It might be useful to point out what Gloria *didn't* do at this stage.

In this, and other parts of the Venus case, the parallels between teacher and student learning are useful to consider. For instance, in Part 1, Venus says she offers a key words strategy to which Gloria responds, "I always include the wrong key words to throw them off." At this stage, neither the teacher nor the students are sure what operations to use, and so in this way, Gloria is coaching on a variety of levels.

Setting participants up to analyze the case by looking carefully at Gloria's moves and the ways (and on what basis) she begins to establish a learning partnership with Venus will support a lens for the overall experience of working with the Venus case and materials. As the participants continue their work throughout both Sessions 1 and 2, paying careful attention to Gloria's coaching and evolving learning agenda for Venus will offer important images of the potential for coaching.

Case Reading and Related
Focus Questions Discussion

Participants read Part 2, You Mean You're Not Going to Tell Me? and again work in small groups to respond to related focus questions. If you have time in your session, you might give a few more minutes to this reading period so participants can take a short break before they begin their small-group discussion.

This section of the case introduces readers to Phil and Bruce, two seventh grade boys who are currently struggling with mathematics. The focus questions draw participants' attention to the students' confusions and to Venus's interactions with the boys. Small-group discussions will draw reader's attention to the differences in the ways Gloria interacts with the students and Venus's responses to their work and their questions. This section of the case also offers an image of coaching in lines 133–155 that are at the heart of Gloria's pedagogical skills.

Whole-Group Discussion

Bring the groups back together for a whole-group discussion focusing on several fronts. The participants will have a chance to consider the math Bruce and Phil struggle with and the implications for learning based on the ways Venus and Gloria interact with the two students. In addition, the discussion will highlight the way Gloria elicits Venus' ideas about her own teaching.

Begin by asking participants to describe how they interpret what is happening mathematically for Bruce and Phil. Then you can move the discussion to the ways Gloria and Venus interact with the students. As participants offer comments on types of moves Gloria and Venus make, remind everyone that backing up general comments with the line numbers is an important way to stay focused on what is actually happening in this case. Participants will note the ways Gloria and Venus are beginning to partner in their observations and interactions with the two students such as in lines 97–103 and 105–112. If not, ask them to characterize the relationship of Gloria and Venus in the case and insist on line number evidence. In following the back and forth between Venus teaching and Gloria teaching, participants will see Venus' questioning skills emerging. In lines 108, 117, and 128, Venus asks questions that, indeed, are targeted at both focusing the students' attention on their own work and on eliciting students' ideas as a path toward understanding her students. In contrast to the directive teaching she has described to Gloria in Part 1, Venus is engaging in the students' learning just as Gloria has engaged in Venus's learning.

Ask participants to take a moment and underline each of Gloria's remarks in this section. Then, ask for two volunteers who will read aloud the part of Venus and the part of Gloria in lines 133–155. Now open the whole-group discussion for a consideration of the nature of Gloria's questions and what these questions afford. What do both Gloria and Venus learn in this exchange, and what does it say about a stance of coaching? Parts 1 and 2 end with Gloria assigning a specific homework task for Venus as they gear up to continue learning about the students and to dig into a study of subtraction.

As you wrap up the discussion for this session, ask participants to comment on how this case helps them think about interactions with teachers in their own coaching, and in particular, how they might be thinking about the goals they have in mind for the teachers with whom they work.

Session 2 Agenda—120 minutes

1. Review: Part 1 of the case Encountering Venus and Part 2, You Mean You're Not Going to Tell Me? (Skip this review for a single four-hour session, instead use the time for a brief break.)

2. Case Reading—Part 3 of the case, Investigating With Venus: 25 minutes

3. Focus Questions Activity in Small Groups: 35 minutes

4. Whole-Group Discussion: 15 minutes

5. Case Reading—Part 4, Debriefing With Venus and Focus Questions Activity: 30 minutes

6. Whole-Group Discussion and Wrap-Up Activity: 30 minutes

Case Reading

In this second session, begin by offering participants a chance to reread and review the issues highlighted in Parts 1 and 2. The small-group discussion that follows will narrow in on Part 3, Investigating With Venus, where Venus describes her next steps with Bruce and Phil. She recounts the math problems she wrote for them (based on the homework assignment Gloria had set up at the end of Part 2) and describes the ways the two boys tackled the problem. Again, in this section of the case, Gloria presents new perspectives on ways of thinking about subtraction strategies and describes a visit to Venus's classroom and the ideas raised by Phil and Bruce's classmates.

Focus Questions Activity and Small-Group Discussion

A discussion of these focus questions helps participants move between the mathematical ideas raised in the class and the coaching moves Gloria makes that influence the new type of classroom experience the students have. Bring the participants back to their own work in Session 1 on issues of subtraction. These themes offer learning on three levels for participants. In analyzing the student thinking, they pay close attention to the ways Bruce, Phil, Karen, and Natalie—and likely students they have in their own classes—understand subtraction. In considering Gloria's moves in the classroom and the stance with which she poses questions of both the students and of Venus, participants have a lens on effective coaching in process. And again, participants will continue to develop insights into the mathematics for themselves.

Whole-Group Discussion

Begin by asking participants to discuss the ideas and reasoning offered by students in Venus' classroom. Ask, "How do these students view subtraction?" Remind individuals to refer specifically to students by name or by line number. In this section of the case, we now see Bruce and Phil contributing to a discussion about the operation. Bruce sees that you can add up; he suggests that he'd "go 2 + ? = 7. It's an addition problem." It is interesting to note the difference of this kind of engagement with ideas about math given his previous experiences as Venus described them in Part 1 (lines 19–23). The group might discuss the difference in the characteristics of this lesson. What is it that Venus is doing that matters? What's the nature of Gloria's interventions and contributions with regard to the class and with regard to Venus?

Next, turn the group's attention to lines 291–315. Ask participants to talk about the question, "What do all the different types have in common?" You might refer the group back to the story problems in the math activity they solved prior reading the case.

After the group discusses this question for a few minutes, ask participants to spend a few minutes writing their own subtraction problems. Ask them to consider a range of problems and to discuss, back within their small group, the ways their problems are related to subtraction. This activity is similar to the assignment Venus assigns the students at the end of class.

Case Reading

The participants now read the last section of the Venus case, Part 4, Debriefing With Venus. In this section, Gloria describes a quick debrief with Venus after class. Inherent in the case, but perhaps most transparent in Part 4, is a portrayal of coaching as making thoughtful decisions about when to be directive or explicit, when to reflect together, and when to push and probe. Gloria is equally assertive in her questioning as she is in providing explicit directions or explanations.

Focus Questions Activity in Small Groups

The focus of the final reading and discussion will be on Gloria's coaching and the way her perception of the role, coupled with her beliefs about learning, influenced her moves, her questions, and Venus's learning. Participants should be encouraged to focus first on the dialogue between Gloria and Venus in Part 4. As you circulate among the groups, you might ask participants to underline or circle line numbers where Gloria is asking questions, where she is offering advice, and where she is giving answers. A next step for their discussion is to consider the implications of Gloria's moves for Venus' learning.

Whole-Group Discussion

In this last discussion of the Venus case, the participants will explore the focus question, "If we can say that a coach makes moves based on her understanding of the mathematics, the students' ideas, the teachers' ideas, and her beliefs about both learning and her role in it, what do we learn from Gloria about coaching?"

Ask the group to take a few minutes to go back through all sections of the case and choose two excerpts that capture a particularly significant coaching move. Give the group a few minutes to do this and then solicit from about five participants just the line numbers they chose without comment. Write these up on the board and give yourself and the group a few more minutes to find these sections and to read them. Then ask the same volunteers to share why they chose these excerpts. Invite the whole group to either comment on these same excerpts or to offer a new one for the group to consider.

One participant chose lines 205–235. She said, "Right here, Gloria is doing this thing where she dances back and forth between being really explicit in her answers, and then instead of being explicit in responses, she asks explicit questions. So she answers Venus' question about negative numbers and even gives an example of how Venus could think about it. But in the next turn, she could have answered Venus's question, 'What's going on with Phil?' and instead she asks her very direct types of questions. It's so interesting to me that she constantly makes these decisions about what Venus can take in directly and what Venus should consider for herself."

Another offered lines 272–305. She said, "I think this is really important here. Reading this part of the case, Gloria describes places where she and Venus are both interacting with the students, and you really see how they have a partnership going. Gloria could have just come in and modeled the lesson and then ask Venus what she thought of it. And I've done that before. But this strikes me as not only a really solid back and forth kind of co-teaching, but you also hear how Gloria respects Venus. She says in line 287, 'Venus takes the reins.' And then a couple lines down, Gloria says she's asked the kids way too many questions and that 'Venus picks up the important one and repeats it.' So often I think, either we coaches or even the teachers think of us as 'the knowers' and the teachers as the ones who 'don't know.' I mean I get that Gloria really knows what's she's doing, but she also participates with Venus in all this."

Comments like these will reveal what the participants think is important about this case and also what they are learning about coaching in their analysis of it. Take some time to elicit from the group what they consider salient to their own work and focus on a reflective discussion. Before you close the session, ask participants to spend a few minutes writing an extended exit card about how the discussions about coaching relate to decisions and learning agendas they have in their own work.

Chapter 10
Facilitation Notes

Maintaining a Focus
on Mathematics

2-Hour Session

Session Goals

- Learning about coaching and facilitating with a focus on mathematics
- Considering successful classroom debriefs
- Navigating complaints and other obstacles to learning in group settings
- Considering successful strategies for including the principal in professional development settings

Case Description: Struggling to Keep Math at the Center

The case Struggling to Keep Math at the Center describes a coach's efforts to facilitate productive and math-centered dialogue with teachers and with the principal. In her writing, the coach, Ivy, describes two different teacher team meetings; one she deems a failure, the other a success. Sorting out her reflections and ideas as she writes, Ivy uses case writing as a tool for analyzing and affirming the features of a successful classroom debrief. In addition, she explores strategies for maintaining an effective facilitation stance even in the face of potentially undermining distractions. This case reminds readers of the importance, and the complexities, of "keeping the math" in math coaching.

Session Overview

Participants first engage in a mental-math activity related to the math ideas in the case and structured to go beyond sharing strategies to opening up ideas about the operation of subtraction. Once the group is oriented to the math ideas in the case, the facilitator describes the goals of the session and the context for the case. Before reading the case, participants respond to a set of writing prompts designed to surface facilitation and decision making in their current coaching contexts. Reading Struggling to Keep Math at the Center next, participants are reminded of an important principle of effective coaching: mathematics and students' ideas are central to learning in post-observation discussions. A Focus Questions Activity, during which participants discuss the differences between issues raised in the case, is followed by a whole-group discussion.

Materials for the Session

- Prepare two charts: one that describes the session goals and one that lists the two writing prompts (see the Writing Activity and Case Reading section)
- Provide extra chart paper for recording mental-math strategies and the participant responses to Focus Question 2
- Provide counters or small cubes for exploring the math problems and the focus questions
- Provide writing materials, or a coaching journal, for the Writing Activity

Session Agenda

1. Whole-Group Mental-Math Activity: 25 minutes

2. Writing Activity and Case Reading: 30 minutes

3. Small-Group Focus Questions Activity: 30 minutes

4. Whole-Group Discussion: 35 minutes

Math Activity

Begin the session by jumping in to a mental-math activity with a subtraction problem before describing the session goals or the agenda. As you write the problem on the board or chart paper, ask participants to mentally solve $143 - 87$. In addition to calculating the answer, explain to participants that you are going to ask them to share "images" of the problem: either a story or visual images that illustrate or help them in solving the problem. Give the group a few minutes to think, and then ask for volunteers to share their ideas.

In one group, a coach named Cheryl responded to the mental-math problem by saying, "At first I think of it being in the 60s because of the 14 and the 8, but then I check on the ones and see that the 7 is higher than a 3. I immediately switch to a 50 and see the difference between 7 and 3 as 6. Then I know the answer is 56. I know," she said a bit apologetically, "it sounds like it takes forever, but it's really efficient for me." While the group took a minute or so to consider the problem from Cheryl's point of view, the facilitator asked them to also think about how this description might be explored on a number line. The participants spent some time, with one volunteer illustrating their ideas on the chart paper, to sort out the model of the distance between 87 and 143 following the logic that Cheryl had offered.

Participants will come up with a variety of methods; some will be very familiar to the others in the group and some, perhaps, unexpected. Engage participants in sharing descriptions of their strategies and, most importantly, ask individuals to go further by including an analysis of how they "see" the math solution unfolding. Let the group know that it will be helpful to also look at how the strategies, problems, and visual models might be related. This more elaborated version of a mental-math activity will enhance the participants' view of subtraction and the variety of ways the operation can be illustrated or modeled. Also, discussing each other's points of view and looking for relationships helps the coaches appreciate what it takes to facilitate in ways that reach beneath the surface of a problem.

Writing Activity and Case Reading

Move from the Math Activity to a brief description of the session goals and the agenda. Next, before reading the case, participants will spend a few minutes reflecting on their own recent coaching experiences as facilitators. Explain to the group that the writing exercise is intended to bring to mind two particular issues embedded in the work of facilitation: connecting to an important focus and engaging participants with their own ideas at the center. Each coach should spend 5 to 10 minutes responding to the following writing prompts that are posted on chart paper:

- Describe two recent coaching experiences when you were responsible for facilitating the discussion. Describe the purpose of these meetings.
- Describe, in some detail, the goals you had in mind. What sorts of things—questions, ideas, or insights—did you think through to support your goals *as* you were facilitating the discussions in these meetings?

Let participants know that they should consider writing about facilitation in any of the contexts within the scope of their work. They can choose to write about a meeting with a single teacher or with a group in a grade-level meeting or at a math workshop. Tell the group that the writing is intended to help them connect on a personal level with the case they will be reading; Ivy, the coach, describes the details of two meetings in much the same way. Explain that the purpose of this reflective writing is to describe the real experiences as they unfolded—whether the meetings met the coach's expectations or not. Decide ahead of time if you are going to collect this writing and let participants know.

When you sense that participants are ready to begin reading, end the writing time and let the group know you will refer back to their writing in a whole-group discussion later in the session. Distribute the focus questions for their small-group discussion. If anyone finishes reading the case before the rest of their small group members, they might go back to their written reflection and add new thoughts.

Focus Questions in Small Groups

Participants will spend about 30 minutes in their small groups of four discussing the focus questions. You might circulate with your own copy of the case and ask participants what evidence they have found and what ideas they have about what helps Ivy make her coaching decisions. If participants are responding generally to this, your question will prompt a more in-depth look. There are several questions that require paying attention to students' logic. In Question 4, participants are encouraged to consider how students might approach a subtraction story problem. Having a set of about 20 cubes or other counting objects at each table will support an exploration of this problem.

Case Discussion

Before leading the case discussion, review the case for your own responses to Questions 3 and 7. It is useful to have your own sense of Ivy's stance as a coach. In this way, you can prepare to follow two lines of thinking, one is to briefly consider the math in the case and the other, then, is to follow the decision making process of the coach.

The case discussion can begin with a question that helps illustrate Kwame's idea and the logic behind laying out two piles of cubes when solving $13 - 5$. Ask, "What story problem might easily prompt a young child to place a pile of 13 and a pile of 5 on the table to solve this subtraction problem?"

Next, move on to consider the decisions that underlie day-to-day work in coaching. In this case, we hear quite clearly Ivy's frustration with the pace of progress at the school. Coach participants will relate to these feelings. One coach said that her greatest challenge is to deal with her own patience; "I know that I am there as a support and as a teacher which should, by definition, mean that I am a patient person. But I'm not always. On some days, I just want to say, 'Come *on* now. Can't you see we are getting nowhere with the complaints and the roadblocks? Don't you care as much as I do?'" Another participant nodded her head and said, "I feel like this is such an urgent agenda that means all of us have to dig in, and sometimes, I don't know what to say when I feel stymied in the conversation. I know what Ivy is talking about, and I feel it a lot at my school."

In facilitating these discussions, it seems easy to get into the position of sympathizing or commiserating. In the end, though, the conversation needs to help coaches build their frameworks for coaching principles. What principles drive the participants' decision making when times are tough or the conversations are unproductive? On what do they rely as they press for more accountability or more engagement? Toggling back and forth between Ivy's assertion that "math at the center" is what matters for her, and participants' central ideas might be a possible discussion for your group. If the group has less experience, it is particularly important that they begin to define the principles upon which they make choices and decisions. Sometimes, as we see in Ivy's case, positioning oneself to press forward, based on a firmly held belief and principle regarding deepening math teaching practice, is what will make the difference between work that is unproductive and work that is generative.

Some participants note that the teachers may not know what is expected of them at such meetings. One math specialist pointed out, "If you are just told what the meeting's about, then how do you know how to behave in such a new way?" If no one suggests this in the session, you can raise this as a thought to consider. Ask what work the participants do, very consciously, to help teachers and principals appreciate the nature of the meetings—the cultural norms coaches are striving for—as they facilitate. Ask how teachers and principals understand the nature of the collaborations coaches are working to build.

Before you bring the discussion to a close, ask the participants to share, in pairs, the gist of their previous writing activity. Ask them, in light of the whole-group discussion, how they are thinking about the ideas in their writing. Before the session closes, ask participants to write an exit card responding to a question such as, "How does the idea of math at the center play out in your day-to-day work? What new ideas do you have about facilitating based on principles of coaching and learning?"

Chapter 11
Facilitation Notes

Framing the Connection Between Coach and Teacher Goals

2-Hour Session

Session Goals

- Explore facilitation as an aspect of coaching
- Learn about setting clear learning goals for participants
- Consider the intersection of participants' ideas and beliefs with the goals of professional development
- Learn to balance learning goals, participants' ideas, and participants' perceived needs

Case Description: Unsatisfied in the Seminar

The coach-author, Bonita, describes her efforts to facilitate meaningful and challenging math professional development for teachers. She describes her struggles in reaching two resistant teachers and in connecting the seminar to their beliefs and concerns. Bonita includes specific examples of her correspondence between the teachers and her efforts to reframe the professional development goals to meet the teachers' perceived needs and so that the teachers can appreciate and connect to the purpose and direction of the seminar. In this way, Bonita's case also highlights the use of written correspondence as a useful coaching strategy.

Session Overview

The session begins with a brief description of the goals and the context for the case, Unsatisfied in the Seminar. Participants read the case and the focus questions before moving into small-group discussions that focus on an analysis of the coaching and facilitation issues Bonita's case highlights. Participants will next engage in a reflective writing and planning activity designed to support the articulation of a series of steps toward a more effective and successful collaboration with a teacher or administrator with whom they are currently "out of synch." A final facilitator-led discussion follows.

Materials for the Session

- Create a poster of the Session Goals
- Provide writing materials, or a coaching journal, for the reflective writing during the Planning Activity

Session Agenda

1. Introduction: 5 minutes

2. Case Reading and Focus Questions: 15 minutes

3. Small-Group Focus Questions Activity: 25 minutes

4. Whole-Group Discussion: 20 minutes

5. Planning Activity: 35 minutes

6. Whole-Group Discussion: 20 minutes

Introduction

Begin the session by offering a brief description of the agenda and the learning goals of the session. Set the stage for the case by describing, in just a few words, the context of this coaching case written by Bonita.

Case Reading and Focus Questions

Participants should read the focus questions before they read this case. The questions will provide a useful lens with which to read Bonita's professional development facilitator journal and her coaching questions. Let participants know that they have about 15 minutes for reading the Focus Questions and the case.

Focus Questions Activity in Small Groups

Participants work together in small groups to zero in on important issues of facilitation of a seminar—and coaching in general. Preface the small-group work by helping make the connections between the participants' coaching work and Bonita's case. While the coaches in your group may not facilitate math seminars, they are likely charged with facilitating workshops, grade-level meetings, and other professional development experiences where they may find the learning goals are in conflict with the participants' perceived needs. Even though you are asking the group to stay focused on *Bonita's* experience, this careful analysis of her struggles and decisions will provide new and thoughtful perspectives for coaches to bring to bear on their own facilitation dilemmas.

The first question is aimed at clarifying what sort of math seminar this is and how the goals may differ significantly from previous experiences—and expectations of professional development—that Bonita's and Sylvia's participants have had in the past. Being clear about the seminar goals will help small-group participants appreciate the importance of Bonita's dilemma about how to respond. She wants very much for her seminar participants to find satisfaction in learning about students' thinking and in developing their own math content knowledge; she knows that deep engagement with both will offer more robust learning for teachers than dropping her seminar agenda to respond to the more teacher practice issues the participants raise after the first session. Bonita wants the teachers to feel heard and to understand that their questions and beliefs are important, but at the same time, she needs to figure out how to incorporate these issues in such a way that does not diminish the important and, to Bonita's way of thinking, more fundamental, goals of the seminar.

Participants should investigate the issues Bonita raises through the context of this seminar and the beliefs and ideas unearthed in the teachers' homework assignments. Coaches will have a chance to talk about the specific ways Bonita manages to help the participants find purpose in her seminar while "staying the course." If there is time for the groups to address Question 7, they will have a chance to talk together about the implications of these issues in their own work.

Whole-Group Discussion

Open the whole-group discussion by asking participants to frame the facilitation issues Bonita grapples with in this case. One response to this question might be that while Bonita appreciates the tenor that change can affect for teachers in her district, she begins to appreciate this much more deeply as the seminar begins. In fact, even as she and her co-facilitator, Sylvia, plan and prepare for the seminar by studying the ideas and the work incorporated in the materials, Bonita describes, "I hadn't realized how much time I would spend thinking about the learners' experience, about what it means to engage someone—and engage people coming from lots of different traditions and beliefs."

Inexperienced facilitators may not realize the skill involved in incorporating teachers' beliefs into an already focused agenda. Throughout the series of cases in this book, the themes of working at the level of participants' ideas, focusing on mathematics, students' thinking, and analyzing implications for next steps are evident in and explored through coach-written cases and activities. Bonita's case serves as an example of someone wrestling with the way she perceives the teachers' ideas and wishes, while at the same time, believing that staying the course with the seminar material—even as it doesn't first appear to the teachers to meet their needs—will be the appropriate learning opportunity for them.

One participant pointed out this same excerpt about teachers' beliefs and said, "I spent so much time planning the workshop, it never occurred to me that they would not be engaged or that I would have to fight for their engagement. I was so flustered; it was a flop." New to a facilitation role, it is easy to get caught in studying the session materials, or designing the workshop, without considering how the materials or plan intersects with current teacher beliefs or experiences. The facilitator thoughtfully responded by acknowledging the similarity between Bonita and Sylvia's preparation and the way teachers new to a math curriculum might prepare. She added, "Inexperienced with new material, it is easy to focus preparation on finding the exact wording, making copies, setting up an agenda, etc. All the while we've forgotten there are actual students involved!"

Bonita believes that by studying students' voices and their work, by reading authentic accounts of classroom experiences written by teachers, and by investigating related math activities, the teachers' concerns will actually be addressed. The effort she makes to frame the seminar so that the teachers feel heard and feel confident that the work is worth engaging in are at the heart of Questions 4, 5, and 6. Ask participants to describe the actions Bonita takes and how these support her goals. It will be important for participants to pinpoint line numbers in the case so that the whole-group can focus their attention on specifics.

In closing the discussion, ask coaches to talk for a few minutes about when, in their own work, they need to call on facilitation skills similar to those that Bonita describes. Point to the line where Bonita asks, "How do I stay centered when the going gets tough? What do I rely on as the facilitator that will help me stay the course and push through resistance to a place where people want to 'come to the table'?" Ask the participants on what principles they rely as they move through difficult facilitation experiences. Here, you are not asking necessarily for descriptions of what they do, rather you are asking about the principles of the work that center them. New coaches may not yet be able to answer this question about principles but will be able to answer what they do in these situations. This question can be asked over the course of any of the case sessions in the book. As coaches develop their practice, they come to recognize and articulate the principles that guide their decisions.

Planning Activity in Small Groups

Set up the Planning Activity by assigning small groups of three. Because the first part of the activity requires that each person in the group reflect and talk with the others in the group, limiting the size to three also limits this part to no more than 15 minutes. Launch the activity by describing how the activity will unfold. First, each person in each small group will have a few minutes to reflect before describing the challenging coaching collaboration to the others. As each person talks in the small group, the others listen. It is not a time for offering advice or suggestions; rather this is a time for each person to work at articulating the challenge. Remind participants that there is a great deal they can learn from each other and that this careful listening is one very important way of taking advantage of this time together.

Next, participants respond to the writing prompts. These prompts are designed to give coaches a chance to think carefully about these challenges of facilitation and of relationship building in the context of coaching and fulfilling important math-focused goals.

The Planning Activity ends with a small-group discussion, during which each participant has a chance, once again, to describe his or her thoughts and ideas. Ask groups to pay careful attention to their listening skills and to ask each other questions with the intent of helping the other person think more deeply or productively without resorting to simply offering advice.

Whole-Group Discussion

The whole-group discussion is fairly brief. Participants have had ample time to discuss Bonita's ideas, to articulate their own and to listen carefully to each other. Ask for sharing about the implications of this case and the discussions in the session on ideas about their own facilitation and decision making in coaching. What came up in the Planning Activity discussions and reflective writing that offered new insights? What did they hear from other participants that helped them think about their own contexts? One of the advantages of coming together in a coach group and discussing ideas at this level is to gain new perspectives from others engaged in similar work and who struggle with similar challenges. Open the conversation so that coaches are encouraged to talk with each other in this whole-group discussion.

Save a few minutes for participants to write exit cards. You might ask coaches to describe the most important new idea that came from the session and to explain how the session will specifically influence their facilitation practice.

Chapter 12
Facilitation Notes

Examining the Role
of Authority in Coaching

3-Hour Session

Session Goals

- Cultivate a reflective coaching practice
- Explore what it means to claim the authority to make decisions about the learning needs of other adults and to design experiences with these goals in mind
- Explore the authority we negotiate with others and how to maintain one's authority while not usurping others
- Examine the links between teaching and coaching and analyzing the shift from a *teacher of children* to a *teacher of teachers*
- Learn from other coaches' experiences and perspectives

Case Description: Claiming Authority

Claiming Authority, written by a math coach in her third year of coaching, provides participants with a view of the trajectory of one coach's developing practice. The author describes connections between her developing coaching practice to the early developing years of her classroom teaching. The author tackles the issues of authority in coaching, an important theme that will have resonance for all coaches and teacher leaders. She considers ways she might have moved more quickly toward a stronger practice, including taking advantage of the wisdom of coach colleagues.

Session Overview

The session begins with a brief introduction of the goals and the context for the case, Claiming Authority. Participants will read the case then move into a small-group discussion of the themes and issues the author raises followed by a facilitator-led whole-group discussion. Next, participants work in new small groups on a Planning Activity. This activity is designed to help coaches examine their own trajectory of learning, to explore their own principles of practice, and to articulate ways they plan to continue refining their coaching practice. The session ends with a whole-group sharing and discussion focusing on insights about coaching practice and claiming authority in the role.

Materials for the Session

- You will need enough chart paper and markers for participants to complete the Two Posters Activity and, in the event that you decide to, chart ideas that emerge from the two whole-group discussions.
- Participants will be in two different groupings for small-group activities, thus, writing up a chart with two sets of assigned seats will save transition time.

Session Agenda

1. Introduction: 5 minutes

2. Case Reading and Focus Questions: 15 minutes

3. Focus Questions Activity in Small Groups: 35 minutes

4. Whole-Group Discussion: 30 minutes

5. Two Posters Activity: 60 minutes

6. Whole-Group Discussion: 35 minutes

Introduction

Begin the session by offering a brief description of the agenda and the learning goals of the session. Set the stage for the case by describing, in just a few words, the context of this coaching case written by Carina.

Reading Case and Focus Questions

Claiming Authority is a rich case where the author compares her developing sense of authority as a coach to the way a similar sense of confidence and authority developed in her first three years of classroom teaching. Suggest to participants that reading Carina's writing will be like reading a journal of a colleague's reflections. Ask them to then review the case by underlining particularly important passages; they will want to easily locate lines that have particular resonance during both small-group discussions. For this session, ask participants to peruse the focus questions ahead of reading the case.

Focus Questions Activity in Small Groups

After reading the case, participants will have approximately 35 minutes to discuss the focus questions in small groups. If there is not enough time to get to the last question, let the group know they will have a chance to talk this one through in one of the two whole-group discussions. The goal of this activity is two-fold; the focus questions are designed to help the participants make sense of Carina's developing coaching ideas and the principles that drive her work. The discussions also set participants up to do the Two Posters Activity while using Carina's ideas as a springboard for thinking about their own.

The first focus question points to a powerful passage in the opening of the case. Here, Carina describes her entrée to establishing coaching partnerships with teachers. There are four or five separate statements of coaching moves she made in her new position. This section is also where Carina provides readers with the noteworthy insight that drawing on her "deep respect and admiration for children's thinking" appears to be what enabled her to manage teacher criticism. During one small-group discussion in this section, a participant looked at her colleagues and commented, "It's really true. It's not just about what we say or do; it's also about how teachers perceive what I value. I think Carina's saying that, in the end or, in fact, in the beginning, we can do *this*. We can *meet here*. We can all come together in this place we all value."

As you circulate among the groups, unless participants are discussing Question 6, encourage them to stick with the details of the case. It sometimes happens that the case provokes so much about what happens in day-to-day coaching that individuals might veer off to discussing mostly their own experiences. If so, they will be missing this opportunity to learn from a very reflective and experienced math coach. It is important that the small-group discussions take advantage of learning from these particular sentiments and principles Carina describes. Again, they will have a chance to work on ideas about their own coaching trajectory during the Two Posters Activity.

Whole-Group Discussion

The aim of the whole-group discussion is to elicit main ideas from Carina's case and offer the participants an opportunity to explore how they understand the issues of cultivating a practice. Ask volunteers to offer line numbers of particularly important sections of the case that they would like the whole group to have a chance to discuss. Ask, "What really stood out for you? Look through the case and note a section that resonates in your own coaching or that points to an issue that you wrestle with in your practice or that you particularly would like to hear discussed in the whole group."

Give the group a minute to review the case, and then ask for four or five sets of line numbers. Tell participants that you want to get a list of the sections on a chart; discussion will follow once a list is noted. Explain that this way, if there isn't enough time to discuss the whole list at this point, there might be time to go back to these before the end of the day's session. You can then begin the whole-group discussion by asking all participants (i.e., your question is not aimed at the one who volunteered but rather, opened to everyone) how they understand the section listed first on your chart. Variations of useful framing questions are: Why is the section important in understanding more about coaching? What about this section stands out for you? What seems to be complex about the issue(s) raised in this section? How does this section help us understand the role more clearly?

Two Posters Activity in Small Groups

Before the participants set to work, preface the activity by reminding the group of the norms of these sessions. It will be helpful to have the group talk for a minute about what it means to talk about one's developing practice as honestly as Carina has in her case and about the importance of confidentiality and safety in the group. Assure participants that it is the intention of the group—and an important aspect of your job as a facilitator—to create an atmosphere of trust and a place for open discussion about cultivating a coaching practice.

First, each participant makes his or her own version of the poster reflecting one's own stages of coaching. The second poster can be created either by pairs or by individual participants. As the facilitator, you will want to review this activity and make careful choices about the make up of the small groups and whether the second poster should be a solo or pair activity.

The first poster is a self-reflective piece of work. The participants might represent a mix of very novice to very experienced coaches; they should be assured that the stage of coaching they describe on their posters and the items they list are not compared for speed of trajectory. On the contrary, looking for comparisons should be through a lens of learning more about coaching as a practice, learning about themes across the group, learning about the complexities, and learning from each other's experiences.

The second poster will describe guiding principles, next questions, and ways to continue learning about coaching practice. There should be some consideration for pairing coaches or having each coach create a poster. If your whole group represents a wide range of experience, you may choose to partner the more novice coaches with each other. You might choose to have pairs of coaches discuss and brainstorm ideas, and then ask each coach to make a poster that represents only his or her own principles and questions. The balance is in helping coaches dig deeply to create meaningful posters to share, sometimes more easily accomplished by having a brainstorming partner, while at the same time, allowing each coach to create a very personal list without being influenced by a partner or without deferring to a partner's ideas.

You will need to act as timekeeper. Ask participants to create straightforward posters that clearly display their thinking. (Sometimes people might need to be encouraged to add words to their more pictorial representations!) Remind them that they have one hour to consider and create posters; it will be important to plan their time accordingly. Be sure that participants have 30 minutes to plan and to create the first poster. If any participant has not completed Poster 1 by then, have them move on and spend the rest of the time on Poster 2. As charts are created, group them by first and by second poster and tape them to the wall in a gallery style. When the hour is up, let participants know that it is time to take a break, and then carefully review each poster on the wall. Remind participants that the posters have been created with real care and that each one deserves their thoughtful attention. All participants should then quietly read and review as they do a gallery walk.

Whole-Group Discussion

The final whole-group discussion is aimed at the ideas revealed in the two posters. These will reveal a variety of perspectives on coaching and themes of coaching practice, a central goal of the activity. Ask participants to describe what's typical about the beginning stages of coaching ideas. Ask the group to compare the themes from participants' first charts to their previous reflections regarding Carina's trajectory. Are they similar? If so, what might that mean? If not, what might account for the difference? What did you learn by looking at your practice through the lens of your developing ideas?

Ask participants to take a few minutes to review the posters that describe, guiding principles, next steps, and ways to continue learning. Take time to discuss the lists of guiding principles. Again, look for commonalities and for new ideas. Choose a well-framed principle from a list and ask participants to comment on the implications of the principle for the work that they do. Ask how this principle is important and in what way their work is more successful or effective when grounded with this principle in mind. Review the lists with an eye toward bringing forward principles that are aligned with a strong coaching vision. You may find that, given the personal and revealing nature of the reflective work participants have been engaged in, they will welcome your reassuring leadership in the facilitation of this discussion of principles and a focus on strengthening and refining practice.

End the discussion by asking for comments on the last section, Ways to Continue Learning. You may have particular structures or strategies in your setting that coaches can use to their advantage. Perhaps coaches want to attend coaching seminars, intend to write (or continue writing) their own cases of practice to share with colleagues, or partner with another coach to observe each other and debrief their work. Look for promising examples such as these, and ask coaches how these ideas might be accomplished.

As the session comes to a close, ask participants to respond to a set of exit card prompts. You might ask coaches to describe the most important new idea that came from the session, to explain how the session will specifically influence their coaching practice, or to articulate one next step in cultivating a coaching practice.

CORWIN

A SAGE Company

The Corwin logo—a raven striding across an open book—represents the union of courage and learning. Corwin is committed to improving education for all learners by publishing books and other professional development resources for those serving the field of PreK–12 education. By providing practical, hands-on materials, Corwin continues to carry out the promise of its motto: **"Helping Educators Do Their Work Better."**

Education Development Center, Inc.

Education Development Center's mission is to enhance the quality and accessibility of education, health, and economic opportunity worldwide.